MY PROPER
GROUND

MY PROPER GROUND

A Study of the Work of

Philip Larkin

and its Development

A.T. Tolley

Edinburgh University Press

©Carleton University Press Inc. 1991

First published by
Carleton University Press Inc.
Ottawa, Ontario, Canada

First published in UK by
Edinburgh University Press
22 George Square, Edinburgh

Printed and bound in Canada

British Library Cataloguing in Publication Data
Tolley, A.T.
    My proper ground: a study of the work of Philip Larkin and
    its development
    I. Title
    821

ISBN 0 7486 0311 5 (cased)
ISBN 0 7486 0326 3 (limp)

Cover design: Aerographics Ottawa, Canada

Acknowledgements:

This book has been published with the help of a grant from the Canadian Federation for the Humanities, using funds provided by the Social Sciences and Humanities Research Council of Canada.

To Glenda

Other books by A.T. Tolley

The Early Poetry of Stephen Spender: a Chronology
The Poetry of the Thirties
The Poetry of the Forties

Edited by A.T. Tolley

John Lehmann: a Tribute

Contents

Acknowledgements

My first debt is to the late Dr. P.A. Larkin, who read and commented on some parts of this book in an earlier form. He kindly corrected misinformation, provided new information and generously granted permission to use previously unpublished material.

The book has benefited from conversation with Bernard Bergonzi, John Heath-Stubbs, Anthony Thwaite, John Wain, and Frank Wilson. Anyone who writes about Larkin must owe a great deal to B.C. Bloomfield's *Philip Larkin: A Bibliography* and to Anthony Thwaite's edition of *Collected Poems*. I also owe much to Jenny Stratford's bibliographical work on the manuscript notebook in the British Library. Other debts and admirations will, I hope, be clear in the text.

Michael Gnarowski of Carleton University Press has, as ever, been steadily and generously supportive of my work. Mary Ford, Gordon Wood and other colleagues at Carleton University drew my attention to pieces I might have missed. I had the opportunity of discussing many of the ideas in this book with the students in my graduate seminars and with Paul Keeler and Pat Scrimingeor. Mrs. I.D. Edrich found me a hard to get item.

The Ontario Arts Council made me an award in their Works in Progress Competition for 1985. The Social Sciences and Humanities Research Council gave me a Research Grant for early research on the Larkin Notebook in the British Library. The Canadian Federation for the Humanities made a grant in support of publication.

My thanks are due to the Curator and staff of the Manuscript Room of the British Library, to the staff of the English Literature Section of the Birmingham Reference Library, and to the staff of the MacOdrum Library at Carleton University.

I am grateful for permission to reprint material that previously appeared in *Arc*, *Agenda* and *Aquarius*. The executors of Philip Larkin's estate and his publisher, Faber, kindly permitted me to quote from his work.

Once again my wife freely gave up time from her own research to read and comment on my text.

Lyane Groulx, Dina Migoel, Heather Parks and Cathy Schmueck of the Comparative Literature Program at Carleton University typed the text for me. Christina Thiele, of Carleton University's Journal Production Centre, prepared the text for printing.

Abbreviations of Titles

Intro. to	=	Introduction to
NS	=	*The North Ship* (London: The Fortune Press, 1945; 2nd ed., Faber, 1966)
Jill	=	*Jill* (London: The Fortune Press, 1946; 2nd ed., Faber, 1975) (paging from 2nd ed.)
AGW	=	*A Girl in Winter* (London: Faber, 1947) (paging from paperback edition of 1975)
IGL	=	*In the Grip of Light* (unpublished, 1947)
XXP	=	*XX Poems* (Belfast: privately printed, 1951)
LD	=	*The Less Deceived* (Hessle: Marvell Press, 1955)
WW	=	*The Whitsun Weddings* (London: Faber, 1964)
AWJ	=	*All What Jazz?* (London: Faber, 1970; 2nd ed. (with new material) Faber, 1985) (paging from 2nd ed.)
HW	=	*High Windows* (London: Faber, 1974)
RW	=	*Required Writing* (London: Faber, 1983)
CP	=	*Collected Poems* (London: Faber, 1988)

References for quotations from the above works are given in the text, using the above abbreviations. References for quotations from other works are given at the end of the book. Quotations from poems are all from *Collected Poems* (except for unpublished material) and their provenance or the volume in which they were originally published is indicated contextually.

INTRODUCTORY

In praising the poetry of John Betjeman, Larkin quoted with approval the remark of Oscar Wilde that "Only mediocrities develop". As with many of Larkin's asides, it has the air of being directed against something rather than of asserting something for its own sake. He went on to argue that "if Betjeman could hit the target so unerringly at 25 he clearly had no need to change".[1]

Larkin's own career would hardly compel such a remark. If he had died in 1950 at the age of 28, he would have left behind two minor novels and a volume of adolescent poetry; while the writer we knew — if we knew him at all — would bear only a small resemblance to the one we have come to admire. He was 33 when *The Less Deceived*, the first book of poems entirely in the manner that became distinctively his, was published.

Larkin's remark was in keeping with his dislike of the notion that the artist is concerned with developing a vision of the world: as though he were at every stage of his career groping forward to a sense of things that he may or may not eventually attain, with every work a step towards his *Duino Elegies* or his final string quartets. Such a view would have been startlingly at odds with Larkin's own sense of the artist's direct responsibility to experience.

Yet, if the artist is to be the honest servant of experience, he has to discover the idiom in which to do so. For Larkin, that process — the finding of his "proper ground" — involved a number of indirections. One is reminded of his telling summation in "Aubade", at the end of his poetic career: "An only life can take so long to climb/ Clear of its wrong beginnings". Climbing clear was a long process; and the study of that process importantly enhances our sense of his total achievement. This is particularly true for Larkin, whose poems are frequently occasioned by moments of self-recognition and one of whose major themes is how we come to be what we are.

It is easy to see Larkin's life as uneventful and exerting no pressure for artistic change. Following school and university, he went to work in a libarary; and, after three early posts, he spent his mature life in

Hull as Librarian of a provincial university. Larkin encouraged the picture of himself as someone to whom nothing happened. However, if we look at the changes in the culture of which he became eventually the admired, unofficial laureate, it is clear that he lived through times of great cultural reversals and that the changes touched him closely.

He began writing in the nineteen-thirties, when contemporary poetry was dominated by the work of Auden and the left-wing literary movement with which Auden was associated. The coming of the war in 1939 marked the end of that movement and of the emotional and cultural attitudes to which it gave voice. The war brought a humbled attitude to the modern intellectual panaceas of the nineteen-thirties and a return to traditional forms and attitudes in the arts in Britain. To these changes, Larkin, a young imitator of Auden, responded, switching his allegiance to Yeats. After the war, with the decline of the romantic and traditionalist impulses, there was a period of doldrums in literature that was, in part, a symptom of the decadence of the reigning upper-middle-class social and artistic hegemony. The philistinism of the Movement, in which Larkin was such an important figure, finally broke that hegemony and its associated high-minded sense of what literature should be or should deal with. A significant change at that time was the growing recognition of the important cultural role of popular arts, among them jazz, to which Larkin had been a pioneering devotee.

The Movement became the dominant literary voice of the newly affluent nineteen-fifties; but the affluence was succeeded by a much more disruptive and anarchic ambience in the late nineteen-sixties. The aggressive emphasis on artistic freedom of that period, which seemed to push to extreme the experimentalism of early modernist artists, was clearly uncongenial to Larkin, and he reacted to it very strongly. Despite great acclaim and popularity, he seemed unhappy with the world into which he had lived on, and this manifested itself in a hardening conservatism and, eventually, poetic silence.

That conservatism was no doubt reinforced by the changes that had taken place in Larkin's own situation. *The Less Deceived* had been written by an assistant librarian in a provincial university whose poetry had consistently been refused by commercial publishers and whose efforts to write a third novel had not born fruit. *High Windows* was written by a very successful Librarian of what had become a large university, whose work as a poet and a librarian was widely acclaimed. The rejected outsider had become a member of the Establishment.

Chapter 1

BEGINNINGS

Philip Larkin's childhood and youth were so aggressively utilized in his earlier poetry that for many readers it must be hard to disengage the facts of his biography from the personal mythology of which he made it a part. Many of his poems project a persona awkward, diffident, unable to participate in the conventional activities of youth, or looking back on earlier days that seem no more than "a forgotten boredom" ("Coming"). "My childhood was all right," Larkin in fact recalled, "comfortable and stable and loving, but I wasn't a happy child, or so they say. On the other hand, I've never been a recluse. . ."("An Interview with *Paris Review*", *RW* 66) His youth he remembered as having a similar uneventful quality: "It now seems strange to me that all the time I lived in Coventry I never knew any girls, but it did not at the time. . . I never knew anyone in Coventry who was interested in writing".[1]

In these respects his experiences were perhaps no different from those of the majority of artistically inclined grammar school boys of his day; and his reflection that "Until I began to meet grown- ups on more or less equal terms I fancied myself a kind of Ishmael"("The Savage Seventh", *RW* 111), must have been made by many who disliked the barbarity of boyhood. Nonetheless, that dislike remained with him, even if it is not noticeably felt in his writing; while the fact that he "never knew any girls" seems to have left a permanent mark on his attitudes to the opposite sex that is felt in many of his poems.

His father was town-clerk of Coventry, so that the family into which Larkin was born on August 9th, 1922 was of comfortable, fairly well-to-do middle class. He attended King Henry VIII School — both the preparatory and the senior sections. A great friend of these school days was James Ballard Sutton, to whom he dedicated *Jill* and the early poem, "Conscript", and in whose company artistic exploration began:

> He was a year older than I, and left after taking Matric to become a master-builder's apprentice, but he somehow go interested in painting.

Together we took our education in hand: I lent him Lawrence, he retal-
iated with Cézanne. On Saturday afternoons we sat, frowning intently,
in the glass cubicles at Hanson's, trying to decide whether both sides
of the latest Parlophone Rhythm-Style Series or Vocalion Swing Series were sufficiently good to justify expenditure of the record's stiffish
price of three shillings.[2]

These sessions marked the beginning of a life-long passion for Larkin.
Jazz was not popular music then; and those who liked current dance
music found it repulsively cacophonous. It had a far smaller following
than conventional "serious" music. It was something one could call
one's own — music that gave articulation to feelings that seemed ignored by the official culture. It was an art worthy of serious attention,
yet concerning which there was nobody to tell one what one *ought* to
like. The cultural iconoclasm involved in liking jazz was to re-emerge
frequently and importantly in Larkin's work — not least in the period of the Movement; and the sense that one valued something, not
because it was felt to be culturally important, but because it spoke to
one with immediacy, was to remain for him a touchstone of the arts.
    The other major source of artistic nourishment was his father's
library:

> Thanks to my father, our house contained not only the principle [sic]
> works of most main English writers . . . but also nearly-complete collec-
> tions of authors my father favoured — Hardy, Bennett, Wilde, Butler
> and Shaw, and later on Lawrence, Huxley and Katherine Mansfield.
> Not till I was much older did I realise that most boys of my class
> were brought up to regard Galsworthy and Chesterton as the apex of
> modern literature, and to think Somerset Maugham 'a bit hot'. I was
> therefore lucky.[3]

It was evidently from his father that Larkin derived his abiding love
for Lawrence; and the later crucial encounter with the poetry of
Thomas Hardy was in fact a re-encounter.
    Larkin's earliest publications were in the school magazine, *The
Coventrian*: "all my early contributions were in the manner of 'The
Humorist', and all excruciating,"[4] he recalled. The first appeared
in December, 1934, when he was twelve. The first poem was in the
issue for December 1938, when Larkin was 16 and in the Sixth. It
is conventional, as one would expect from a boy of that age, though
replete with imagery that Larkin was to find congenial for many years
to come — darkness, rain, wind. The sophisticated handling of the
movement of the poem, and the spacing of its sense groups to make

the first twelve lines of the sonnet a unity are quite remarkable in a poet so young:

> Mantled in grey, the dusk steals slowly in,
>   Crossing the dead, dull fields with footsteps cold.
> The rain drips drearly; night's fingers spin
>   A web of drifting mist o'er wood and wold,
> As quiet as death. The sky is silent too,
>   Hard as granite and as fixed as fate.
> The pale pond stands; ringed round with rushes few
>   And draped with leaning trees, it seems to wait
> But for the coming of the winter night
>   Of deep December; blowing o'er the graves
> Of faded summers, swift the wind in flight
>   Ripples its silent face with lapping waves.
> The rain falls still: bowing, the woods bemoan,
>   Dark night creeps in, and leaves the world alone.
>   ("Winter Nocturne")

This must mark the beginning of the period in which Larkin "wrote ceaselessly. . . now verse, which I sewed up into little books, now prose, a thousand words a night after homework. . ."[5]

By the following year he had evidently discovered Auden. The first poem to show the new influence was from early in 1939 when Larkin was still sixteen. He shows that he had already learned from Auden the trick of social placing by the use of significant detail: "He smiles demurely at his uncle's jokes,/ And reads the *Modern Boy* in bed at night" ("Having grown up in shade of Church and State"). A little later there seems to be evidence of admiration for Eliot: "Let me accept the role, and call/ Myself the circumstances' tennis-ball" ("When the night puts twenty veils"). Some echoes of an earlier conventional taste are still evident in 1939; but in the following year Auden is clearly the model in every surviving poem: in "Spring Warning", published in *The Coventrian* in April, we encounter "The muffled boy, with his compelling badge,/ On his serious errand riding to the gorge." In "Nothing significant was really said" and "Schoolmaster" Larkin tries the sonnet as portrait sketch that Auden had used in an already celebrated poem "A shilling life will give you all the facts"; while, as a farewell to the school, in collaboration with Noel Hughes, he contributed to *The Conventrian* a stylish "Last Will and Testament", in clear imitation of the poem of that name with which Auden and MacNeice closed their *Letters from Iceland* (1937):

Item, our school reports we leave the Staff,
To give them, as we hope, a hearty laugh;
And Kipling's "If" to hang upon their wall.

There was, however, no published evidence of the "thousand words a night" of prose: his contributions to *The Conventrian* in his final year include editorials and reports, but the only creative writing, aside from the poems, is in the manner of the "Humorist".

By the late thirties, Auden was the most admired poet in England among readers of modern poetry. The poem that had established "modern" poetry in the nineteen-twenties was T.S. Eliot's *The Waste Land* (1922); but with *Ash Wednesday* (1930), Eliot had seemed to abandon contemporary themes and evince a taste for more conventional poetic imagery; and his only non-dramatic poem of any length during the nineteen-thirties was "Burnt Norton". He no longer presented an attractive example for the aspiring poet. The books that would have invited admiration by Larkin when he started to read contemporary poetry were Auden's *Poems* (1930) and *Look, Stranger!* (1936); Stephen Spender's *Poems* (1933); and Louis MacNeice's *Poems* (1934) and *The Earth Compels* (1938). It is clear from Larkin's poems that he had read Auden and MacNeice's poetic travel book, *Letters from Iceland* and Auden and Isherwood's *Journey to a War* (1939). Newer and less well known were David Gascoyne, with his surrealist *Man's Life is This Meat* (1936); George Barker with *Poems* (1935) and *Calamiterror* (1937); and Dylan Thomas, who had two books, *18 Poems* (1934) and *Twenty-five Poems* (1936). Of these, only Thomas's *Twenty-five Poems* had achieved any fame; and Larkin seems not to have been influenced by these younger writers, who were more involved with romantic styles of modernism (such as surrealism in Gascoyne's case). Larkin appears to have been drawn to the realist style of modern poetry practiced by the poets of the left-wing literary movement of the thirties. There are no echoes of their political concerns in Larkin's early work; but he was undoubtedly attracted by the acclimatization of the modern world to poetry that he encountered in their work — and particularly that of Auden. John Betjeman, whose *Mount Zion* (1931) was an obscure rarity, and whose *Continual Dew* (1937) got little attention when it appeared, seems to have been discovered by Larkin only when he went up to Oxford.[6] As Larkin later put it, he "had been educated in the Auden tradition — objective, outward-looking, poltical, materialist, unpretentious."[7]

In much of Larkin's early work it is possible to point to the particular poem by Auden that is being imitated. "Midsummer Night, 1940" (from June, 1940) begins "The sun falls behind Wales", echoing the beginning of the peroration of the final poem by Auden in *Journey to a War*, "Night moves over China". In its panoramic social vision of England, "Midsummer Night, 1940" also recalls the "Prologue" to *Look, Stranger!*. "Tomorrow in the offices the year on the stamps will be altered;/ Tomorrow new diaries consulted" (from "New Year Poem", December 1940) recalls the conclusion of Auden's "Spain". The opening line of "Out in the lane I pause: the night" echoes Auden's "Out on the lawn I lie in bed", both in phrasing and rhythm; while the stanza form of the poem seems to have been inspired by "Brothers, who when the sirens roar", also from *Look, Stranger!*.

In these imitative poems we encounter hints of Larkin's later themes: "What was the rock my gliding childhood struck" asks the speaker of "Nothing significant was really said". In the long "After-Dinner Remarks", in its form also reminiscent of Auden's "Out on the lawn I lie in bed", Larkin's brand of self-doubt and regret emerges: "Think what I could have won today/ By stretching out my hand"; "And am I one of these?/ A keyhole made without a key,/ A poem none can read or say. . ." He already seems to have arrived at a position concerning fate that was to remain with him throughout his life: "We do not make ourselves".

The most effective of these youthful Audenesque poems was written in Larkin's first term at Oxford, after his home town Coventry was partially obliterated in one night of bombing in November 1940. "New Year Poem" utilises the proporties of the derelict landscape of Auden for the expression of personal feeling, which, however, only partially extricates itself from the Audenesque poses:

> These houses are deserted, felt over smashed windows,
> No milk on the step, a note pinned on the door
> Telling of departure: only shadows
> Move when in the day the sun is seen for an hour,
> Yet to me this decaying landscape has its uses. . . .

In the summer of 1940, before his departure for Oxford, Larkin sent four poems to *The Listener*. They accepted "Ultimatum", a piece that answers to his description of it as one he "had put in to make the others seem better".[8] It takes us again into the doom-ridden landscape of Auden's early poetry:

> Remember stories you read when a boy
> — The shipwrecked sailor gaining safety by
> His knife, treetrunk, and lianas — for now
> You must escape, or perish saying no.

When it appeared in the issue for 28th October, Larkin was already in Oxford and "ready for an injection of self-esteem."[9] Ironically, "Ultimatum" was to be his only poem in a national periodical until 1953.

The Oxford at which Larkin arrived in October, 1940 was one in which a prop to poetic self-esteem must have been helpful. In 1940 and 1941, *Cherwell*, the principal undergraduate weekly for poetry and other literary contributions, published poems by Keith Douglas, John Heath-Stubbs, Sidney Keyes, Drummond Allison, Norman Hampson, Michael Meyer, J.A. Shaw, Roy Porter, David Wright — as well as three by P.A. Larkin. Douglas had already left Oxford by the time Larkin came up. Meyer was one of the editors of *Cherwell* from October 1940 to March 1941, and Keyes replaced him in June 1941. Keyes and his friends had a firm hold on the poetry scene at Oxford. Larkin was at St. John's; and as he later wrote "fortunate enough to have chosen the same College as Kingsley Amis, Alan Ross, John Wain and Bruce Montgomery ("Edmund Crispin"). . . the accepted poets of the University — Sidney Keyes, John Heath-Stubbs, and Drummond Allison, for instance — were all at Queen's."[10]

During Larkin's first year (which was also Keyes's first year) Meyer and Keyes conceived the project of bringing out an anthology of young Oxford poets. They at first approached T.S. Eliot, who declined, but suggested Herbert Read, then with Routledge. In June 1941 Read came to Oxford to discuss the proposal with them. Meyer and Keyes showed him a selection from the work of eight young writers. This was to become the basis for *Eight Oxford Poets*, which appeared later that year. It included poems by Keyes, Heath-Stubbs, Meyer, Keith Douglas, Drummond Allison, Gordon Swaine, J.A. Shaw and Roy Porter. The following year Read published the first books of Heath-Stubbs and Keyes, *Wounded Thammus* and *The Iron Laurel*, which were well received.

Meyer and Keyes had published poems by Larkin in *Cherwell*; and Meyer, who was also "under the spell of Auden", wanted to include Larkin in *Eight Oxford Poets*; but Keyes, possibly with the encouragement of Drummond Allison, did not go along. As "it was he (Keyes) who did the choosing", Larkin was left out.[11] To Kingsley Amis it seemed "that Keyes, who may well have known that Philip considered him a third-rate personage, left him out with some deliberation."[12]

In his "Foreword" to *Eight Oxford Poets*, Keyes wrote: "We. . . have confined ourselves to a fairly liberal selection from the work of those writers who seem to us most interesting, most typical, and most hopeful for the future"; and went on to characterize his contributors as "*Romantic* writers" with "little sympathy with the Audenian school of poets".[13] Larkin's admiration for Auden had been clear in all his poems published in Oxford up to that time, and this may have contributed to his absence from Keyes's anthology.

Larkin gave his own sense of those days in the "Introduction" to the second edition of *The North Ship* (1966): "I remember looking through an issue of *Cherwell*. . . and coming across John Heath-Stubbs's 'Leporello': I was profoundly bewildered. I had never heard of Leporello, and what sort of poetry was this — who was he copying? And his friend Sidney Keyes was no more comforting: he could talk to history as some people talk to porters, and the mention of names like Schiller and Rilke and Gilles de Retz made me wish I were reading something more demanding than English Language and Literature."(*RW* 28) The self-deprecating humour masks an acute characterization of Keyes's weaknesses as a poet; but Larkin does not attempt to hide the fact that Heath-Stubbs, in particular, had found a recognizable style of his own.

Larkin had come to Oxford to read English ("what else!").[14] In those years English seemed the dominant cultural subject; though the nine compulsory papers in English finals included only one devoted to authors after 1700, while half an undergraduate's time was given to Old English, Middle English, philology and the History of the English language. Kingsley Amis recalls, "Nobody had a good word to say for *Beowulf*, *The Wanderer*, *The Dream of the Rood*, *The Battle of Malton*. Philip had less than none. If ever a man spoke for his generation it was when, mentioning some piece of what he called in a letter to me 'ape's bumfodder', he said, 'I can just about stand learning the filthy lingo it's written in. What gets me down is being expected to *admire* the bloody stuff.'"[15] Nevertheless, Larkin showed over the years a very full scholarly knowledge of English literature of all periods in his reviews. The recollection of another friend of those years might seem to confirm that Larkin was already set in his preference for a literature direct in appeal, without the need for explanation or any other mediating considerations. Michael Hamburger, then the youthful author of a translation of the poems of Hölderlin and an admirer of T.S. Eliot, wrote to Larkin about "tradition". He got for reply: "To me the 'tradition of poetry' is, quite simply, emotion and honesty of emotion, and it doesn't matter who it is written by or how, if this is conveyed."[16]

The most important meeting for Larkin came in his third term, with Kingsley Amis. The friendship was to be then and later one of the most fruitful for both of them. In those days "Kingsley's 'serious side' was political. . .he became editor of the University Labour Club

Bulletin and in this capacity printed one of my poems" ("Observation"). A second poem ("Disintegration") was found "morbid and unhealthy" by the Club committee — perhaps a measure of Larkin's distance from politics at the time. But about "jazz we had no disagreement. . .I suppose we devoted to some hundred records that early anatomizing passion normally reserved for the more established arts."("Intro. to *Jill*", *RW* 21–22) In the uninhibited ambience of this "unofficial" culture the important literary friendship was formed. Larkin's "main intention was to become a novelist"[17] at that time; and Amis saw the parts of *Jill* that already existed in those Oxford days, and was later consulted about Larkin's third novel that was never completed.[18]

However, it was as a poet that Larkin was known publicly at Oxford. "Looking back", he later wrote of the poetry of his early years, "I find . . . not one abandoned self but several — the ex-schoolboy, for whom Auden was the only alternative to 'old-fashioned' poetry; the undergraduate, whose work a friend affably characterised as 'Dylan Thomas, but you've a sentimentality that's all your own'; and the immediately post-Oxford self, isolated in Shropshire with a complete Yeats stolen from the local girls' school."("Intro. to *NS*", *RW* 28) Auden is the mentor in all the poems Larkin published in 1941. Among these was "Conscript", the earliest poem in his first book *The North Ship*. It appeared in *Phoenix*, whose principal editor seems to have been Norman Hampson, one of the most promising undergraduate poets of his day, though now largely forgotten: unlike Keyes, he modelled himself on Auden and the poets of the thirties. Three other poems, "Story", "A Writer" and "May Weather", appeared in *Cherwell* in 1941. They were again characteristically Audenesque in style:

> 'Interesting, but futile,' said his diary,
> Where day by day his movements were recorded
> And nothing but his loves received inquiry;
> He knew, of course, no actions were rewarded,
> There were no prizes: though the eye could see
> Wide beauty in a motion or a pause,
> It need expect no lasting salary. . .
>
>   ("A Writer")

The form, as for "Conscript" and "Story", is the Audenesque potted-narrative sonnet encountered in *Look, Stranger!* and *Another Time* (1940). The poem contains many all-or-nothing statements characteristic of Auden's poetry in the thirties; while the "furniture" of the poem ("There were no prizes") and the self-regarding concerns of the character depicted ("nothing but his loves received inquiry") are equally Audenesque. The poetic gestures have been skillfully mastered; and, while there is little individuality, one must admire the fluency of movement (always a feature of Larkin's poetry) and the naturalness of the diction.

In a poem printed in *Cherwell* in the February of the following year, we still see the influence of Auden in the luckless conclusion:

> will you greet your doom
> As final; set him loaves and wine; knowing
> The game is finished when he plays his ace,
> And overturn the table and go into the next room?

However, earlier in this sonnet there is a passage of sensitive observation that has the voice of Larkin's later poetry, reminding one of "Lines on a Young Lady's Photograph Album":

> sunbeams are prodigal
> To show you pausing at a picture's edge
> To puzzle out the name, or with a hand
> Resting a second on a random page. . .

Not long after, there may have been for Larkin a break in writing, deriving perhaps from a sense that he could no longer go in this direction. He said that in 1942 he "gave up the whole business" — though it was not to be not for long.[19] A new direction is taken by the three poems he contributed to *Oxford Poetry 1942–43*:

> Planted deeper than roots,
> This chiselled, flung-up faith
> Runs and leaps against the sky,
> A prayer killed into stone
> Among the always-dying trees. . .
>
> ("A Stone Church Damaged
by a Bomb")

The subject was one close to his personal experience and one to which he was capable of responding movingly, as can be seen from the description of the bombed city in *Jill*, evidently based on seeing the devastation of his home town, Coventry. The poem's exaggerated diction and the violent figurative use of language ("A prayer killed into stone") seem to indicate a conversion to the romanticism of the forties. The change must have taken place early in 1943, as two of the

poems in *Oxford Poetry* had appeared in Hilary term in *Arabesque*,
published by the Oxford University Ballet Club — a periodical that
included work by John Heath-Stubbs and Roy Porter. Among the
evidence of a new orientation are echoes of Yeats's rhythm and diction:

> I have looked on that proud front
> And the calm locked into walls,
> I have worshipped that whispering shell.

All this points to the fact that the most important event of Larkin's
final months at Oxford had been a visit to the English Club by Vernon
Watkins. It began a lasting friendship and marked an important
change of direction for Larkin. He adopted Yeats as his model, and
this set the tone of his poetry for the first three years after he left
Oxford. This was to prove a wrong direction for him, and one that
he had to abandon before he was to find either his own style or public
recognition. It led to a prolific period of writing that produced two
books of poetry, one of which was never published. These books will
be the subject of a later chapter.

Larkin's years at Oxford had seen the beginning of a transition in
English poetry. Writers like Drummond Allison, Alan Ross, Kingsley Amis and Norman Hampson were all admirers of Auden; but the
beginnings of the romanticism that was to be so dominant in the mid-
forties were to be seen in the work of John Heath-Stubbs and Sidney
Keyes and in the *Eight Oxford Poets* that Keyes edited. Nonetheless, it would be misguided to suggest that Larkin had been wrong in
choosing Auden as his early model. Alan Ross and Norman Hampson wrote and continued to write in a manner that derived from that
of Auden and MacNeice and similar poets of the thirties; and by
1942 both were appearing in *New Writing and Daylight*, one of the
leading periodicals of the decade. While Larkin did not appear in
Eight Oxford Poets — an omission that John Heath-Stubbs, Sidney
Keyes's great friend, later saw as a mistake,[20] he did get his Audenesque poems published regularly in *Cherwell*, even under Keyes's
editorship. However, though these poems are, for a young writer,
accomplished performances in the Auden manner, there is nothing
particularly memorable about them —nothing as memorable or distinctive as Heath-Stubbs's "Leporello", which also appeared in *Cherwell*. As Larkin wrote in a note to himself of the time: "almost any
single line by Auden would be worth more than the whole lot put
together."[21]

Indeed, Larkin's undergraduate poems, both to contempory eyes and in retrospect, were overshadowed by the youthful work of his Oxford contemporaries, John Heath-Stubbs, Alan Ross, Drummond Allison, Norman Hampson and Sidney Keyes. His early poems afford no sense of a personal voice; and the completeness with which he switched from the Audenesque mode to that of Yeats points up how unformed his idiom was at that time. Ironically, except for two poems that appeared in 1946 in *Mandrake* — a magazine started at Oxford by Larkin's friend John Wain — Larkin's undergraduate publications were to be his last poems to appear in periodicals for ten years.

However, the cultivation of Auden as a model was not to prove detrimental for Larkin in the long run; indeed, much that he imbibed from Auden was to become important to his poetry in later years — the ready evocation of details of modern life; the handling of colloquial speech; and a fresh and modern use of traditional forms. These were to become part of his idiom when he had turned his back on Yeats as a model to find his own voice at last in the 'fifties.

Chapter 2

THE YOUNG NOVELIST

Larkin went down from Oxford in June of 1943. Medically unfit for military service, he nevertheless faced the certainty that he would be directed into some sort of approved work, if he did not find something himself. He was turned down twice by the Civil Service, and started applying for jobs indiscriminately. "The imminence of a directive from the Ministry of Labour spurred him into picking up a copy of *The Birmingham Post* and perusing the Situations Vacant column. A librarian's position was advertised in Shropshire. He applied for it, and got it — 'there was no opposition in those days'."[1] The post was in a one-man library in Wellington. He went there in December, 1943. It must have seemed a lonely assignment; and he evidently made frequent visits to Oxford, where John Wain, still an undergraduate and editing the periodical *Mandrake*, remembers him as an absent leader:

> It took the trumpet-call 'Philip's coming up!' to bring together a motley crew who did not associate at any other time, and who were connected simply by a common admiration for one whom we already considered a Flaubertian saint of letters. Kingsley Amis, appearing on his leaves from active service, was one of the nebulous group, and my first casual meetings with him came about because we were both, so to speak, swimming in the thin fluid that solidified only when Philip Larkin arrived. It was Kingsley who sold me my copy of Philip's first novel, *Jill* . . .[2]

Perhaps the most important of his former Oxford friends at this time was Bruce Montgomery, the "Edmund Crispin" of mystery stories, who had already written *The Case of the Gilded Fly*, and who was teaching at Shrewsbury School while Larkin was in nearby Wellington: "I sometimes wonder if Bruce did not constitute for me a curious creative stimulus. For . . . three years we were in fairly constant contact, and I wrote continuously as never before or since." ("Intro. to *Jill*", *RW* 24) Although Larkin continued to compose poems in the large green manuscript book that he started to use shortly after coming to Wellington, he "thought of himself then primarily as a novelist, and continued to do so for several years subsequently."[3]

During his months at home waiting to find where he would go, Larkin had worked on his first novel, *Jill*, parts of which had been written at Oxford. *Jill* was completed in the autumn of 1944 and *A Girl in Winter* in July 1945.[4] They are thus the products of the wartime period, and it is hard to see in them the beginning of a curve of sensibility that was to manifest itself a decade later as the "Movement". They were written with a poetic care for detail — particularly *A Girl in Winter*; and this approach to writing is much more in harmony with the manner of novelists of the nineteen-forties, such as Denton Welch, L.P. Hartley or William Sansom, than with the cultivation of the demotic that was the mark of "Movement" novels like John Wain's *Hurry on Down* (1953) or Kingsley Amis's *Lucky Jim* (1954).

Jill follows a young scholarship boy from the North, John Kemp, through his first term at Oxford. He arrives to find that he is sharing rooms with a rather vulgar, self-indulgent product of a minor public school, Christopher Warner, who has already opened Kemp's luggage and is serving tea to his friends from Kemp's china. Warner's lack of regard for other people and their property extends to borrowing Kemp's notes and his money, and even to poking fun at him with other people in his presence. Yet Kemp, despite this treatment, longs to be accepted by Warner, and finds himself trying to imitate Warner and to enter his world of drinking, loafing and not giving a damn. One day, when he feels he is succeeding, he hears Warner and his girl-friend laughing at him.

In reaction, on impulse, he invents a sister "Jill", who is away at school. From being an invention to impress Warner, she grows to be a counterpoise to Kemp's inability to enter Warner's world. He begins to write letters to her, in which he figures with the ease and the attitudes that he envies in Warner. Then he writes a story in which she too behaves with the same panache. From there he moves to keeping a diary, supposedly hers. One day, in one of the startling scenes of the novel, he sees "Jill" in a bookshop and speaks to her. After days of hunting to meet her again, he sees her go into his own college and finally into his own rooms. She is the young cousin, Gillian, of Warner's girl-friend, Elizabeth. He invites her to tea, preparing by war-time standards a feast, only to be visited by Elizabeth, who tells him that it is inappropriate for him to have invited the fifteen-year-old Jill.

Hurt deeply by this defeat, he hears of the bombing of his home town, and gets permission to visit it. His family is not there; but amidst the devastation they and their home are safe. He returns to Oxford numb to the idea of his earlier caution. One evening he gets drunk and arrives at a party where Warner and Gillian are present, just as Gillian is leaving. He kisses her and is thrown by Warner and his friends into a fountain. He contracts pneumonia: and, in the delirium of his illness, becomes unsure whether Jill accepted him or not. He comes to a sense of resignation before the course of events. The novel ends with Warner and Elizabeth, who has indicated that she is now willing to go to bed with Warner, leaving for London.

Kemp confronts what for Larkin must have been the common struggle of a young adolescent male to find himself or assert his individuality. In presenting this, Larkin explores three central themes of his writing: the roles of choice and of fate in determining the directions of our lives; the loneliness that accompanies failure or unfulfilled longing; and the response to that loneliness, especially in the tendency towards the creation of illusions which themselves inhibit fulfilment. At Huddersford Kemp looks into the window of his locked home to find nobody there. Powerful images and incidents of exclusion and loneliness fill the book; and the sense of being excluded from a world where fulfillment is taken for granted — particularly sexual fulfillment — is the basis of Kemp's actions and his fantasies.

The introduction into the story of the imaginary sister Jill is critical to the resolution of the issue of loneliness in the book. For Kemp, the creation of Jill was unplanned and spontaneous; but he became entrapped by the imagined figure he so carelessly and off-handedly created. The tale of the imaginary Jill itself offers possible responses to loneliness: the forging of a bond with another human being, as in Jill's friendship with Patsy Hammond; the compromising of one's individuality by becoming a member of a group, as in the case of the girl Rosalie; or the acceptance of loneliness as part of existence — the reaction of Minerva, who "simply went her own way" (*Jill* 141). For the Jill of Kemp's story, "Minerva's remote indifference she could not capture" (*Jill* 142). Minerva is a touchstone figure in the book. That "loneliness was not to be to be abandoned at the first chance of friendship, but was a thing to be cherished in itself" (*Jill* 148) is at the heart of the "Jill" story. This, however, is not the conclusion that Kemp is drawn to: he is betrayed by his fantasies into an unreal relationship with a real girl whom he takes to be the imagined Jill.

Jill has rightly been seen as concerned not only with loneliness, but with the role of illusion and with the deceptions that illusions create — a theme much to the fore in Larkin's first major volume of poetry, *The Less Deceived* (1955). *Jill* shows how our illusions, and the deceptions to which they give rise, play as important a part in shaping our lives as do chance and circumstances. Kemp is betrayed by his fantasies because they become confused with reality when he sees in a bookshop a girl he thinks is Jill, but who is, in fact, Gillian, the cousin of Warner's girl-friend. He never gets to know her, but develops an infatuation for her that has its origin in his fantasies. The feeling of fatalism that pervades the book is shaped by the perception that Kemp is trapped as much by his illusions as by his personality or his social status. One such illusion is that he has become a friend of Warner. As Larkin remarked, looking back on the book forty years later: "*Jill* was based on the idea that running away from life, John's fantasy about an imaginary sister, might lead you straight into it — meeting the real Jill . . ." ("An Interview with *Paris Review*", *RW* 63)

However, Kemp's final meditations are not concerned with self-deception, but with a more profound yet related theme to which Larkin often returns — that of choice and the extent to which we choose our lives.

> He grew confused whether she had accepted him or not, since the result was the same: and as this confusion increased, it spread to fulfilment or unfulfilment, which merged and became inseparable. The difference between them vanished.

> He was watching the trees, the tops of which he could just see through the window. They tossed and tossed, recklessly. He saw them fling their [sic] way and that, throwing up their heads like impatient horses, like sea waves, bending and recovering in the wind. They had no leaves. Endlessly, this way and that, they were buffeted and still bore up again to their full height. They seemed tireless. Sometimes they were bent so low that they passed out of sight, leaving the square of white sky free for a second, but then they would be back again, clashing their proud branches together like the antlers of furious stags.

> Then if there was no difference between love fulfilled and love unfulfilled, how could there be any difference between any other pair of opposites? Was he not freed, for the rest of his life, from choice?

> For what could it matter? Let him take this course, or this course, but still behind the mind, on some other level, the way he had rejected was being simultaneously worked out and the same conclusion was being reached. What did it matter which road he took if they both led to

the same place? He looked at the tree-tops in the wind. What control
could he hope to have over the maddened surface of things?

(*Jill* 242–3)

The role of "choice", and of what "behind the mind" is being "worked
out" without our knowing, is a concern to which Larkin would return
in *A Girl in Winter* and throughout his work. The implied longing
to be "freed . . . from choice" and from the concern with what one
is or might be, is to appear again in the poetry — in "Absences", in
"Wants" and above all in "At Grass". This theme of the self and its
relation to the past, also emerges when Kemp visits his home after
the bombing of Huddersford:

> It was as if he had been told: all the past is cancelled: all the suffering
> connected with that town, all your childhood, is wiped out. Now there
> is a fresh start for you: you are no longer governed by what has gone
> before. (*Jill* 219)

The movement of the wind outside Kemp's window is clearly associated with the acceptance of change, of "the maddened surface of
things". In *The North Ship*, compiled a little after *Jill* was completed,
the wind suggests destructive impulses, but also suggests breaking
free, which can be dangerous though desirable. It is contrasted there
with images of control and containment. For Kemp, his restricted
finances and his social uncertainty point to the type of control that
had been a feature of his background and that, inhumanly, had been
the basis of his scholarly success. He must plan his very meagre
amount of money week by week, and entering Warner's world means
the breaking of such plans. Yet the lack of need for such planning is
what attracts him to Warner:

> . . . no one felt this lapsing, lifting, turning and returning motion like
> a crowd of gulls. Knowing their desires they went straight for them.
> And although he knew his, going straight for them was like firing a
> gun in a dream: things locked and jammed, every possible bewildering
> mistake interfered. (*Jill* 189)

In contrast, when he visits Whitbread and his scholarship friends:
"All their actions were characterized by this scrupulous convention
. . . There was no luxury or waste or freedom in their company . . ."
(*Jill* 124) Pressures for control and for freedom compete in all of
Larkin's work.

Whitbread shows clearly what Kemp's life could have been at Oxford and what the basis of his sense of identity could have been. The

outcome of the novel is carefully hinted at in Kemp's initial reaction
to Whitbread:

> He had a pale stubbly head, queerly like a doormouse, and thick steel-
> rimmed spectacles: he spoke with a flat Yorkshire accent that made
> John suppose wrongly that he had a sense of humour. John could tell
> by his clothes that he was not well-off, and he remembered a phrase
> from one of his mother's letters . . . that said that she hoped he had
> made some friends "of his own standing". With a gust of indignation
> he realized that she meant people like Whitbread.   (*Jill* 51)

Whitbread's educational success is as firm an assertion in the novel as
Warner's eventual sexual conquest. Whitbread has as decided an individuality as Warner, though the fullness of his character is achieved
with an astounding parsimony of words compared with the development of Warner's character, which is perhaps overdone in terms of
the economy of the book as a whole.

Carefulness with food is a feature of Kemp's regimen as it was of
his background; and nervousness about eating gives us the novel's first
notable scene. In contrast, Warner eats with abandon and vulgarity
and makes free with other people's food. When Kemp, towards the
climax of the novel, feels himself crossing over into Warner's world,
he defaces Whitbread's rooms with his valuable rations. Food, in the
form of a gesture of love, is what Kemp offers Gillian, extravagantly.
Andrew Motion has suggested that those scenes are "a means of expressing what is predominantly a sexual anxiety".[5] Visiting rooms
with food as sociability was the pattern of Oxford undergraduate life;
and those who remember 1943 will perhaps feel that no explanation
for a preoccupation with eating was then necessary. Nonetheless, the
suggestion is compelling that the incidents with food are a means
of putting before the reader attitudes to appetite and indulgence —
and, by implication, sexual appetite and indulgence. Indeed, the
contrast between the attitudes of Warner and Whitbread to food is
one between selfishness and scrupulousness; and this contrast is at
the root of Kemp's relation to his own appetites. Warner's ability to
"go straight for" what he desires is, for the reader, clearly an aspect
of his selfishness; but for Kemp this ability of Warner's seems something of a mystery. The nexus between selfishness and fulfilment —
particularly sexual fulfilment — is obscured by Kemp's awareness of
his shyness and his envy of Warner's *savoir faire*. The novel does
not bring a clear focus to this area of feeling; and this was to be true
of Larkin's treatment of it in later work, such as "Self's the Man",
"Places Loved Ones" and "Life with a Hole in It".

What distinguishes Kemp is his plasticity. In contrast to the assertiveness of Warner and Whitbread, he is easily moved to experience embarrassment, humiliation, dejection and fear of failure. The changes in his response to Warner and Whitbread constitute an important thread in the development of the book. Yet Kemp is not *trapped* in his relation with Warner, and rejects offered opportunities to escape, such as the opportunity to have tutorials alone. Although Kemp is the "hero" of the book, he is somewhat pitiable, somewhat a victim: he has a passive, reactive relation to experience frequently encountered in Larkin's work.

It is questionable whether the tensions of the novel arise from Kemp's trying to get above his class, or whether the characteristics of Whitbread and Warner are manifestations of class or of contrasting human values. In fact, there does not seem to be any strong element of class conflict in the book. To see the book as a precursor to "Movement" novels (*Jill* 11) can hide the book's real concerns. Even an examination of the themes in *Jill* that are to reappear in Larkin's later work can obscure the novel's true quality through the emphasis they suggest.

The book is extremely funny, and the fun is not all associated with the antics of Christopher Warner: the opening scene, in which the nervous John Kemp is afraid to eat his sandwiches in public on the train and retires to the lavatory, only to end up thrusting his lunch out of the window as soon as someone bangs on the door, is one of the best in the book and highly characteristic. It has the same tone as Christopher Warner's description of how he smashed up someone's room looking for something to eat in the middle of the night when dead drunk. Such scenes have little in common with the unhistrionic realism of a book like *The Senior Commoner* by Julian Hall, a novel about Eton that both Larkin and Amis have said was important to them at the time. The humorous scenes clearly owe a great deal to one of Larkin's lasting admirations — Evelyn Waugh. Kemp's purchase of the bow tie; the drunken scene in which he smears Whitbread's room with food (a scene that would embody, in a different idiom, the most vicious action in the book); the climactic scene where he ends up thrown into a fountain; the over-lavish tea he prepares for Jill, only to find Elizabeth at his door; and the treatment of Kemp's nervousness in many of the Oxford scenes: all have the flavour of Waugh. In many respects, Warner, a Waughian character, is the best achieved in the book.

Jill is the work of someone twenty-one and twenty-two, drawing on the experiences of life and fiction that he has gathered up to that time.

It is conventionally realistic in the presentation of its material and directly sequential in narrative, except for a section where it goes back to establish the background of the hero. Nonetheless, the mechanics of its construction do obtrude. Certain aspects seem to spring from intimately known experience: the shyness and attendant loneliness that Larkin has described as being part of his youth; the ambience of undergraduate experience; the telling description of Huddersford (Coventry) after the blitz; or the description of the sensation of entering a different world that stepping into the Oxford market from the High gave in those days. Christopher Warner, a type common enough in Oxford, is more consistently presented than Kemp himself, whose working class background was alien to Larkin. Indeed, the contrast between Kemp after he invents Jill and the inhumanly dour person he was before that, has been remarked upon. It is often argued that Kemp could never have developed the fantasies of upper-middle class girls' school life that he suddenly escapes into. As Kingsley Amis has reported, "the Willow Gables fantasy had come to independent life as a kind of pastiche of schoolgirl stories. When the book finally appeared I was amazed at the skill that half concealed the utter incongruity of that episode with the rest of the material."[6]

If *Jill* does not leave the reader so clear about the experience of the novel as does *A Girl in Winter*, this is a constructional fault not unusual in a first novel, where experiences and attitudes may be taken too rawly from life. Yet it gives us the whole entanglement of Puritan feeling: concern for others; control; scrupulousness and suspicion of appetite; withholding and exclusion. With these feelings it associates a sense of unavoidable exclusion. Such feelings are to be encountered and explored throughout Larkin's work.

Again, in *A Girl in Winter*, Larkin draws, with cunning economy, on the material of his immediate experience. His home city of Coventry gave him the topography of his town; but the experience of being alone, cut off from friends and his former life, belongs to his time at Wellington. Katherine, like Larkin, works in a library, though not from choice. Exiled in wartime England, she is faced with the problem that must have been pressing for her author: what to make of a life of work that did not arise from one's aspirations. The long-flash back to a pre-war summer of innocent assurance must have had a powerful personal significance for Larkin; while his own nervousness and insecurity with people is used in the wartime scenes. Even Katherine's emerging sense that marriage might not be her destiny may have corresponded to Larkin's own sense of what life might hold for him. Yet, in contrast with *Jill*, everything is perfectly subdued to its role in the economy of the novel.

Katherine has escaped from wartime Europe to England and is working in a library in a small provincial town. The story takes place on one day in winter when she is waiting for a letter from Robin Fennel, who was her pen-pal before the war, and with whose family she had stayed one summer. Seeing by chance an announcement in the paper that the child of Robin's sister Jane had died, she was finally prompted to get in touch with the family again. She is puzzled as to what to expect from the revival of the relationship; but the expectation of Robin's letter and possible visit is what her life is moving towards throughout the story — a revelation or a turning point. It exists as a focus of hope in a life in which she is extraordinarily isolated among people who are, both for her and the reader, depressingly petty and ordinary — and also strange.

Much of the first part of the story is taken up with Katherine's escorting a junior at the library, Miss Green, to a dentist, because she has an infected tooth. Locked in her pain, Miss Green seems more distant to Katherine than she normally would; yet sympathy for her has the effect of bringing Katherine out of herself. The dentist they find in somewhat run-down premises is deaf and does not fully understand what Katherine says to him, increasing the sense of isolation in human relationships that gives the predominant tone to the novel. The removal of the tooth is rather brutally described. Katherine takes Miss Green home, to find Robin's letter announcing his arrival within the hour. Shortly thereafter she realizes that she has taken someone's else's bag in mistake for Miss Green's at the dentist, and that she must recover the lost bag. Looking for some identification in the bag she has, she finds an envelope addressed to a woman, and has the impression that the handwriting is that of Mr. Anstey, the pettifogging head of her branch of the library.

This concludes the first part of the novel. The second part is concerned with Katherine's visit to the Fennel's before the war. Physically, it seems a long idyll of English rural life, with punting on the Thames and a visit to a gymkhana that is like a precursor of the poem "Show Saturday". Yet it proves to be fraught with irony; for it is not Robin who has wanted to invite Katherine, but her sister Jane, who is unable to find anything to do with her life. The section ends with Robin clumsily attempting to embrace an unwilling Katherine, and with Jane accepting an offer of marriage for which she had given no previous hint of interest.

The third section returns to the wartime day, with Katherine aware that Robin may arrive at any time, yet forced to go looking for Miss Green's missing bag. She decides to leave the outcome of the afternoon to chance, and goes to the address, in a poorer part of town, that she has found in the bag. There she meets Miss Parbury, who quite clearly is involved with Mr. Anstey, but who cannot accept his offer of marriage because of her duty to her ailing mother. Katherine retrieves the bag and returns to the library, where she is sent for by Mr. Anstey who gives her a message that Robin is not coming. He berates her for her long absence, and she explodes at him, revealing her knowledge of Miss Parbury. When she returns home after the library has closed, she finds a slightly drunk Robin waiting at her door. He is no longer the poised young man she knew and she is disappointed. He, for his part, seems to expect to go to bed with her; and, after making him a meal, she does so, without feeling anything for him. The novel ends with them in bed, waiting for it to be time for Robin to catch a late train back to his unit, with which he is soon to embark for service overseas.

Katherine's life is one of acute uneventfulness, subject to a routine of eating, work and unrewarding leisure, with its attendant boredom: "She ate, slept and worked . . ." (*AGW* 181) The physical setting is in every instance drab. Katherine lived in "an old-fashioned building, with extinct gas-brackets on the walls, and no light on the narrow flights: carpets gave way above the first floor to linoleum . . . on the top landing . . . a sink . . . had been converted from a primitive laboratory to a primitive kitchen." (*AGW* 50) There is no joy in human contact: Miss Feather had an "untidy grey head" (*AGW* 13); Miss Green "looked pale and badly-fed: her thick-lensed spectacles stretched over her ears . . ." (*AGW* 28); while Mr. Anstey was "a thin, wizened man of forty" with "hair carefully oiled" who "resembled a clerk at a railway station who had suffered from shell-shock" (*AGW* 16). Even the beautiful summer holiday of the past had been a procession of activities that took her close to boredom.

Several important themes of Larkin's later work are made explicit in this novel, written when Larkin was only twenty-three. Most obvious is the pervasive loneliness of people inhabiting "their separate ugly worlds" (*AGW* 233) — something that links *A Girl in Winter* with *Jill*. However, in *Jill* loneliness and the attendant awkwardness of John Kemp are felt as an affliction — a sense of things that is qualified only by the attitude of the character Minerva in the Willow Gables fantasy. In *A Girl in Winter* we have a carefully structured fable of loneliness and renunciation, in which their meaning is explored.

Loneliness is perceived both as a possible destiny and as a necessary consequence of other human impulses. In *Jill*, Kemp sees himself as unable to make the direct step from desire to action and fulfilment that seems to come naturally to Warner. In contrast, towards the end of *A Girl in Winter*, Katherine reflects on the problem of selfishness and happiness: "Having tried for so long to live for herself alone, having concluded that not even the maximum selfishness would secure the happiness she felt herself entitled to, it was disturbing to meet one who valued these things lightly." (*AGW* 205) These reflections are occasioned by her encounter with Miss Parbury, who refuses to set aside her duty to her mother (whose condition is such that she frequently does not know who her daughter is) in order to accept Mr. Anstey's offer of marriage. She accepts instead a life of loneliness and deprivation; and her comment on that choice enunciates a key moral position for Larkin: "I can't understand . . . what people mean by a duty to oneself." (*AGW* 201) Here, for once, there is a clear focussing on Larkin's abiding concern with selfishness. It is noteworthy that, in contrast with *Jill* and some of the poems he wrote later in life, the problem is distanced from any concerns with sexual gratification with which the reader (or the author) might have any involvement.

These revelations of Mr. Anstey's feelings for Miss Parbury play an important part in the development of the novel: Katherine finds the figure of Mr. Anstey "blurring in her mind, no longer a sharply-cut target for loathing." (*AGW* 189) Later "she realized with annoyance that she could not hate him as simply as she had done, now that she had come across this part of him that had no bearing on her. For her conception of him as a hostile cartoon she had to substitute a person who had and could evoke feelings, who would undertake the support of an old woman, and on whose account she had seen another crying." (*AGW* 204–205) As with the sympathy she feels for Miss Green in her pain, this revelation is part of the maturing process that Katherine undergoes — a part of her escape from her sense of the importance of what is happening in her own world.

As a person, Miss Parbury does not convey the impression that she is destined for a rich fulfilment: "From the gawkiness of youth she was passing to the grotesqueness of old age, and at no point would she touch the handsomeness of maturity." (*AGW* 196) We are reminded of the misshapen fortunes met in "Faith Healing" or of the pathetically slight hold on destiny of the mothers in "Afternoons", who are being pushed "to the side of their own lives". The sense that our destinies are revealed to us as much as chosen is something discovered by Katherine in the course of her day: ". . . she had believed for a long time that a person's life is directed mainly by their actions, and these in turn are directed by their personality, which is not self-chosen in the first place and modifies itself quite independently of their wishes afterwards." (*AGW* 185) This is a truth offered in "Dockery and Son"; and it is not presented here as a passing reflection.

The story of the book is the unfolding of Katherine's hopes concerning the renewal of her acquaintance with the Fennels. The events of the summer that form the middle section of the book constitute a centre of incipience. In themselves they are ironical, for Katherine discovers that it was not Robin who invited her, but the bored Jane; and that Jane's presence at all times was not an attempt to prevent Robin from falling in love with her (as she had imagined) because he had no wish to. Entrapped in her illusion, she missed an opportunity to derive pleasure from the visit and to discover a kindred spirit in Jane: "Now that the surface of their relations had quietened in her mind, she saw that only her inquisitive imagination had prevented the holiday being like this from the evening she arrived — an untroubled expanse resembling a lake between hills . . . Now that it was too late, she felt that all the time she had been paying attention to the wrong things." (*AGW* 167) The depth of Jane's longing for a friend, which had gone unnoticed, is revealed in Katherine's final meeting with Robin, when she learns that Jane had named her daughter after her — "Lucy Katherine".

The final outcome of the pre-war summer, Robin's visit to her in the war-time winter, is also a thing of irony. She had dreamed that he might marry her, or at least carry her off from the empty life she led. Instead, when she meets him, he is not what he had been, and she does not want him; yet she gives herself to him, merely because he begs her to, with no sense that their relationship might have a future. At the close, as in *Jill*, there is an acceptance of the movement of destiny, though it is much more explicit: "Unsatisfied dreams rose and fell about them, crying out against their implacability, but in the end glad that such order, such destiny, existed." (*AGW* 248) The ticking of the clock and the falling of the snowflakes mark the inexorability of this process.

The misunderstandings of the pre-war summer and the ironies of Katherine's re-encounter with Robin, only exacerbate the sense of isolation and entrapment within her life that she feels, and that so many characters exemplify. The misunderstanding and ironies also convey Larkin's sense of the deceptiveness of experience — a theme later dominant in *The Less Deceived*. This deceptiveness is something that obtrudes between us and the implementation of our choices and between us and the discovery of what we are destined to become. Opportunity is not always what it seems to be, or it goes unnoticed; while often we are, ourselves, not what we take ourselves to be.

Looking back, Larkin said "*A Girl in Winter*, which I always think of as *The Kingdom of Winter* . . . I do think it's remarkably . . . *knowing* . . . not really mature, or wise, just incredibly clever. By my standards, I mean." ("An Interview with *Paris Review*", *RW* 63) Like *Jill*, it is about a loneliness that leads to acceptance after a dreamed of transforming event fails to fulfil its promise. However, it is much better constructed than *Jill*. The control of pace and rhythm, so crucial to the success of narrative, is sensitive and unfaltering. If the novel has any technical failing, it is its proclivity for metaphor:

> She was angry with herself for behaving unreasonably and for the knowledge that she was still not quite controlled. What was wrong, to make her rush away from her lodging, leaving no message and making no arrangements? . . . Her feelings were like a flight of birds that swoop over to one corner of a field and then stop, all trembling equidistantly in the air, and then come streaming back, like a banner tossed first one way, then the other. Had there been anything more exciting than the thought of this letter?   (*AGW* 178)

The presentation of her emotional predicament is much more effective in terms of what she had done than in the form of the double layer of metaphor that is so grandly offered. This reaching for metaphor is frequent in the latter part of the book; yet it is more impressive than effective.

Such "poetic" writing was fashionable with some novelists in the days when *A Girl in Winter* was written, though Larkin said of his tastes at that time: "My favorite novelists were Lawrence, Isherwood, Maugham, Waugh — oh, and George Moore. I was on a great Moore kick at that time: probably he was at the bottom of my style, then . . . I hadn't read Elizabeth Bowen." ("An Interview with *Paris Review*", *RW* 64) Moore's *Ester Waters* is a story of loneliness told from a woman's perspective by a male author. Elizabeth Bowen is among the writers who have been suggested as models for the author of *A Girl in Winter*. So too has Henry Green; though his mannered prose, his imagistic construction and his use of speech to place people socially, have little in common stylistically with *A Girl in Winter*. Mention by Larkin of Waugh reminds one that the poised, sensitive, poetic second novel is not devoid of the humour of the first. Mr. Anstey's four page ticking-off of Katherine is a *tour de force*, while

Stormalong's account of a tiger hunt is in the Christopher Warner manner:

> You'd imagine you'd feel safe as houses up on an elephant . . . At least you do till our friend stripes comes along. But you see it's like this. The tiger goes for the elephant. . .right up on an elephant's head —clinging, you know, with the claws in. And then it all depends how the elephant behaves. It's liable to get bothered, and anything may happen. It may try to shake the tiger off, and only succeed in shaking the poor bloke out of the howdah . . . What it ought to do is stand still and let the guns pot the tiger till it drops off. But they don't always see it that way.   (*AGW* 168)

A Girl in Winter was, in fact, extremely sophisticated in its construction for an English novel of its day — not to mention a novel by a young man of 23. What is immediately notable is the unobtrusiveness of the author, whose presence is felt largely through the steady control of tone. The action of the story grows out of the development and interplay of the feelings of the characters, and is revealed to the reader through the expression of those feelings. The author in fact allows himself to know directly only the feelings of his principal character: this steady maintenance of narrative viewpoint not only gives concentration to the story, but is in itself rather unusual in an English novel of the period. It is through the feelings of the central character that the story is interpreted to us — though devices of juxtaposition of event and character, such as the contrast between Robin's letter and Mr. Anstey's letter, are utilized to lead the reader to a fuller perspective than that achieved by the leading character. The viewpoint of that character is a developing one, conditioned by her own knowledge of events and by her reaction to them. This is most notable in the matter of the misunderstandings that are so important to the book's development. The reader is drawn into these misunderstandings, while through their unravelment the import of the book is revealed. The chief character is the one with whose valuations we are led to sympathize, though these valuations are discovered through the action of the story. She is what Henry James called a "fine central intelligence" — one to whom the action occurs and through the quality of whose awareness it is interpreted.

All of this gives to the novel great concentration. The unity of action is not achieved, however, merely by focussing it all through the sensibility of Katherine. The central action takes place in one town in one day, and the one expected event with which it concludes, the coming of Robin, dominates the day. Into the story of this day

is interpolated the flash-back that relates the story of the holiday
that is the source of the anticipated meeting and the meaning it is
hoped it will reveal. The relationship of the parts reminds one of
Virginia Woolf's *To the Lighthouse*, not because the third part takes
the characters to a fulfilment they have always sought, but because
the meaning of the past is revealed in the final encounter, and because
that encounter has been looked forward to throughout the book as
a completing of the present through contact with a meaningful past.
There is something in Larkin's book of Woolf's sense of the past
completing itself in the present; and, in the flashback, of the past
awaiting a future that will complete it. In *A Girl in Winter*, however,
that completion is ironic and dubious, involving the revelation that
expansive developments are not what one is to expect of life.

Mention of Virginia Woolf reminds one how powerfully scene and
weather are utilized by Larkin to create moods. The opening is reminiscent of two scene-setting passages in Virginia Woolf's *Orlando*
(1928):

> There had been no more snow during the night, but because the frost
> continued so that the drifts lay where they had fallen, people told each
> other there was more to come. And when it grew lighter, it seemed
> that they were right, for there was no sun, only one vast shell of cloud
> over the fields and woods. In contrast to the snow the sky looked
> brown. Indeed, without the snow the morning would have resembled
> a January nightfall, for what light there was seemed to rise up from it.
>
> It lay in ditches and in hollows in the fields, where only birds walked.
> In some lanes the wind had swept it up faultlessly to the very tops
> of the hedges. Villages were cut off until gangs of men could clear a
> passage on the roads; the labourers could not go out to work, and on
> the aerodromes near these villages all flying remained cancelled.
>
> (*AGW* 11)
>
> The Great Frost was, historians tell us, the most severe that has ever
> visited these islands. Birds froze in mid-air and fell like stones to the
> ground . . . The mortality among sheep and cattle was enormous.[7]
>
> (*Orlando*)
>
> The great cloud which hung, not only over London, but over the whole
> of the British Isles on the first day of the nine-teenth century stayed, or
> rather, did not stay, for it was buffeted about constantly by blustering
> gales, long enough to have extraordinary consequences upon those who
> lived beneath its shadow. A change seemed to have come over the
> climate of England. Rain fell infrequently, but only in fitful gusts,

which were no sooner over than they began again. The sun shone of course, but it was so girt about with clouds and the air was so saturated with water, that its beams were discoloured and purples, oranges, and reds of a dull sort took the place of the more positive landscapes of the eighteenth century. Under this bruised and sullen canopy the green of cabbages was less intense, the white of the snow was muddied.[8]

(*Orlando*)

The debt to Woolf — if there is one — lies as much in the conception of orchestrating the novel in this way as in the phrasing itself. Larkin's opening is drawn to our attention as a set piece by the fact that it constitutes the entire first chapter. Its note is taken up again at the conclusion of the novel and in the opening words of its third section.

But the snow did not come. The sky remained as immovable as a pebble frozen in the surface of a pond. (*AGW* 177)

Again, this opening chapter of the final section is purely descriptive and does not involve any of the characters of the novel. This is not true of the opening of the middle section, though the contrasting evocation of summer is as intense as the descriptions of the winter scenes:

The morning when she came to England for the first time had been still and hot: not an accidental fine day, but one of a series that had already lasted a week. Each had seemed more flawless than the one before it, as if in their slow gathering of depth and placidity they were progressing towards perfection. The sky was deep blue as if made richer by the endless recession of past summers: the sea smooth, and when a wave lifted the sun shone through it as through a transparent green window. (*AGW* 67)

While the passage is a set piece, it is worth remarking that there is nothing so evocative and lacking in mannerism to be found in Larkin's poetry up to that time. Equally, there is to be found in the novel a rendering of the provincial urban scene, as the poetic ambience of human lives and human feeling, that is not achieved in the poetry for some years to come.

Both novels are narrated from the viewpoint of the central character, though the narrative voice is that of the author, who looks over the shoulder of his main character. In *Jill*, in particular, Larkin tells his story with great verve, skillfully manipulating the intensity of detail and the length of incident to control pace — something facilitated by there being no division into chapters. However, there are shifts

and waverings of viewpoint such as are not found in *A Girl in Winter*.
Having got his hero in bed with pneumonia, Larkin is forced to han-
dle his conclusion as third person narration, giving concluding scenes
to Kemp's parents and to Christopher and his girl-friend; though the
final image of the small dog who growls at Elizabeth when she tries
to coax him has a powerful if elusive focussing effect. Similarly, after
the intoxicated Kemp has kissed Jill, he is taken to be dumped in
the fountain, but the reader remains behind to hear the reactions of
Elizabeth and Jill, and the drop into the fountain is off-stage. The
flashback to Kemp's schooldays takes up one tenth of the novel, and
is told from the point of view of Kemp's teacher, Mr. Crouch. It
establishes Kemp's background in a way that is later useful, but it
constitutes a severe interruption of focus and a diffusion of the established tone. In contrast, the narrative viewpoint is sustained without
blemish in *A Girl in Winter*.

Both of Larkin's novels were completed by the middle of 1945, and
while Larkin was still in Wellington. He continued to regard himself
as a novelist after the publication of *A Girl in Winter*. In 1945 he
had in mind "a third book in which the central character will pick
up where Katherine left off and develop *logically* back to life again."[9]
In 1947, he told Alan Pringle of Faber and Faber, "I have made an
infinitely tentative start on another book."[10] The novel was evidently
"a seriocomic account of the gradual involvement of a rising young
executive in the motor industry, Sam Wagstaff, with a working-class
girl he knocks down in his car coming home from the factory", a
description that suggests a Movement flavour.[11] In 1948 he reported
that "The novel becomes clearer to me in conception as time to work
on it becomes shorter";[12] while in February 1950, he confessed that
he had "been trying to write novels and failing either to finish them
or to make them worth finishing . . ."[13] In 1953 he confirmed that this
was still the case. By then he had come to see that he had "to leave
uncompleted" the novel he had been working on "after five years of
fruitless toil. Giving it up meant giving up also the ambitions with
which he had begun his career as a writer."[14]

The process involved in the recognition that he was not to find his
way with the novel, but that the concerns that he had had as a novelist would find expression in poetry, is one that probably remained
mysterious to Larkin and is likely to remain so for his readers. Looking back on his published novels, he said "I think they were over-sized
poems. They were certainly written with intense care for detail. If
one word was used on page 15 I didn't re-use it on page 115. But
they're not very good novels."[15] Possibly he had in mind the taste

for metaphorical flights evinced in *A Girl in Winter*. The idea of the novel as poem was in the air when Larkin was trying to write the novels that never got published, and it evidently appealed to him. "When I was young, *Scrutiny* ran a series of articles under the general heading of 'The Novel as Dramatic Poem'. That was stimulating, an exciting conception. Something that was both a poem and a novel." ("An Interview with *Paris Review*", *RW* 63) The series began in *Scrutiny* in the Spring, 1947 issue with F.R. Leavis's essay on *Hard Times*, though several of the other essays that made up Leavis's influential *The Great Tradition* (1948) had appeared in earlier issues. For Leavis, the novel as conceived by Henry James and Joseph Conrad provided a touchstone of what fiction should be; and, as we have seen, *A Girl in Winter* measures up well in this respect, with its scrupulously sustained point of view and narrative viewpoint and its careful orchestration of scene and image.

This does not seem to have continued to recommend itself to Larkin as the ideal form of the novel. In 1982 he said "I think a novel should follow the fortunes of more than one character." ("An Interview with *Paris Review*", *RW* 63) His favourite novelists then included Anthony Powell and Barbara Pym, both of whom wrote novels with large castes of characters. Barbara Pym's *A Few Green Leaves* (1980) presents a picture of a village, and its principal character, Emma, is more a centre of focus than a heroine. Her books have a quality that brings to mind the "studied circumstantial irrelevancy" that Larkin saw as contributing so much to the sense of life in Julian Hall's *The Senior Commoner*, a novel he had discovered in his younger days and continued to admire throughout his life. ("The Traffic in the Distance", *RW* 276) Barbara Pym's style of novel is decidedly English, and has little place for the Jamesian control of narrative viewpoint. It has far more in common with the novel as written by Trollope. This would seem to have been Larkin's mature idea of what a novel should be; and this is consonant with his saying, in 1973, that "he thinks that the successful novelist must be interested in other people and he does not think that he is."[16] It is a very English attitude to the novel; yet many great works of fiction have been written at the length of *A Girl in Winter* and after its pattern, particularly by American and European writers. Whether these later attitudes had anything to do with Larkin's ceasing to write fiction it is hard to say. Many will be glad he came to devote all his creative energy to poetry. For him, at the time, it involved a hard disappointment.

Whether Larkin's ambitions as a novelist were a misdirection of his talents and whether, if his fiction had been better received, he might have continued to write novels are questions that cannot be answered. Certainly, there is every sign that, had he been drawn to attempt a "Movement" novel on the lines of John Wain's *Hurry on Down* (1953) or Kingsley Amis's *Lucky Jim* (1954) — picaresque novels with a large caste of minor characters — he might still have been led to his later stricture that the novelist is interested in many other people and he was not. His novels remain, in any case, the product of his younger years; and, apart from their intrinsic value, they invite examination in terms of their contribution to the development of the idiom of his mature poetry.

We encounter, consciously developed, major themes of Larkin's later work: loneliness; the role of illusion and the deceptions associated with it; misunderstanding; and, above, the role of choice in determining our destinies. There exist, too, pressures that seem not to be fully understood, especially in *Jill* — pressures associated with what one might term a puritanism of feeling: control and suspicion of appetite; withholding and exclusion. Such concerns come into clear focus in the role that the recognition of her selfishness has in the maturing of Katherine in *A Girl in Winter*; but they were to remain somewhat intractable for the mature Larkin, particularly where sexual relations or sexual gratification were concerned.

The idiom of the novels, despite the deft handling of flashback and narrative viewpoint in *A Girl in Winter*, is that of straightforward realist narrative by a third person narrator. We encounter none of the innovations of modernism, such as the interior monologue or distortions of form. The humour of *Jill*, often at the expense of the autobiographically based hero, points forward to the self-deprecating humour of poems like "Poetry of Departures" or "Reasons for Attendance".

Above all, the novels seemed to provide a place in which, at that time, Larkin could be himself more than in his poetry. In them there is hardly any sense of a manner that must be attained, a mode of dealing with material that is mandatory; whereas, in the poetry, the manner of Yeats imposes itself as a model, intruding between the writer and his experience. Within the novels — and especially in *A Girl In Winter* — an individual sense of things was developed that could later be carried over into the poetry, when the example of Hardy showed Larkin the possibilities for poetry contained in his own world. The realistic, contemporary idiom of the fiction linked up, at that point, with the poetry of his earlier admirations, Auden and MacNeice, making them again available as models. In addition, it linked up with the poetry of John Betjeman, the master of contempory detail, who became so important to Larkin.

But that was all still well into the future when he completed *A Girl in Winter* in 1945 at the age of 23. He was to continue to try to write novels for another four years.

Chapter 3

THREE YEARS TRYING TO WRITE LIKE YEATS

The years in Shropshire also saw a great deal of poetry written. Shortly after arriving in Wellington, Larkin began using the "large dark green manuscript book", the first of a long series that he was to use throughout his life. With his "complete Yeats stolen from the local girls' school", he "used to limber up by turning the pages", though the volume he had was the "1933 plum-coloured Macmillan edition, which stopped at 'A Woman Young and Old'" so that he "never absorbed the harsher last poems". (Intro. to *NS*, *RW* 28–29)

The visit of Vernon Watkins to the English club early in 1943 had been decisive, and Larkin was to spend "the next three years trying to write like Yeats" (Intro. to *NS*, *RW* 29): "it wasn't so much enthusiasm for Yeats as for Vernon — he has such tremendous sincerity, and more purity of feeling for poetry than I've ever met in anyone else since".[1] Larkin recorded that "his likes became my likes, his methods my methods, or attempted methods". ("Vernon Watkins", *RW* 41) He was taken by Watkins into a different world of poetry from that of his earlier admiration, Auden. As he wrote, when Watkins's *Cypress and Acacia* was published in 1959, "The visible world is for him both text and symbol, and his prevailing mood is present ecstatic."[2]

Born in 1906, Watkins was sixteen years older than Larkin. He had written something like a thousand poems during the late twenties and early thirties without publishing any of them, until he met Dylan Thomas in a Swansea bookshop. After that, a few poems began to appear in periodicals; but he gained attention with his first book, *The Ballad of the Mari Lwyd*, published by Faber and Faber in 1941, when he was thirty-five. Its acclaim was presumably the reason for his being asked to address the Oxford English Club. It gained considerable attention, and was one of the first books brought out by a publisher of standing in a manner that came to be called "the New Romanticism". In the same year, poems by Watkins appeared in *The White Horseman*, the second anthology brought together by the Apocalypse Movement; though Watkins's controlled serenity has

nothing in common with the inflated rhetoric of most of the contributors to that anthology. Watkins belonged to the same generation as
Auden, MacNeice, or William Empson. What distinguished his poetry most noticeably from theirs was the absence of irony — a tone
quite inimical to Watkins. His reading of Yeats to the English Club
had been "unashamedly sonorous". ("Vernon Watkins", *RW* 40)

The encounter with Watkins was a conversion of the type not unusual for young men of twenty-one. Nor was the direction of that
conversion surprising. The coming of the war and the Hitler-Stalin
pact of 1939 had brought an abrupt end to the left-wing literary movement that had dominated the writing of the thirties, and with which
Larkin's earlier model, Auden, had been associated. Many of the
younger poets declared themselves to be "Romantics", as had Sidney
Keyes in *Eight Oxford Poets*; and a cultivation of the eternal verities
and respect for commonplace emotions replaced the knowing Marxist
and Freudian interpretation of action and motive characteristic of the
previous decade. Christianity was rampant in the Oxford of the day.
David Wright found himself drawn into the ambience of the Romanticism of Keyes and Heath-Stubbs; and, among the young poets in
Oxford in the early forties, only Alan Ross and Norman Hampson
made a mark in a manner inspired by the poets of the thirties.

Watkins affected Larkin in one other important way. He had left
Cambridge in the late twenties — the Cambridge of I.A. Richards and
William Empson — in disgust at the prevalent rationalism. After an
emotional breakdown, he returned to Swansea, where he remained a
bank clerk for the remainder of his working life, refusing promotion
for a life dedicated to poetry. As Larkin later wrote, "To anyone who,
like myself, was on the edge of the world of employment his example
was significant." ("Vernon Watkins", *RW* 42) How far that example
remained a guide for Larkin one cannot say; though, like Watkins, he
pursued a career from which his writing was in good measure isolated.

Larkin's first appearance in print after coming to Wellington was
in *Poetry from Oxford in Wartime*. As he was to explain, "the late
William Bell, then an undergraduate at Merton College, . . . set about
making up a collection which he eventually called *Poetry from Oxford
in Wartime*. Oxford poetry was reputedly in the ascendent again following the scarlet and yellow *Eight Oxford Poets* in 1941 . . . and Bell
no doubt thought it was time for another round-up. When his anthology came out in 1944 it had Allison, Heath-Stubbs and Roy Porter
from the earlier collection, and the new names of Bell himself, Francis
King, myself, Christopher Middleton and David Wright." (Intro. to
NS, *RW* 27) Bell was a friend of John Heath-Stubbs. He was killed

climbing the Matterhorn in 1948; and Heath-Stubbs edited a posthumous collection of his poetry *Mountains Beneath the Horizon* (1950). Bell was called up in 1944, so that the requests for contributions may have gone out in 1943 or early in 1944. The book is marked "first published in 1945"; but long delays were not unusual in the war years.

Poetry from Oxford in Wartime contained ten poems by Larkin, all of which were reprinted unchanged in *The North Ship* a year or so later: "I see a girl dragged by the wrists" (*NS* xx); "Love, we must part now" (*NS* xvi); "The bottle is drunk out" (*NS* xvi); "Heaviest of flowers" (*NS* xxvii); "The horns of the morning" (*NS* vii); "All catches alight" (*NS* i); "The moon is full tonight" (*NS* iii); "I put my mouth" (*NS* viii); "So through that unripe day" (*NS* xxx); and "Morning has spread again" (*NS* xxxv). None of these had appeared in print before; and none is to be found in his earliest notebook, the first poem in which is from October, 1944. They would seem then to have been written between June 1943 and October 1944, and were probably sent to the publishers before the latter date.

The mark of Larkin's new admirations is on all those poems. The longest, "I see a girl dragged by the wrists", is written in eight line Yeatsian stanzas, and built, after the manner of Yeats, around a set of contrasting images — "girl" and "snow" set over against "mortar and bricks" and "two old ragged men . . . with shovels and a spade". "Nothing so wild, nothing so glad as she/Rears up" for the speaker, and she represents a condition he would want to attain. Instead, he must "live the fact/That everything's remade/ With shovel and spade;/That each dull day and each despairing act//Builds up the crags from which the spirit leaps"; though he prays that "a snow-white unicorn,/ . . . may for sanctuary/Descend at last to me". The sense of exclusion from spontaneous fulfilment, set beside the need to accept everyday experience, offers a contrast encountered in Larkin's mature poetry. What makes the poem creak are the imported Yeatsian gestures: "Never in seventy years be more a man/Than now — a sack of meal upon two sticks"; "All that's content to wear a worn-out coat,/All actions done in patient hopelessness"; and "Damn all explanatory rhymes!"

Not all the poems echo Yeats so heavily; yet the limited emotional repertoire of up-beat feeling (with up-beat rhythms) or a drifting gloom, coupled with the lack of individuality of imagery ("Gulls" and "girls", "light" and "dark", "heart" and "head") cloys and defeats the reader's attempts to focus the feeling. Best are the more lyric moments:

I put my mouth
Close to running water:
Flow north, flow south,
It will not matter,
It is not love you will find.

I told the wind:
It took away my words:
It is not love you will find,
Only the bright-tongued birds,
Only a moon with no home.

It is not love you will find:
You have no limbs
Crying for stillness, you have no mind
Trembling with seraphim,
You have no death to come.

The movement of the poem, with the refrain shifted through the stanzas, has individuality and delicacy. The water and the wind, that go hither and thither, do not lead to love: though what will is not quite clear from the last stanzas, whose dated stage-properties — "Trembling with seraphim" — contrast with the transparency of the remainder of the poem. What leads to love, what breaks isolation, would be an important question in the later poetry.

Poetry from Oxford in Wartime led to greater things: "Before it appeared . . . the proprietor of the small but then well-known house that was producing the book wrote to some of its contributors enquiring if they would care to submit collections of their own work." ("Intro. to *NS*", *RW* 27) The "proprietor" was the notorious R.A. Caton of the Fortune Press; and his approaches seem to have resulted in a number of books that included Anthony de Hoghton's *24 Poems* (1945), W.J. Harvey's *The Uncertain Margin* (1946), Christopher Middleton's *Poems* (1944) and *Nocturne in Eden* (1945), and Roy Porter's *World in the Heart* (1944). Drummond Allison's *The Yellow Night* was also published posthumously by the Fortune Press in 1944; while William Bell had a volume of his own, *Elegies* (1945) (quite distinct from the group of poems of that name in *Mountains Beneath the Horizon*). Of the others in *Poetry from Oxford in Wartime*, John Heath-Stubbs already had a publisher; while David Wright was waiting for Tambimuttu to bring out his *Poems* in *Editions Poetry London* (submitted in 1943 but actually published in 1949).

The Fortune Press, because of some of the authors that went to it, gained quite a reputation, having published the first books of Roy Fuller, Julian Symons, Henry Treece and Ruthven Todd, and having

acquired the right to republish Dylan Thomas's *18 Poems* for fifteen
pounds. It was however essentially a vanity operation, and Caton
had no interest in modern poetry. He had started out in fine editions
and unusual erotica — something in which he had a real interest; and
seems quite accidently to have moved into publishing contemporary
poetry on commission in the late thirties with the approach of Julian
Symons and his friends from *Twentieth Century Verse*. A frequent
arrangement was for the author to agree to buy a certain number of
books; and, judging from the loose sheets remaining when the press
was sold, this would be all that was bound in some cases. Binding
was done at need, as the many "states" of most Fortune Press books
show; and the quality declined as years went by. Caton kept the books
in cartons in his Buckingham Palace Road quarters; and few Fortune
Press books ever appeared in bookstores. Larkin was evidently assured by him "that no agreement was necessary" (Intro. to *NS*, *RW*
27), and received and was charged nothing for the publication. The
wartime poetry boom must have given a fillip to Caton's activities;
and a book like *Poetry from Oxford in Wartime* would have sold well
enough, as each contributor would have generated a number of sales.

The North Ship was published in July, 1945 in an edition of no more
than 500 copies and at a price of six shillings — a usual price for a
book of poems in those days. It contained all the poems from *Poetry
from Oxford in Wartime*, but only three of the poems published while
Larkin was an undergraduate — "This was your place of birth . . .",
"Conscript" and "I dreamed of an out-thrust arm of land". On the
evidence of the notebook in which many of the new poems were first
drafted, Larkin must have typed out *The North Ship* on his "father's
portable Underwood" (Intro. to *NS*, *RW* 27) in November, 1944, in
his last days at home before going to Wellington.

Among the new poems there are a few that recall Larkin's earlier
more realistic style:

> Like the train's beat
> Swift language flutters the lips
> Of the Polish airgirl in the corner seat.   (XII)

However, particularly those poems from the autumn of 1944 have a
decided and consistent Yeatsian style, though some of the echoes are
rather gross:

> To write one song, I said,
> As sad as the sad wind
> That walks around my bed . . .   (XVII)

Nonetheless, the idiom is bent to the expression of concerns that are recognisably Larkin's and with an imagery that gives the book its character:

> Kick up the fire, and let the flames break loose
> To drive the shadows back;
> Prolong the talk on this or that excuse,
> Till the night comes to rest
> While some high bell is beating two o'clock.
> Yet when the guest
> Has stepped into the windy street, and gone,
> Who can confront
> The instantaneous grief of being alone?
> Or watch the sad increase
> Across the mind of this prolific plant,
> Dumb idleness?   (VI)

The "high bell" is redolent of Yeats; but the central feeling, loneliness, is a characteristic concern and is confronted with directness.

The use of the wind as an image of harshness and desolation is the most decided stylistic feature of the poems of this period. The wind blows through almost every one of them — "sad" (XVII), "wild" (XXII), "deafening" (IX) — and several images, such as the movement of branches or clouds, derive from it. It is associated with exultance as well as exposure and destruction: "Let me become an instrument sharply stringed/For all things to strike music as they please" (IX). It belongs to a pattern of imagery that involves escape, destructiveness and abandonment, against which are made gestures of control and protection.

> If hands could free you, heart,
>   Where would you fly?
> Far, beyond every part
> Of earth this running sky
> Makes desolate? Would you cross
> City and hill and sea,
>   If hands could set you free?
>
> I would not lift the latch;
>   For I could run
> Through fields, pit-valleys, catch
> All beauty under the sun —
> Still end in loss:
> I should find no bent arm, no bed
> To rest my head.   (XXIII)

Despite the lack of particularity of imagery, the poem is beautifully achieved, with its controlled movement supportive of the emotional changes. It follows, in its rejection of going away, the same pattern as the later and more celebrated "Poetry of Departures", though with a very different tone. Taken in the context of *The North Ship*, its circular, protective pattern suggests that departure is associated with abandoning oneself to energies over which one has no control. This tension between energy and control remained an important one for Larkin. At least three poems involve loss and estrangement in a dream, as though this were an obsessive psychological concern. Among them is the poem John Wain considered the most beautiful in the book:[3]

> Within the dream you said:
> Let us kiss then,
> In this room, in this bed,
> But when all's done
> We must not meet again.   (X)

The poems from which the book takes its title, a sequence "The North Ship: a Legend", are the only ones in which Larkin comes close to what he called "the undergrowth of *Poetry Quarterly* and *Poetry London*" (the principal organs of the "New Romanticism") (Intro. to *NS*, *RW* 28).

It has been usual to search *The North Ship* for evidence of some turning towards Larkin's mature style, since many of the poems in the next published volume, *XX Poems* (1951), show that manner fully attained. However, Larkin continued to write steadily in his notebook throughout 1945, and while there is an assured manner, it is still that of the later poems of *The North Ship*. He stayed with this style in the following year.

There are twenty completed poems from 1945 in the notebook, only two of which were published in Larkin's lifetime. At times the manner and the poetic furniture are too derivative from Yeats:

> I have loaded my soul
> With a malediction,
> And for beef and a big house
> Would sink it in a pool:
> *The black cowl and the white cowl*
> *Will not show us their faces.*

(from "Beggars":   5 Feb. 45
and 6 Oct. 46)

However, the poetry has its own personality, asserted most notably through the recurrent images of wind, cold, darkness and isolation found in *The North Ship*. If it returns too frequently to characteristic scenes of desolate renunciation, there are passages of arresting power:

> In a trap's teeth
> What are the words
> That break in a shriek,
> That break against death?

> (from "The Cry I Would Hear":
> 24 Oct. 45)

In nearly all the poems, one senses the impressive rhythmic control that was to be one of Larkin's abiding gifts.

In May, 1946, two of these poems, "Plymouth" and "Portrait", appeared in *Mandrake*, then still an undergraduate periodical, which had been started by John Wain at Oxford in 1945. The choice was a good one. "Plymouth" has a delicate particularity of detail that sets it apart from many of the other poems of the period:

> A box of teak, a box of sandlewood,
> A brass-ringed spyglass in a case,
> A coin, leaf-thin with many polishings,
> Last kingdom of a gold forgotten face,
> These lie about the room, and daily shine
> When new-built ships set out towards the sun . . .

> The hands that chose them rust upon a stick.
> Let my hands find such symbols, that can be
> Unnoticed in the casual light of day,
> Lying in wait for half a century
> To split chance lives across, that had not dreamed
> Such coasts had echoed, or such seabirds screamed.

These were in fact to be the last poems by Larkin to appear in a periodical until 1953. He apparently submitted five poems to *Canto*, a magazine whose "putative editor was called Arthur Ley". *Canto* never appeared; and Larkin later said that "Canto" was an earlier title for his book *In the Grip of Light* — though he subsequently corrected himself: "I should not like it to be thought that I should ever call a collection of my poems *Canto*, even when young."[4]

Between the end of 1945 and September 1946, composition was not so steady, and, in a long apparently unfinished piece, Larkin seems less sure of his idiom. Among the poems from this time is "Going" (not then so titled), one of Larkin's early successes, carried forward into *XX Poems* in 1951 and *The Less Deceived* in 1955.

> There is an evening coming in
> Across the fields, one never seen before,
> That lights no lamps.
>
> Silken it seems at a distance, yet
> When it is drawn up over the knees and breast
> It brings no comfort.
>
> Where has the tree gone, that locked
> Earth to the sky? What is under my hands,
> That I cannot feel?
>
> What loads my hands down?

As has been remarked, the poem "with its impassioned tone and its shadowy subject-matter might readily be mistaken for a *The North Ship* poem".[5] It has a symbolistic, impressionistic relation to experience, such as is encountered in Yeats's earlier work. It fitted easily enough into the context of *The Less Deceived*; yet, encountered in the notebook, it clearly has the same emotive feel and the same type of imagery as the poems that precede and succeed it, though it is free of Yeatsian mannerisms and its form does not derive from Yeats.

In September, 1946, Larkin moved to be sub-librarian at the then University College of Leicester. There followed a surprising burst of composition: in two weeks he completed seven poems — among them "The dedicated" and "Wedding-wind"; and followed this by writing a poem of a hundred and four lines in the next two weeks. In the following month he wrote a scene from a poetic drama set in the seventeenth century — "Night in the Plague"; and he continued to produce poems steadily until the end of the year. To these poems Larkin added six from *The North Ship* and eleven others written in the previous twelve months to make up a collection with "the portentous title of *In the Grip of Light*".[6]

It has become customary in writing about Larkin's early years to refer to his growing admiration for Hardy's poetry. Larkin has recalled how he began reading Hardy with a new respect in the early part of 1946; but there is nothing about *In the Grip of Light* to suggest this. While the style of the book is derivative, Larkin employs it with an assurance and facility that gives no sense that the writing has been disturbed by a new influence. He made only one draft of "Wedding-wind" for instance; and, while there is considerable alteration of detail, many lines stand in the printed version as they were first written. Indeed, the fluency of the month at the beginning of the autumn of 1946 is quite out of keeping with any sense of insecurity in his idiom. Yeatsian cadences and a Yeatsian choice of phrase are encountered throughout the book (though there are no poems that so deliberately cultivate Yeats's manner as there are in *The North Ship* or among the unpublished poems of 1945):

> Coming at last to night's most thankful springs,
> I meet a runner's image, sharply kept
> Ambered in memory from mythology;
> A man who never turned aside and slept,
> Nor put on masks of love; to whom all things
> Were shadowlike against the news he bore,
> Pale as the sky. . .

The emotional pattern is characteristic, with its tension between a longing for hope and consolation and the demands of a lonely, deprived but inescapable condition. The phrase "thankful springs" evokes the intense yearning for fulfilment that underlies many of the poems. The poem concludes with the image of the "full moon travelling through her shepherdless fields", suggesting a consolation on which the runner may not look — though the image itself is one of loneliness. Both the longing and the consolation are vulnerable to the calls of a dedication for which "all things/ Were shadowlike against the news he bore". The syntax is "poetic" in a somewhat old fashioned way, and the poem is rather aggressively high-toned; but its music is memorable — as is that of most of Larkin's early poetry.

The tone of courageous exultance — the "present ecstatic" — is the one evidence, perhaps, of the influence that Vernon Watkins still had on Larkin at the time. It is the tone of several of the poems from the productive month at the end of the summer of 1946:

> Draw down the window-frame
> That we may be unparted from the darkness,
> Inviting to this house
> Air from a field, air from a salt grave,
> That questions if we have
> Concealed no flaw in this confessional,
> And, being satisfied,
> Lingers, and troubles, and is lightless,
> And so grows darker, as if clapped on a flame,
> Whose great extinguishing still makes it tremble.

Though Watkins's serenity seems alien to Larkin, there is something of his hushed reverence for the incipient in the passage quoted.

The forced exultant tone is encountered in the poem that, by its place at the centre of the book, and by its length (104 lines), was clearly intended to be the most weighty and to carry what theme the book had:

> Many famous feet have trod
> Sublunary paths, and famous hands have weighed
> The strength they have against the strength they need;
> And famous lips interrogated God
> Concerning franchise in eternity;
> And in many differing times and places
> Truth was attained (a moment's harmony);
> Yet endless mornings break on endless faces . . .

The diction and rhythm alert one to the Yeatsian inspiration, as does the eight line stanza, though nothing could be further from Yeats than the bleakness of the final line: its juxtaposition with the heroic quality of the opening exemplifies such individuality of tone as *In the Grip of Light* possesses. Impressive as the poem is in its control of argument and of movement in so long a piece, it is marred by its Yeatsian mannerisms and Yeatsian strategies, which stand between the poem and the emotions it explores rather than serving to focus them:

> Annals of men who fought
> Untiringly to change their hearts to stone,
> Or to a wafer's poverty,
> Or to a flower, but never tried to learn
> The difficult triple sanity
> Of being wafer, stone, and flower in turn.

"Wedding-wind", which stands apart in recalling, in its movement, the poetry of Edward Thomas, is one of Larkin's strongest poems. Like so many later poems, it is built out of a single incident. The ever present wind, so harsh in the night of joy, bodies forth that joy in the day. It evokes the details of the scene with a firmness and particularity that contrasts with the feel of the other poems of the period. In "Going" too, this rootedness in the actual is maintained, despite the strongly metaphorical treatment of the evening scene. Yet, both poems are cut from the same idealistic poetic cloth as their fellows from *In the Grip of Light*:

> Can it be borne, this bodying-forth by wind
> Of joy my actions turn on, like a thread

> Carrying beads? Shall I be let to sleep
> Now this perpetual morning shares my bed?
> Can even death dry up
> These new delighted lakes, conclude
> Our kneeling as cattle by all-generous waters?

This concluding passage evokes the exultance and hope encountered throughout the book; and its details are conventionally poetic.

"Wedding-wind", in the clash of joy and desolation, carries one of the principal themes of *In the Grip of Light* and of Larkin's poetry as a whole. He used the poem to open *In the Grip of Light* and again *XX Poems*. The closing poem of *In the Grip of Light* is "And the wave sings because it is moving": its first line reappears as a refrain at the end, asserting the poem's sense of the power of joy. Solitude and separation are again the disturbing emotions:

> And the wave sings because it is moving;
> Caught in its clear side, we also sing.
> We are borne across graves, together, apart, together,
> In the lifting wall imprisoned and protected,
> And so devised to make ourselves unhappy.
> Apart, we think we wish ourselves together,
> Yet sue for solitude upon our meetings,
> Till the unhindered turning of the sea
> Changes our comforts into griefs greater
> Than they were raised to cancel, breaking them.

These feelings are perceived in terms of a vision of death as total loss that has always been with Larkin, though there is an attempt in this early poem to invest the desolation with the traditional grandeur of tragedy:

> Death is a cloud alone in the sky with the sun.
> Our hearts, turning like fish in the green wave,
> Grow quiet in its shadow. For in the word death
> There is nothing to grasp; nothing to catch or claim;
> Nothing to adapt the skill of the heart to, skill
> In surviving, for death it cannot survive,
> Only resign the irrecoverable keys.

The poems from *In the Grip of Light* were written after Larkin had completed *A Girl in Winter* in July, 1945. In that novel are encountered events and themes common in Larkin's mature poetry — deprivation, misunderstanding, gestures half-meant and half-completed. In contrast with the early poems, the novel is striking in its feeling for the provincial urban scene. Towards its close, it articulates a sense of life not to be found for some years in the poetry: "in most lives there had to come a break, when the past dropped away and the maturity that it had enclosed for so long stood painfully upright . . . life ceased to be a confused stumbling from one illumination to another, a series of unconnected clearings in a tropical forest, and became a flat landscape, wry and rather small, with a few unforgettable landmarks somewhat resembling a stretch of fenland . . ." (*AGW* 183). That the vision is first encountered in a novel rather than in the poetry is in part a measure of the fact that, throughout the forties, Larkin thought of himself first as a novelist; though it also shows how resistant was the poetic idiom of the forties to feelings and observations such as are encountered in everyday experience.

In the Grip of Light marks the end of an era both in style and in the attitude to poetic fluency: from then on his poems came less prolifically and, after 1949, were subject to more extensive drafting. Yet its vision is consonant with the vision of the later poetry. There is what Dan Jacobson, in his profile of Larkin in *The New Review*, called "a hunger for transcendence".[7] As in so much of Larkin's later work, the speaker of many of the poems is isolated and reflects on his isolation. Harshness and disappointment are recurrent features. Some of the poems, such as "Träumerei", recreate dreams and are visionary in intent, in contrast with the realism and daytime clarity of the later poetry. The imagery of light in an affirmative role is alluded to in the title of the book: it is more pervasive than it was later to be, though it was to emerge again importantly in "High Windows". Its contrasting companion is the ever present wind, which is associated, conventionally, with all that is harsh and destructive. "Portrait", one of the poems in *Mandrake*, begins "Winds are her enemies": the wind reappears in a similar role in the much later "Afternoons", "ruining" the "courting-places" of the suburban mothers.

What may have contributed to the book's continued rejection is the pervasive lack of particularity in its imagery. A poem by Larkin from this period is not without individuality, and would be immediately recognisable; yet the overall effect of the book is a certain lack of character. Particularity and character were abundantly present in the novels, especially in *A Girl in Winter*. The change in the poetry that was to come after *In the Grip of Light* involved a painful movement towards a greater particularity through the abandonment of a visionary idiom in favour of one rooted in the realistic treatment of everyday events. The change was undoubtedly a very personal one for Larkin; but it also reflected a widely felt need to break with the "romanticism" of the forties, with its compulsory exultation, its pre-occupation with myth and the "eternal verities", its high valuation of "sensitivity".

In the Grip of Light "went round the publishers in the middle and late forties".[8] It was sent in 1947 to Faber and Faber, who had recently published Larkin's second novel. They returned it within a month: T.S. Eliot probably saw it. It was apparently also rejected by John Lane, Dent, Macmillan, Methuen and John Lehmann.[9] Larkin was to comment later: "thank God nobody accepted it".[10] It remained only for the author himself to reject it and its stylistic orientation, allowing himself to move towards the discovery of his true idiom.

Chapter 4

THE MAKING OF A STYLE

At the end of 1946, Larkin once again "gave up the whole business" of writing poetry.[1] It seems in fact to have been quite usual for him to stop writing after the completion of a volume of poetry. However, the immediate refusal of *In the Grip of Light* by his own publisher, Faber, and its continued rejection by other houses, must have affected his attitude towards the whole enterprise. Twelve months separate "Thaw", the last poem selected for *In the Grip of Light*, from the next completed poem "Sunday Morning" (from December 1947). There are no drafts in between in his notebook and no evidence of missing pages. With "Sunday Morning" there is a decided change of style, and the poem seems, both in its character and in its isolated position, to live up to Larkin's contention that it shows "the Celtic fever abated and the patient sleeping soundly." ("Intro. to *NS*", *RW* 30)

The bleak months must have been those in which the influence of Hardy began to take hold. As Larkin has recalled, "I was in some digs which faced east and the sun used to wake me very early in the morning . . . and it happened that I had Hardy's own selection of his poems, and I began to read them and was immediately struck by them . . . by their tunefulness and their feeling, and the sense that here was somebody writing about things I was beginning to feel myself." ("The Poetry of Hardy", *RW* 175) As *In the Grip of Light* shows no sign of this influence, the difficult transition must have begun in 1947.

There is only one poem from 1948 and six from the spring of 1949, though there are some missing sheets in his notebook: "Some missing pages contained material I did not wish to make public . . . others were torn out simply when I wanted a sheet of blank paper. . ." Larkin commented.[2] Nonetheless, this cannot have been a prolific period: it corresponds to the years spent trying to write a third novel. These were years of uncertainty for many writers, when the more romantic idioms of the forties seemed less and less satisfactory: there were hardly any first volumes of poetry of any distinction from the beginning of 1947 to the end of the decade. As T.C. Worsley wrote in 1949, at the demise of *Horizon* (one of the principal literary periodicals of the nineteen-forties): "Five years after the war there is still no sign of any kind of literary revival; no movements are discernable, no trends."[3] Indeed, periodical after periodical ceased publication. Larkin's own turning away from Yeats can be seen as one manifestation of this more widespread unease. He said that "It was . . . in Belfast. . . that he abandoned the 'Yeatsian properties' of *The North Ship*, and began to find a voice of his own. The process was a painful one: 'the unhappiest part of my life, creatively'. . ."[4] In fact, he arrived in Belfast in September 1950, having already written "At Grass" and "Deceptions", poems as decidedly his as anything he ever wrote: the difficult years would seem to have been those between 1946 and 1950, spent at University College, Leicester.

"Sunday Morning" was certainly a turning point, though not so signal a mark of change as it has been taken to be. As Andrew Motion has said, "the characteristics of both his mentors are strongly evident: the poem provides an important early example of the tension between distinct qualities which appears in much of his later work."[5] Motion points out that the conclusion of the second stanza, "Turning, I kissed her,/Easily for sheer joy tipping the balance to love" echoes Hardy's "At the Word 'Farewell'", with its lines "Even then the scale might have been turned/ Against love by a feather". In Larkin's phrasing, the two participles, with the pair of adverbials preceding the second, gives a formalized and slightly unnatural syntax we often encounter in Hardy. The opening details are presented with a realism new to Larkin:

> Waiting for breakfast, while she brushed her hair,
> I looked down at the empty hotel yard
> Once meant for coaches. Cobblestones were wet,
> But sent no light back to the loaded sky,
> Sunk as it was with mist down to the roofs.
> Drainpipes and fire-escapes climbed up
> Past rooms still burning their electric light . . .

The second stanza brings an access of joy, but the imagery, conventionally appropriate in tone, is no longer drawn from the scene:

> The colourless vial of day painlessly spilled
> My world back after a year, my lost lost world
> Like a cropping deer strayed near my path again,
> Bewaring the mind's least clutch.

The "cropping deer" could take their place easily in Yeats's world, and the contrast in style is obvious as soon as one is alerted to it. Yet it is hard to believe that it is a controlled contrast. In addition, the poem is elusive in a manner that one feels is not intended. For David Timms, its theme is that "we can only fully feel love towards someone when he or she has left us";[6] while for Motion (and Anthony Thwaite) the poem involves a conflict between the feeling for the girl and the demands of the Muse.[7]

> Will you refuse to come till I have sent
> Her terribly away, importantly live
> Part invalid, part baby, and part saint?

It is hard to get the tone of the last line: there has been nothing in the poem to direct our responses to "invalid . . . baby . . . saint" — all new images. Conversely, the line does not effectively bring what has gone before into focus; and this is true of the poem as a whole, in spite of moments when feeling seems perfectly rendered, such as "the mist/Wandering absolvingly past all it touched,/Yet hung like a stayed breath". There is an ironic reversal and an ironic recognition immediately perceptible in the poem, but what the subject of that irony is, is not clear, as the contrasting interpretations of Timms and Motion show.

An uncertainty of direction is manifest in the poems that Larkin wrote or attempted after "Sunday Morning". It was immediately succeeded by a draft of a poem "Conversion of Saints", where the only touch of irony is in an alternative title (conceivably added later) "57 varieties of religious experience". The opening is altogether too redolent of Dylan Thomas's *Deaths and Entrances*, and it is not surprising that the draft was not brought to completion:

> One night in their floodlit hearts
> The beasts will not lie down.
> Each roars like a town.
> Fresh, urgent labour starts,
> The red beast, the white,
> The black that would swallow both:
> Flesh, spirit, death,
> Convulse the sarcophagal night.   (First of two sections)

The only poem from 1948, "An April Sunday brings the Snow", is conventional but very satisfying in its poise and clarity of visualization, capturing something of the tone of voice of the mature poetry.

Here, for the first time, we have a poem that, like those of Hardy, gets its emotional power from our normal response to domestic detail. It was occasioned by the death of Larkin's father, whose hobby was jam making. Its directness and its firm evocation of detail are perhaps marks of Larkin's emotional engagement.

> An April Sunday brings the snow
> Making the blossom on the plum trees green,
> Not white. An hour or two, and it will go.
> Strange that I spend that hour moving between
>
> Cupboard and cupboard, shifting the store
> Of jam you made of fruit from these same trees:
> Five loads — a hundred pounds or more —
> More than enough for all next summer's teas,
>
> Which now you will not sit and eat.
> Behind the glass, under the cellophane,
> Remains your final summer — sweet
> And meaningless, and not to come again.

However, the poems completed in 1949 are undistinguished and perhaps symptomatic of a writer who is trying to find his way in a new idiom — an idiom posssibly epitomized in the first line of the one poem he chose to publish from those years, "Words plain as henbirds' wings" ("Modesties" in *XX Poems*). Composed of three simple four-line stanzas, it is unpretentious and uningratiating in diction. A sonnet "To failure" deals with a theme that may have touched Larkin closely in these years of little recognition: he returned to it in "Success story" in 1957, and with great sympathy in the later "Faith Healing". Yet the diction and imagery of this earlier poem do not seem to go naturally with the subject, and give the sense of someone straining to turn personally important feelings into poetry:

> You do not come dramatically, like dragons
> That rear up with my life between their paws
> And dash me butchered down beside the wagons,
> The horses panicking; nor as a clause
> Clearly set out to warn what can be lost,
> What out-of-pocket charges must be borne,
> Expenses met; nor as a draughty ghost
> That's seen, some mornings, running down a lawn.

Another shot at self-recognition, the rather monotonous "On Being Twenty-six", in contrast opens in a manner that could almost be taken as a parody of Larkin's later style:

> I feared these present years,
>   The middle twenties,
> When deftness disappears . . .

Yet these poems are perhaps important signs of how Larkin was turning away from the Yeatsian ambitions for poetry, to write out of his own strong feeling of the failure of those ambitions.

Success and deprivation are among the themes of "At Grass" and "Deceptions". Completed early in 1950, they mark a clear change, both in the orientation of the poetry and in the compositional method. The poetry comes to embrace the life of everyday that made up the world of his novels. It is content, as is so much great art, to take for its material emotions shared by everyone. Metaphor is now incidental, rather than rhetorically dominant, as in some of the poems from *In the Grip of Light*. The details of scene and event carry the emotional charge of the poetry, and the movement of feeling is achieved in terms of these details. This concern with contemporary detail is shown by one of the few extraneous pieces in Larkin's notebook — an advertisement from Millets Army Surplus Store that he drew upon for detail in an uncompleted poem, "Last of all, when a great war has ended. . ." "At Grass" and "Deceptions" also mark a change in the compositional process, in that they are much more intensely worked over and subject to many more drafts than were most of the earlier poems, suggesting a rejection of any Romantic idea of inspiration. The drafting of "At Grass" occupies twelve pages in the notebook.

"At Grass" , with its intimate evocation of contemporary England, is one of Larkin's first characteristic triumphs, and, with the partial exception of "Wedding-wind", the earliest poem in which we encounter the manner we have come to associate with his mature poetry. He was later to recall, "I wrote my first good poem when I was 26"; and, as Peter Ferguson pointed out, the reference is probably to "At Grass".[8] Its composition was prompted by seeing "a news reel film of Brown Jack, the famous old race horse, peacefully at grass".[9] The obscure and seemingly idyllic pastoral present of the retired horses is contrasted with the brief glamorous races of their days of fame. No direct statement is made about that contrast; though the question is asked "Do memories plague their ears like flies?" The relationship of past and present is insinuated through the details of the poem and through changes in perspective. In the opening, the horses are seen obscurely, at a distance: "The eye can hardly pick them out"; at the end we get the homely detail of the "groom, and the groom's boy" coming at evening, the light again obscure, the scene tranquil. In contrast, the details of the days of fame are loud and brilliant:

> Silks at the start: against the sky
> Numbers and parasols: outside,
> Squadrons of empty cars, and heat,
> And littered grass . . .

The poem is not, of course, about the treatment of horses, nor even about the way they feel: it rightly reduces any presentation of their feelings to a question or a qualified statement "gallop for what must be joy". The career of the horses becomes a means of isolating the passage of time and the way time takes everything away a theme involving fame, its passing and the possibility of accepting this, and the related question of the relative attractions of fame or tranquillity.

> Summer by summer all stole away . . .
> Almanacked, their names live; they
>
> Have slipped their names, and stand at ease . . .

"Stand at ease" the exact phrasing for a familiar human posture insinuates a human perspective into the passage. The criticism that the poem offers "a nostalgic re-creation of the Platonic (or *New Yorker*) idea of the English scene, part pastoral, part sporting" and that the horses "emotionally. . . belong to the world of the R.S.P.C.A."[10] is wide of the mark, so far as its main pressures are concerned. A more interesting and relevant question is whether the poem is vulnerable to the suggestion that it distances human pressures to permit an indulgence in nostalgia by treating those pressures in terms of the lives of the race horses. The answer would depend in part on one's response to the feel of the poem as a whole. Nonetheless, the concern with the passage of time and the fading of fame arises unforcedly from the contemplation of the horses. The final serenity of the poem is the serenity of contemplation, implied in the earlier visual distancing: there is a very real sadness for the passing of the glories of the racetrack; but, in the pivotal phrase at the end, "they//Have slipped their names", there is an equally strong feeling for the relaxation associated with the tranquillity with which the poem both opens and concludes.

The phrase is strikingly placed. One of the last alterations Larkin made in drafting the poem was to introduce the line "And stands anonymous again". The pastoral tranquillity of the conclusion can be seen as offering a freedom from the concern with what one is or might be — a concern that forms the theme of so many of Larkin's most characteristic poems, such as "Reasons for Attendance", "Dockery and Son" and "Ignorance". It must have been a pressing concern in those years of no publication and self-questioning.

"Deceptions" also took as its starting point something outside Larkin's own experience — the entry from Mayhew's *London Labour and the London Poor* used as epigraph. What sets it apart, like "At Grass", from most of the earlier poetry, is its development in terms of images associated with a specific incident. We are reminded that Larkin said that, at this time, he "had to find a way of bringing into his poetry the interests and range of emotions which he had previously believed could be expressed only in novels. . .".[11] The poem's title was to have been "The Less Deceived" until this was taken for the book in which it appeared; and its presentation of the drugged girl as "less deceived" than the man who raped her involves one of Larkin's recurrent themes — the way in which appearances and our perception of things can mislead us. The poem also makes use, very obliquely, of the sense of rejection and disappointment that Larkin had experienced as a poet.

The experience is distanced, not merely by time (as the poem says) but by the fact that it is that of a woman, as in "Wedding-wind". The quality of suffering is rendered with a starkness and lack of circumspection not found in poems where the feeling is attributed to an authorial speaker:

> Even so distant, I can taste the grief,
> Bitter and sharp with stalks, he made you gulp.
> The sun's occasional print, the brisk brief
> Worry of wheels along the street outside
> Where bridal London bows the other way,
> And light, unanswerable and tall and wide,
> Forbids the scar to heal, and drives
> Shame out of hiding. All the unhurried day
> Your mind lay open like a drawer of knives.

The sense of how, to the sufferer, the world seems busy with its own business, and how at such times, light that normally beautifies, is a scourge, is acutely rendered.

There are many potent images, some appetitive, associated with eating and swallowing: "sun's occasional print"; "open like a drawer of knives"; "Bitter and sharp with stalks"; and the metaphor of tasting, explicit in the first line and transferred from the poet to the girl in the second. The phrase "light, unanswerable and tall and wide" has an Audenesque daring in its application (so right here) of "tall and wide" to "light" (that has no dimensions). Audenesque, too, is the conjunction of those two concrete words with the abstract "unanswerable". Such startling adjectival juxtapositions were to become characteristic of Larkin, as in "the endless, altered people" of "An Arundel Tomb".

The second half of the poem is different in tone — contemplative, sad, but withdrawn. Its first observation that "suffering is exact, but where/Desire takes charge, readings grow erratic" has a "Movement" tone, (especially in the clinical word "readings") and could almost be from a poem by John Wain: it was not part of the poem as it stood in the notebook in 1949, but emerged in *XX Poems*. Less acceptable to some have been the last four lines:

> For you could hardly care
> That you were less deceived, out on that bed,
> Than he was, stumbling up the breathless stair
> To burst into fulfilment's desolate attic.

The speaker has already said "I would not dare/Console you if I could"; and the phrase "For you would hardly care" seems to reinforce his acknowledgement of the irrelevance for the girl of anything he may have to say. Indeed, this sense of irrelevance might be seen as giving an added sadness. Yet the conclusion, that she was "less deceived", does *conclude* the poem; and this device of qualifying a conclusion in the act of presenting it was to be a frequent one with Larkin, as in "Mr. Bleaney" or "An Arundel Tomb". Here, however, despite the qualification, the observation involves a changed angle of vision, and the girl's grief is no longer the centre of attention. In addition, the final phrase "fulfilment's desolate attic" has an ambiguity that is not really resolved within the tensions of the poem, and that may be symptomatic of pressures personal to Larkin, though not inherent to the subject. The rape, we presume, occurred in an "attic", the place of the "desolate" "fulfilment"; yet, it has been pointed out, the phrase, in conjunction with the immediately preceding remarks about suffering and desire, could be read with a greater generality, implying an emptiness in fulfilment generally. The veiled suggestion (reminiscent of Emily Dickinson's "Success is counted sweetest") that fulfilment destroys our power to appreciate it, is encountered elsewhere in poems like "Reasons for Attendance" or "Sunday Morning"; yet it is not a reflection to which one might be led by the girl's experience, which forms the heart of the poem.

Larkin has recalled "When I came to Hardy it was with the sense of relief that I didn't have to try and jack myself up to a concept of poetry that lay outside my own life — this is perhaps what I felt Yeats was trying to make me do. One could simply relapse back into one's own life and write from it. Hardy taught one to feel rather than to write . . . and he taught one as well to have confidence in what one felt." On the same occasion he said of Hardy that he was "not a transcendental writer . . . not a Yeats. . . not an Eliot: his subjects are men, the life of men, time and the passing of time, love and the fading of love." ("The Poetry of Hardy", *RW* 175–6) The words have a particular point as applied to "At Grass" and "Deceptions". From Hardy, one senses, Larkin learned to dramatize his own feelings concerning fame, rejection and the passing of his life without any certainty of achievement, in a novelistic way through the experiences of imagined characters and in terms of everyday detail related to those experiences. Other influences, too, must have been brought into operation by this change of direction. His early admiration had been Auden, who, like MacNeice and the other poets of the thirties, did so much to bring the details of the modern world into poetry. One feels too the influence of John Betjeman, who meant so much to Larkin, in the description of the race meetings in "At Grass". There also appears to have been a turning away from any grandiose ambitions for literature ambitions that may in fact have seemed to Larkin a source of failure for *In the Grip of Light*.

Such a limitation of literary aspiration was later to be regarded as characteristic of the poetry of the Movement. A long, diffuse, uncompleted draft, "When I see literature", involves confrontations between the speaker of the poem and a character who is given remarks like "Life is? . . . More serious than *Lear*?" The piece is not finished, and the handling of tone is such that one cannot with any certainty gauge the attitude of the author to the speaker of the poem. Nevertheless, there must have been some engagement with the positions voiced:

> Great literature puts a premium on dishonesty
> Great literature is something that gives its writer a great kick
> And its reader a great kick too . . .
> "I want Truth!" they insist, but it's usually truth of detail . . .
> Greatness in that sense, as I understand it, means
> Ability to make your reader *ultimately* complacent
> To tell him that *finally* all's for the best,
> That the thunderclouds clear *in the end*,
> That God — yes, there is one — plaits all the threads
>   at the close . . .

The passage is echoed in "Fiction and the Reading Public", published in 1954, but composed in 1949 and 1950:

Give me a thrill, says the reader,
Give me a kick;
I don't care how you succeed, or
What subject you pick . . .

But that's not sufficient, unless
You make me feel good —
Whatever you're 'trying to express'
Let it be understood
That 'somehow' God plaits up the threads,
Makes 'all for the best',
That we may lie quiet in our beds
And not be 'depressed' . . .

Just please me for two generations
You'll be 'truly great'.

This was one of his first satirical poems, and he told Dan Jacobson that, at this time, one of the things he felt he had to gain for his poetry was "the right to be 'colloquial. . .funny or flippant' if he felt like it"[12] — qualities already encountered in the poetry of Kingsley Amis.

1950 saw Larkin writing fluently again after "Five years of an irresistible force meeting an immoveable object" ("The Literary World"). In that year he completed nine poems that he was to keep in print for the rest of his life. It would be wrong, however, to see too decided a change of direction on the basis of the pieces so far discussed. As Larkin later remarked of the developments that took place in that period: ". . . it wasn't as any conscious reaction. It's just that when you start writing your own stuff other peoples' [sic] manners won't really do for it."[13] "Coming", for instance, would certainly be regarded as a characteristic Larkin poem: its concluding stance "And I, whose childhood/Is a forgotten boredom" seems to offer the undercutting of delight that misguided readers found to be his stock-in-trade. In fact, it comes *after* "At Grass" and was at first called "February"; and it renders with startling delicacy, a throughly conventional theme, a first glimpse of spring, with birdsong echoed in the repeated phrase "It will be spring soon". The conventionally poetic emerges again in a piece that immediately follows "Coming" — a poem, commonsensically deflative, about going to sleep, that seems to fail because of too unqualified a commitment to the "poetic" in its opening stanza:

Child in the womb,
Or saint on a tomb —
Which way shall I lie
To fall asleep?

> The keen moon stares
> From the back of the sky,
> The clouds are all home
> Like driven sheep.   ("How to Sleep")

Although at the end of 1949 we find Larkin "writing" his "own stuff",
the arrival was less definite and certain than the tidied perspective of
the work he later chose to publish would suggest.

Shortly after completing "At Grass" and "Deceptions", Larkin
moved to University College, Belfast as a sub-librarian. There he
compiled his next volume, *XX Poems*, privately published in March
1951. The book received very little attention at the time, the only review being by his contemporary, D.J. Enright, in *The Month*. Larkin
sent many of its hundred copies to "prominent literary figures",[14] who
may not have received them, as the postage rate was raised at the
time of posting, so that the packages were all inadequately stamped.

XX Poems has been regarded as a volume transitional between
The North Ship of 1945 and Larkin's first major collection, *The Less
Deceived* of 1955. Although it comes almost mid-way between the
two books, it contains only four poems written before 1949. Notwith-
standing the statement in the introductory note that the poems were
"written during the last five years", nearly all of them were composed
in the fifteen months before the book was published.

XX Poems was "inscribed to Kingsley Amis", and as late as 1980,
Larkin remembered that one of its poems, "If My Darling", was "the
first poem that made Kingsley think I was some good".[15] It was
completed on May 23rd 1950. Its sophisticated, witty opening was
something new for Larkin and would have appealed to Amis:

> If my darling were once to decide
> Not to stop at my eyes,
> But to jump, like Alice, with floating skirt into my head . . .

The apparently flippant and decidedly iconoclastic treatment of a central "poetic" theme — love — is an early harbinger of the Movement,
as is the "no-nonsense" ending:

> to hear how the past is past and the future neuter
> Might knock my darling off her unpriceable pivot.

"If My Darling" succeeds in part through its skillful creation and
manipulation of tone. The simulation of a particular tone of voice
was to be especially important to Larkin's best poetry throughout his
later career; and in the poems of this period we see the recognition

and development of that dimension. A poem that depends heavily on tone is "Wants", written a week after "If My Darling": bleakly unfigurative, it afronts the poetic expectations of that highly metaphoric decade, the nineteen- forties, when abstract, generalized statements were not felt to be the stuff of poetry. While "Wants" in fact does not offer a grammatically complete sentence, its stance is declarative and uncompromising: "Beneath it all, desire of oblivion runs". It offers a poetry of statement, largely unenhanced by metaphor, that was to be characteristic of the Movement anthology, *New Lines*, in which it was later included.

Indeed, in a number of poems from *XX Poems* we encounter phrases with a Movement flavour: "the figurehead with golden tits" and "bad habits of expectancy" ("Next Please"); "the printed directions of sex" ("Wants"); "A Grecian statue kicked in the privates" ("If My Darling"); "suffering is exact, but where/Desire takes charge, readings will grow erratic" ("Deceptions"). A clinical or iconoclastic pose concerning emotions points forward to the Movement. In "Spring" the speaker adopts a role characteristic of the later Larkin — that of one who cannot participate in the lyricism of the season: "Threading my pursed-up way across the park,/An indigestible sterility."

However, not all the poems from 1950 to 1951 point in this direction. Some of the poems written after "Wants" and "If My Darling" mark a new departure. As David Timms wrote in his *Philip Larkin* (1973):

> The most characteristic poems of *XX Poems* are in fact poems that take an emotional concept, and express it by fleshing it out with an extended metaphor; they are a kind of conceit . . . of the poems of *The Less Deceived* that did not appear previously in *XX Poems*, none is like this.[16]

The poems to which these remarks are most apposite are "Wires", "Next Please", "Since we agreed" ("No Road"), and "Since the Majority of Me" (not included in *The Less Deceived*):

> Since the majority of me
> Rejects the majority of you,
> Debating ends forthwith, and we
> Divide. And sure of what to do
>
> We disinfect new blocks of days
> For our majorities to rent
> With unshared friends and unwalked ways.

The manner has much in common with that of seventeenth-century
metaphysical poetry, as Timms implies. Metaphor had been a dominant feature in Larkin's earlier poetry; but it had been metaphor
with a directly evocative or symbolic function, rather than geared
to argument through the employment of an extended conceit. The
"argued lyric" (with "a tough reasonableness beneath the slight lyric
grace"[17]) is often said to be the characteristic form for metaphysical
poetry. "Latest Face", the last poem of *XX Poems* to be written (in
February 1951) fits the characterization well:

> Admirer and admired embrace
> On a useless level, where
> I contain your current grace,
> You my judgement; yet to move
> Into real untidy air
> Brings no lasting attribute -
> Bargains, suffering, and love,
> Not this always-planned salute.

The tone of voice changes as the poems unfolds, directing our response
to it; and the delicate interplay of wit and lyricism points forward
to "Lines on a Young Lady's Photograph Album". In "Poetry of
Departures" and "Mr. Bleaney", the manipulation of "voice", or of
more than one voice, was to become a key dimension of Larkin's
poetry, and was to remain so.

The more iconoclastic "Next Please" is structured around an argument — one that is worked out in terms of the analogy between
hopes or expectations and approaching or passing ships. However, as
in many later poems by Larkin, the argument is used to badger the
reader out of his normal expectations into disconcerting recognitions:

> No sooner present than it turns to past.
> Right to the last
> We think each one will heave to and unload
> All good into our lives, all we are owed
> For waiting so devoutly and so long.
> But we are wrong . . .

As in the period following "Sunday Morning", the changes evinced
by these poems of 1950 and 1951 were not decisive. Alongside them
we encounter notably conventional poems. Of the two companion
poems written in March 1950, "Oil" and "Drypoint", only the second
was included in *The Less Deceived*. With its unstated but pervasively
"bawdy" subject, "Drypoint" is in line with seventeenth-century po-

etry of a similar genre. There was no doubt intended a contrast with
the rejected companion, "Oils", with its clotted, metaphorical but
reverential opening that seems to look back to earlier admirations:

> Sun. Tree. Beginning. God in a thicket. Crown.
> Never-abdicating constellation. Blood.
> Barn-clutch of life . . .

Heavily metaphorical, too, is the slightly later "Who Called Love
Conquering" (July 1950). It attempts a lyrical ironic treatment of
the theme implied in its opening questions; but the extremely conventional images with which it works — "sweet flower", "Flowerless
demonstrative weeds", "the cloak of dark" — provide too obvious
a target for anything but the somewhat trite ironic treatment they
are given. In these poems we sense an unsureness of touch — the
poet trying out manners in which he does not succeed. We also encounter a decidedly conventional element of sensibility not wholly
"contained" stylistically by these poems — something from which
Larkin was never entirely to free himself.

In *XX Poems*, for the first time in published work, we hear Larkin's
mature voice. Admittedly, the poems of 1950 and 1951 show some
uncertainty of stylistic direction and do not directly develop the manner of "At Grass" and Deceptions", where a particular scene is used
to explore the feelings and concerns of the poems — the manner of so
many of his later major successes, such as "Church Going" or "Dockery and Son". This lack of an assured continuity of style is mirrored
in what was chosen for inclusion in *XX Poems*, where the cloyingly
conventional "The dedicated" from *In the Grip of Light* is retained
alongside poems that must be counted among his best. *XX Poems*
nonetheless constituted an important and innovative poetic achievement; and it is ironical that Larkin had to publish the book privately,
and that, because of the circumstances surrounding its publication,
it received almost no attention and became one of the least known
important volumes of poetry from its period. Larkin may have felt,
after the rejection of *In the Grip of Light* and his failure to complete
his third novel, that his work would not find acceptance. He and
Kingsley Amis used to exchange manuscripts of poems because they
believed that they would never by published; even though, in those
years, *Lucky Jim* was evolving, and we see in the work of both of
them the seeds of what was later to be hailed as "The Movement".
It was to be another four years before some of the poems of these
years, arranged as part of *The Less Deceived*, were to find a wide and
welcoming public.

When *XX Poems* appeared, Larkin was 29. More significant than the lack of attention it received was the comparatively advanced age of its author. If *XX Poems* deserved more acclaim than it got, this cannot be said with any force concerning Larkin's earlier poetry, which had continued to be decidedly imitative when poets of his own age, such as John Heath-Stubbs or Alan Ross, had found manners of their own. This can in part be explained by the fact that the dominant romanticism of British poetry in the nineteen-forties constituted a misdirection for Larkin and was uncongenial to the ironic, realist poetic stance in terms of which he was to find himself. Nonetheless, his startling switch from Audenesque to Yeatsian poetry in 1943 seemed to point to an absence of any secure poetic identity. When that identity emerged in the late forties, it did so gropingly. Even with the publication of *XX Poems*, the moment of full poetic self-recognition was still to come. This was an unusual situation for a poet who, three years later, was to change the course of British poetry and of British poetic taste.

Chapter 5

INTO THE MOVEMENT

In the *Spectator* for August 27th 1954, Anthony Hartley, reviewing work by Thom Gunn, George MacBeth and others, under the title "Poets of the Fifties", concluded his article: "what is certain is that, for better or for worse, we are now in the presence of the only considerable movement in English poetry since the Thirties."[1] The poets whom he particularly named were John Wain, Donald Davie, Thom Gunn and Kingsley Amis. In January of that year he had remarked that these "young academic poets" were the true descendents of Eliot, Auden and Empson, and had contrasted them with the Neo-Symbolists, whom he felt had dominated the poetry of the forties. The new poets were *"ironic, intellectual, rigorous, witty"*.[2] On October 1st, a *Spectator* article called "In the Movement" asserted that: "The English literary scene as we have known it was last transformed in the Thirties"; and went on to say that "nothing dates literary fashions so certainly as the emergence of a new movement, and within the last year or so, signs are multiplying that such a thing is, once again, emerging."[3] "The Movement" had been christened.

What was being hailed as a "movement" was in fact a group of books, most of which had appeared in 1953 and 1954: John Wain's *Mixed Feelings* (1951); Kingsley Amis's *A Frame of Mind* (1953); Thom Gunn's *Fighting Terms* (1954); and pamphlets from the Fantasy Press by Donald Davie and Philip Larkin. These poets were also among those who had appeared in the anthology *Springtime* in 1953. Lending force to their presence on the literary scene was the success of two novels: John Wain's *Hurry On Down* of 1953 and Kingsley Amis's *Lucky Jim* of 1954. The heroes of these novels — of middle-class origin and having university education (then something of a rarity) — go out of their way to dissociate themselves from their class and education. In Wain's novel, the hero attempts to find himself a place free of the expectations implied by his education, which is seen as something of a trap, holding out opportunities yet leading to a pattern of life destructive of his identity. Amis's hero carries on guerrilla tactics against the bogus cultural aspirations of those with whom he

is associated at a provincial university. Their heroes were widely regarded as mean minded and iconoclastic and deliberately preoccupied
with the mundane or the sordid. These books were a reaction to the
"poetic", high-minded, middle-class novel that epitomized the "best
writing" of the forties; and the leading characters did not want to belong to the society pictured in such novels. In contrast, the reader's
nose was pushed up against the realities of everyday life — the re-
strictions that purely economic concerns bring, such as going to work,
or wondering whether you could buy twenty cigarettes, or living in a
furnished room. The Movement novel saw a return to the mode of
the realist novel and a break with conventional, upper-middle-class
images of what consitituted British life.

Wain and Amis were identified as "Red Brick", denoting their association with provincial universities (Reading and Swansea respec-
tively) rather than the Oxford and Cambridge that had been the cultural centres of so many literary movements in England. In fact Wain
and Amis were both recent graduates of Oxford. They represented
the new intellectual class, educated and middle-class in origin, but
no longer enjoying the freedom from basic economic pressures that
higher education had previously brought with it. Indeed, the Movement was early recognized as being associated with wide changes of
thought and feeling that were taking place in the early fifties and
that reflected the sense that power and opportunity remained with
a particular portion of society, the "Establishment" (as it came to
be called), even though the economic structure of society and the av-
enues of social mobility had changed in the immediate post-war years.
Similarly, literary journalism seemed dominated by an establishment
that had its roots in the twenties and earlier: Sir Harold Nicholson,
Cyril Connolly, Raymond Mortimer and others, who lent support to
the type of writing against which the new writers were reacting. Both
Wain and Amis became identified in popular journalism as "Angry
Young Men" — a term given currency by the success of a play by
John Osborne, *Look Back in Anger* in 1956. Wain went so far as
to contribute to a collection called *Declaration* (1957), in which a
number of writers, some of whom had nothing to be angry about in
the reception their writing had been accorded, sounded off about the
current state of affairs. Subsequently, a great deal of writing that
had little or nothing to do with what Wain and Amis stood for came
to be associated with their work, such as the many Northern novels,
like Keith Waterhouse's *Billy Liar* (1959), that appeared in the late
fifties.

All this may seem to have little to do with the Movement considered in terms of a group of poets writing at a particular time. In fact, of course, the awareness that the emotional life is not lived in a social vacuum marked a break with the emphasis, in much of the poetry of the forties, on the eternal verities, on the irrational and on sensitivity of observation. The Movement, as the *Spectator* had put it, was "anti-phoney" as well as "anti-wet, sceptical, robust, ironic".[4] It saw a return of the play of intelligence in poetry, with a scepticism and circumspection concerning feeling. It had a suspicion of "culture" and high-mindedness that was very much part of the climate of the time for those who had grown up on the literature of the forties:

> It seems the poet made a bad mistake.
> How could she know how awful passion was?
> The lesson is that breaking hearts must break.
>
> (John Wain — "Don't Let's Spoil it all")

It was iconoclastic, yet with a nostalgic sense that its members had come too late — that the age of great causes was over. Victory over fascism in World War II, the post-war full employment and the social changes brought about by the first Labour government seemed to have wiped the slate of obvious wrongs that had to be righted. The iconoclasm involved a healthy dismissal of the bogus pieties that many members of society still seemed to find it necessary to subscribe to. Such dismissals were a feature of Larkin's poetry in the early fifties, in "Poetry of Departures", "Toads", and "Places, Loved Ones". If the young writers appeared to many to have their eyes fixed resolutely on their boot laces, their best work of those years seems, in retrospect, to have a notable centrality. Of none is this more true than of Larkin.

Although Larkin, Amis and Wain had been at Oxford in the early forties and had continued to see one another in the succeeding years, the origins of the Movement are to be found in the literary friendships and activities of the forties only in a very unformed way. It is true that D.J. Enright's contributions to *Scrutiny* while at Cambridge mark the beginning of the influence that the periodical and its principal editor were to exercise on the literary ambience of the fifties. However, the outlook of most of the contributors in 1956 to *New Lines*, the defining anthology of the Movement, had little to do with John Wain's Oxford of the early forties, where "every poet I knew, or knew of, was an amateur theologian",[5] and much more to do with the empirical Oxford of 1950, where everyone had read A.J. Ayer's *Language, Truth and Logic*. Though Larkin and Amis and their friends at St. John's were not aligned with the "romanticism" of Sidney Keyes and his *Eight*

Oxford Poets, they were not waiting in the wings for the time when the world would be ready for an alternative conception of literature. After meeting Vernon Watkins in 1943, Larkin himself had taken a "romantic" direction with *The North Ship* and *In the Grip of Light* — one that he was forced to abandon before he could find his own idiom. It is largely fruitless to search those books or the early issues of John Wain's Oxford periodical *Mandrake* for embryonic evidence of the later Movement. Only in places in Kingsley Amis's *Bright November* of 1947 do we find writing that has any clear continuity with what came later. The most notable pointer to what was to come (aside from the humorous fantasies shared by Amis and Larkin, such as the "Yorkshire Scholar", and the anti-heroic humour of *Jill*) was the fervent interest in jazz displayed by Larkin, Amis and Wain — an interest that went along with an unwillingness to be bamboozled into liking something because one ought to. Jazz was not a patrician taste, not a part of the official culture.

Indeed, the involvement of Larkin, Amis and Wain in the romantic ethos of the nineteen-forties importantly influenced the character of the Movement. The New Romanticism of the forties was the last stand in a cultural enterprise that went back at least to the time of Matthew Arnold. For Yeats and for Eliot (despite Eliot's protestations to the contrary) literature was a means of finding or formulating a basis for affirmation and belief that religion had previously provided. Dylan Thomas's "Poem in October", one of the most admired poems of the nineteen-forties, goes about this same business, seeking to find sanctity in the memories of childhood. The "no-nonsense" stance of the Movement, its circumspection concerning emotion, was a reaction to that sort of thing. Its seemingly deliberate lowering of sights reflected a refusal to have anything to do with high-minded consolations that it found bogus. In the same way, much in the Movement stance that seemed outrageous — the dismissal of conventional "serious" music, the down-playing of cultural ambitions for the arts — can be seen as an inversion of the cultural orientations and snobberies of the preceding period.

The first piece of writing to point clearly in the new direction was John Wain's essay on the poetry of William Empson, "Ambiguous Gifts", which appeared in the last issue of *Penguin New Writing* in 1950. As Wain explained later: "After the war there was a great deal of reconstruction to be done in the arts . . . It was rather like being confronted with a smashed-up tangle of railway lines and wondering which one to repair first . . . The 'thirties were no use, at any rate as far as the main line was concerned, the Auden line: it was worn out even before it got smashed, and what smashed it decisively was not the war but Auden's renunciation of English nationality . . . My own answer . . . was that the Empson track was the best one . . ."[6] Wain underplays the importance of Auden's idiom to the poets of the Movement: as Larkin later saw it, the Movement involved "a reversion to the virtues of the thirties."[7] Nonetheless, the achievements of the great modernists such as Eliot and Pound appeared to have pre-empted the major possibilities for innovation in poetry, so that their work not only offered no viable models for emerging poets, but seemed to stand in the way of the development of a new idiom. This sense of things is reinforced by the early novels of Wain and Amis, where there is a deliberate turning away from the experimentation that had characterised modernist fiction and a return to the simple narrative of the realist novel that the modernists had rejected. Along with this went a rejection of the modernist cosmopolitan programme, with its insistence on the importance of an awareness of the culture of the past. "Culture" was a bad word for the Movement writers, and they were aggressively English.

The turning away from modernism and its ambitious programme for poetry appears in retrospect a conservative reaction, even if it seemed the only way forward. Some of the writers associated with the Movement later espoused decidedly conservative attitudes concerning society and the arts and were happy to point to the features of artistic conservatism in the Movement as evidence that they had always been conservative. This was the case with Larkin in his later years. However, the cultural attitudes espoused by the Movement writers, particularly those that at the time were characterised as "philistine", were radical and led to a radical reorientation of British writing.

Indeed, the Movement appears conservative only if viewed in terms of the modernist ideas about the arts against which it was revolting. Its rejection of what immediate predecessors had stood for was something it had in common with all movements of renewal in the arts. The criticism by some of its members of writers who had been canonized — Eliot, Pound, Yeats — and the value it placed on the work of writers who had seemed more marginal — Empson, Hardy, Betjeman — is also charcteristic of revolutions in writing.

We can see important parallels to Movement positions in the work of American writers who certainly cannot be viewed as conservative in their attitude to modernism — in Alan Ginsberg's *Howl* of 1955 and Robert Lowell's *Life Studies* of 1959. In the work of Ginsberg we encounter aggressively anti-establishment attitudes; while in *Life Studies* there is a manipulation of seemingly irrelevant and trivial detail to create the impression that the poems have no design to impose a vision on experience but rather seek at all costs to be honest with experience. Both poets were turning their backs on the notion, for which both Eliot and Pound proselytized, that the poet has an important duty to his culture and to the culture of the past, and that he should shape his poetry in the light of that duty. Both poets sought what Lowell termed a "breakthrough back into life" — an expression very applicable to the Movement.[8]

In the poetry of the Movement the reaction against modernism was seen in the ignoring of one of modernism's chief tenets, that poetry is an autotelic mode of creation that operates quite differently from the declarative statements by which we communicate in normal speech and in discursive prose. Some of Wain's early Empsonian poems seem to be composed almost entirely of general statements:

> Sometimes just being alone seems the bad thing.
> Solitude can swell until it blocks the sun.
> It hurts so much, even fear, even worrying
> Over past and future, get stifled. It has won,
> You think; this is the bad thing, it is here.
>
> ("The Bad Thing")

A poetry of statement became the manner of the poets of the Movement, with a concomitant downplaying of the dominant figure of modernist poetry, the metaphor. These tendencies manifested themselves in Wain's first volume, *Mixed Feelings* (1951) and Amis's *A Frame of Mind* (1953). Both books were marked by anti-romantic attitudes, as in Amis's "Against Romanticism", "A Dream of Fair Women" and "Dirty Story", or an ironic circumspection concerning feeling, as in Wain's "Reason for not Writing Orthodox Nature Poetry". The two books were published in limited editions from the Fine Arts Department at Reading University, where Wain had taught since 1947. They constituted the first sign of the new movement in English poetry.

We also see evidence of a movement taking shape in the publications of the Fantasy Press, a series of booklets of poetry that included the work of Amis, Larkin, Davie and many other new poets. The Fantasy Poets began as a series of pamphlets produced on behalf of the Oxford University Poetry Society by Oscar Mellor on his hand press. The first pamphlet was by Elizabeth Jennings in 1951; and, by the end of 1952, there had been fifteen more, including ones by Donald Hall, George Steiner, Lotte Zurndorfer, Martin Seymour Smith, Geoffrey Hill, Adrienne Rich, Mitchell Raper, Alfred Alvarez, and the first editor of the series, Michael Shanks. Donald Hall took over the series (with Oscar Mellor) from the ninth to the eighteenth number, and was succeeded by George MacBeth for the next six pamphlets in 1953 and 1954. The series continued into 1957, later editors being Anthony Thwaite and Bernard Bergonzi. Six issues of a periodical, *New Poems*, edited by Jonathan Price and Geoffrey Hill, appeared from Autumn 1952 to Autumn 1953.

With the pamphlets by Alvarez (No. 15), Gunn (No. 16) and Thwaite (No. 17), a direction begins to emerge; and in the pamphlets of 1953 and 1954 under the editorship of George MacBeth — those by Davie, Price, Larkin and Amis — we have the whole anatomy of the Movement. At that time, it is clear that MacBeth and Price (both neo-Empsonians), along with Geoffrey Hill, had an important influence on what was published by the Press; and, despite the fact that they did not appear in *New Lines*, their work was regarded at the time as an important part of the Movement. Although by 1954 the new movement had been hailed by the *Spectator*, we see an important focusing of what was going on through the publications of the Fantasy Press.

Indeed, the Movement was a coming together rather than a concerted programme: in 1953 it justified the recognition given it by the *Spectator*; but, by 1958, the grouping had dissipated.

Larkin said in 1964 that "the Movement, if you want to call it that, really began when John Wain succeeded John Lehmann on that B.B.C. programme; John planned six programmes called *First Readings* including a varied set of contributors — they weren't all Movementeers by any means."[9] A further consolidation of this image of a group of young writers of a particular character forming the growing edge of English poetry occurred with the publication in 1953 of *Springtime*, edited by G.S. Fraser and Ian Fletcher. It included poems by Larkin, Alvarez, Amis, Davie, Gunn, Jennings, and Wain; though this group was hidden among over forty other contributing poets, so that the anthology did not have a strong defining effect. More powerful in this way was George Hartley's periodical, *Listen*, which began publication in 1954. The first issue contained nothing by poets normally associated with the Movement; but the second included work by Larkin, Amis, Davie, Wain and Bernard Bergonzi. The third issue had Davie, MacBeth, Amis, Price, Anthony Hartley and Bergonzi; while the fourth included Enright, John Holloway, Jennings, Larkin, Amis and Davie. Shortly after the first issue had gone to press, Hartley came upon *The North Ship* and wrote to Larkin asking for poems: Larkin was to contribute regularly to *Listen* until it closed in 1962.

Larkin first appeared on Wain's programme in July, 1953, reading "If My Darling", from *XX Poems*. This appearance, along with the publication of eight poems in *Springtime* (again all from *XX Poems*) must have been very important for Larkin. His inclusion in *Springtime* was the first appearance in print of his poetry since the two poems in *Mandrake* in 1946 — apart from *XX Poems*, which he had had printed himself and which had gone almost completely unnoticed. For the first time his poetry was in a book published by a regular commercial publisher, and this made his work the object of review in national periodicals. He was 31.

Appearance in *Springtime* and on First Readings was followed by the publication of poems in the *Spectator* and other periodicals in 1953 and 1954. The only poem by Larkin in a periodical in 1953 was "Wires", from *XX Poems*, in the *Spectator* for October 2nd. Larkin in fact continued to draw on *XX Poems* down into 1955: "Latest Face" appeared in the *Spectator* for March 5th 1954; "If My Darling" came out in *Shenandoah* in the spring of 1955; while "Next Please" and "No Road" were in *Departure* in the spring and summer of that year. "Fiction and the Reading Public", published in *Essays in Criticism* in January 1954, did not come from *XX Poems*; but it had been drafted in the Notebook in 1949. Indeed, "Triple Time", which came out in *Poetry and Audience* in January 1954 and then in the *Spectator* in April, was the only new poem by Larkin to appear in a periodical up to June 1954.

One might form the impression that Larkin was short of poems and writing very little at the time. This would not be true. Larkin was perhaps dissatisfied with the poems that he had written in 1951 after he had completed *XX Poems*: "To My Wife", "The March Past", "Best Society", "To put one brick upon another", "The local snivels through the fields", "Maturity" and "Marriages" were never published by him, and it would be hard to fault his judgement concerning some of these poems. However, "The March Past", in particular, contains passages that could be from any period of his mature work: "And all was focused, larger than we reckoned,/ Into a consequence of thirty seconds"; while "Best Society" (about solitude) and "Maturity" treat two of his major themes with the sardonic presentation of himself so characteristic of his later work.

However, with "Arrivals, Departures" of January 1953, he had started to write poetry again, after a gap of a year and a half; and from August until the end of the year he completed eleven poems, among them "Days", "Lines on a Young Lady's Photograph Album", "Whatever Happened?" and "Reasons for Attendance". The best of these he may have seen as pre-empted for periodical publication because he had chosen them for his Fantasy Press pamphlet, which appeared in March of 1954, but which had presumably been assembled earlier. For it he chose "At Grass" and "If My Darling" from *XX Poems* and "Arrivals, Departures", "Lines on a Young Lady's Photograph Album" and "Whatever Happened?" from his recent poems. One or two of the remaining new poems, such as "Autumn" or "Mother, Summer, I", deserved not to be passed over, even if they lack the brightness of the best poems he was now writing; though others, such as "He Hears that his Beloved has become Engaged" or "At thirty-one, when some are rich", are unsuccessful in that they fail to distance appropriately the experiences that are the subject of their irony. Whatever the case, it seems possible that, once Larkin had written "Reasons for Attendance" in December 1953 (the first poem in a new manner of self-reflexive irony), he was dissatisfied with most of the poems that he had written earlier in the year.

The Fantasy Press pamphlet was his first collection to be brought out by a publisher since *The North Ship* nine years earlier; and the poems chosen for it established quite firmly the sense of a new voice. "Arrivals, Departures" has something of the manner of *XX Poems*; while "Whatever Happened?", though freshly sardonic, makes an extended metaphor of its subject, as did "Wires" and other poems from that earlier book. Nothing that went before, however, quite prepared the reader for "Lines on a Young Lady's Photograph Album". It has been recognized as a typical Movement poem in its low-toned, sceptical attitude towards emotion and in its suspicion of art. In its fluent manipulation of tone of voice from the matter of fact to the lyrical, in its utilization of vocabulary for social placing, and in its accommodation of a variety of tones from the satirical to the unqualifiedly lyrical to make its own "tone", it reminds one, as Michael Hamburger has suggested, of Laforgue or the young Eliot,[10] and shows a depth of awareness of traditional and modern poetic resources to which Larkin was often reluctant to admit. It was a characteristic triumph that seemed to establish at one go the mature Larkin manner.

The studiedly old-fashioned formality of the title shows an intention to distance emotion. It is in tune with the titles found in John Wain's first books of poetry, such as the aggressively unpoetic "On Reading Love Poetry in the Dentist's Waiting Room". The title of Wain's first book, *Mixed Feelings*, suggests the scepticism concerning feeling that was characteristic of his early poems. There is a corresponding backing off from emotion in Larkin's poem: "Too much confectionary, too rich:/I choke on such nutritious images", where the references to eating have the effect of lowering the emotional tone. This is reinforced by the insistence on control: "(Faintly disturbing, that, in several ways) —/From every side you strike at my control", where "Faintly disturbing" takes the emotion into the realm of polite understatement.

Much play is made of the contrast between photography and art — at art's expense:

> But O, photography! as no art is,
> Faithful and disappointing! that records
> Dull days as dull, and hold-it smiles as frauds,
> And will not censor blemishes
> Like washing-lines, and Hall's Distemper boards . . .

It is the honesty of photography that is praised, and the truth that it offers that is valued; while "art", characteristically of the Movement, is made to come off second-best. Within the rhetoric of its line, "Dull days as dull" is not merely matter of fact: it emphasises dullness with its repetition and insists that "dull days" be admitted to. The comparison, without any purely comic effect, to "Hall's Distemper boards" suggests that the emotions of the poem belong in the same everyday world as the billboards. The culminating praise of photography is that it "persuades/That this is a real girl in a real place,/In every sense empirically true!" What is praised is again "truth"; but "empirically true" recalls the philosophy of Bertrand Russell and G.E. Moore, the fathers of the linguistic analysis that dominated British philosophy, especially at Oxford, in the nineteen-fifties, and where what was "meaningful" was equated with what was "empirically verifiable". The ambience of the poem as a whole is decidedly Oxonian, with its "sweet girl-graduate" (a phrase from Tennyson's "The Princess") "in a trilby hat" with those "disquieting chaps who loll/At ease about your earlier days". The diction, too, suggests such a social ambience: "Not quite your class, I'd say, dear, on the whole".

While the poem maintains its tone with superb poise, it is given a turn more decidedly Larkin's in its last four stanzas:

> Those flowers, that gate,
> These misty parks and motors, lacerate
> Simply by being over; you
> Contract my heart by looking out of date.

The two oxymorons in as many lines are characteristic of him as well as being in tone with the opening of the poem; while the consolation that "We know *what was*/Won't call on us to justify/ Our grief", introduces a consideration, that of justifying grief, hardly to be found in poetry outside this period (though encountered often enough in the criticism of F.R. Leavis). The "misty parks and motors" modulate into the unqualified lyricism of the last lines — a frequent way of concluding a poem for Larkin after this:

> In short, a past no one now can share,
> No matter whose your future; calm and dry,
> It holds you like a heaven, and you lie .
> Unvariably lovely there,
> Smaller and clearer as the years go by.

The poem may, indeed, have arisen from the same emotional situation as the much less successful but contemporary "He Hears that his Beloved has beome Engaged". "Lines" is one of Larkin's few poems in which personal erotic involvement is handled with poise and delicacy; and it is a poem in which erotic feeling is distanced almost to the point of being completely masked.

"Lines on a Young Lady's Photograph Album" was completed in September 1953. In the following months Larkin wrote "Triple Time" and "Whatever Happened"; and two days before the year's end he seems finally to have hit form with "Reasons for Attendance", which was followed in the next four weeks by "I Remember, I Remember", "For Sidney Bechet", "Born Yesterday" and "Poetry of Departures". "Toads" came in March, "Church Going" in July, and "Places Loved Ones" and "Myxomatosis" in October. With the writing of "Maiden Name" in January of 1955, "Mr. Bleaney" in May and "Reference Back" in August, we have the poems that, in retrospect, seem to define the Movement and Larkin's place in it.

This was the great period of stylistic self-discovery for Larkin. Nonetheless, even after the wonderful burst in January of 1954, we encounter poems that are somewhat humdrum or conventional: "Gathering Wood" (March 1954), and "Long roots moor summer" (June 1954), whose tone is in keeping with their titles, were never collected by Larkin. More interesting are the successes he rejected at the time: "Days" from August 1953; "For Sidney Bechet", from January 1954; and "Water" from April 1954; all of which went unpublished until 1956 or 1957 and were not collected until they appeared in *The Whitsun Weddings* in 1964. These lovely but largely un-ironic poems were evidently not what Larkin wanted to be known for when he brought together *The Less Deceived* in the heart of the Movement period.

The poems from 1954 and 1955 introduce something quite new in Larkin's poetry. The speaker is not the neutral, authorial voice presenting an experience or making a statement about it, as in "At Grass" or "Deceptions". In "Reasons for Attendance", "Poetry of Departures", "I Remember, I Remember", "Mr. Bleaney" and "Church Going", the speaker—quasi-autobiographical—is dramatized through the details of the poem, and in all these poems there is an element of ironic self-deflation. More startling at the time they appeared was the association of this irony with certain attitudes that seemed to contradict conventional pieties: that work is a curse we would and could easily shake off if we didn't have to do it; that if it were not for our circumstances or our lack of courage, we would throw over our everyday lives and reach for something more satisfying; that the relationship with our parents is not one of unwavering joy; that ordinary life is very ordinary; and that religion offers no consolation. Most noticeable to readers of the early fifties would have been the fact that the poems stay with these attitudes, rather than seeking some redeeming mode of transcending them.

The relationship with Amis seems to have been particularly important to Larkin at this time. *XX Poems* had been dedicated to Amis; and Larkin later remarked "I wrote the bulk of 'The Less Deceived' . . . under no particular influence except Kingsley's . . . I'd visions of showing him things he would laugh at."[11] Indeed, it would seem that the emergence of a new manner in "Toads", "Poetry of Departures", "Mr. Bleaney" and "Church Going" had something to do with the influence of Amis. The speakers of these poems, awkward, down-at-pocket, educated to a sense of things to which their situation does not correspond, have a lot in common with the anti-heroes of *Lucky Jim* and *Hurry On Down*. However, the correspondence between the work of Larkin and Amis is most strikingly seen in Amis's "Something Nasty in the Bookshop", which appeared in *A Frame of Mind* in 1953:

> Critical, and with nothing else to do,
> I scan the Contents page,
> Relieved to find the names are mostly new;
> No one my age.

The tone of voice could place it in *The Less Deceived*: one has only to imagine the words being spoken by Larkin to realize this. The self-parodying image of the poet browsing in the anthology and pleased to find none of his contemporaries have made it there before he has, corresponds to that of the speaker in "Church Going" taking off his cycle clips, reading too loudly from the lectern and donating an Irish sixpence. In Amis's poem there is the down-playing of art encountered in "Reasons for Attendance" and "Lines on a Young Lady's Photograph Album":

> . . .*Landscape near Parma*
> Interests a man, so does *The Double Vortex*,
>   So does *Rilke and Buddha*.

> 'I travel, you see', 'I think' and 'I can read'
>   These titles seem to say . . .

In the passage just quoted, we encounter the interpolation of speech by another voice that Larkin made so much of. Amis's anti-romantic diction was innovative: "Should poets bicycle-pump the human heart/ Or squash it flat?" Most striking is the conclusion, where Amis turns round on himself and his readers, calling into doubt everything that has gone before and deflating himself:

> Deciding this, we can forget those times
>   We sat up half the night
> Chockfull of love, crammed with bright thoughts, names, rhymes,
>   And couldn't write.

This is the concluding strategy of "Reasons for Attendance" and "Mr. Bleaney" and, to a lesser degree, of "Poetry of Departures", "Toads" and "I Remember, I Remember" — all anti-romantic poems that share something of the Amis manner.

In 1956, when reviewing Amis's *A Case of Samples*, Larkin wrote:

> The broad farce ("A Dream of Fair Women"), the literary politics ("Against Romanticism"), the deliberate anti-climaxes ("Going well so far, eh?") fall into place as different ways of discrediting the insensitive, the flatulent, and the dishonest: they all blend into a style which (as in "To Eros") is utterly unmistakable . . . a style that will exasperate only those who cannot see when a poem is being funny and serious simultaneously.[12]

The example of a style that could be "funny and serious simultaneously" was a crucial one, and Larkin seems to have incorporated some of Amis's devices into his own repertoire.

"Reasons for Attendance" with its speaker, a self-parody, gawking through the window of a lighted dance hall, uses several of the

devices encountered in Amis's poem. Characteristically of the Movement, the attitudes expressed and the deflative rhetoric take a cal-
culating sight on the expectations of the conventional reader of the
day. The "reason" for the dancers' attendance is given baldly as
"Sex"; and the speaker turns on this with the dismissive comment:
"Surely, to think the lion's share/Of happiness is found by couples —
sheer//Inaccuracy, as far as I'm concerned". The ostensibly low-
toned and rational rejection, strained over the stanza break with
"sheer//Inaccuracy", comes out rather shrill. The argument of the
poem is rehearsed in brisk short phrases with ostentatiously ordered
parallelisms — "Believing this . . . Believing that" — which suggest a
clear structure of logic — an effect intensified by beginning the penultimate sentence with "Therefore". The speaker has the air of being
sure of himself — but with an impatient defensiveness.

Yet the plug is pulled out on everything in the last line: "If no
one has misjudged himself. Or lied." The device of the concluding
reversal throws into doubt the tightly structured argument, which
nonetheless still stands as the body of the poem. It brings to the fore
the insecurity of the speaker that has been felt throughout the poem
and is implicit in the very activity of watching the dancers with such
close concern. The tensions in the poem are reflected in the quality
of the writing. On the one hand, there is the strong feeling for the
experience of ordinary people that was to be a mark of Larkin's best
poetry: "Shifting intently, face to flushed face,/Solemnly on the beat
of happiness" is all too true to the experience described, even in the
contradictory suggestions set up by "Solemnly" and "happiness", and
the uncomfortably insecure feelings evoked by "Shifting" and "flushed
face". The triumph of the poem is the phrase "The wonderful feel of
girls", which makes poetry in the language of the dancers. The very
firmness of the writing here and in the opening "trumpet's voice,
loud and authoritative" contrasts with the slightly stilted talk of the
trumpet as "that lifted, rough-tongued bell . . . whose individual
sound/Insists I too am individual". The passage verges on cliché, and
the protestations are not convincing. The ostensible tension is that
encountered in the earlier "Sunday Morning", where art and sexual
attachment are felt to be in conflict. Yet the poem, one senses, comes
from experiences more strongly felt than was realized: it is permeated
by Larkin's recurrent concerns with the self, with missed experience,
and with the elusiveness of fulfilment. The situation of the speaker
looking in on what is conventionally regarded as satisfaction is typical.

Unease concerning the focus of the poem leads on to questions
concerning the pattern of its rhetoric. There is a notable virtuosity

in the handling of tone and syntax. The syntax of the first stanza fits the stanza pattern, in keeping with the secure tone with which the scene is initially characterized. In the answer to the question "Why be out here?", the syntax overflows the form. As the poem moves to its close with the argued assertions that were to become a customary way of concluding for Larkin, phrases echo one another: "individual sound" — "individual"; "I hear; others may hear as well,//But not for me, nor I for them"; and this mirroring pattern of assertion in fact creates confusion. Into it, the dismissive "they maul to and fro" drops with unmovable certainty. These rhetorical features detract from the categorical quality of the poem's statements and lead up with mastery to the doubting final lines: the speaker emerges as the best candidate for one who has "misjudged himself".

The poet, one feels, must have been aware of this; yet we are left asking how effectively the control of rhetoric reflects a controlled awareness on the poet's part. There is a rather tense closeness to feelings only partially emergent; and the quick *volte face* at the end, which has the air of partially unmasking the speaker, might be seen as functioning protectively in the uncertainty it generates. Such protective gestures of baffling and baffled reversal are to be found throughout Larkin's poetry.

"Toads" was perhaps the most popular poem to come out of the Movement, and its tone too has much in common with that of Amis's poetry. It portrays work as a nuisance, and finds its choices in the contrasting appeals of conforming or living off one's wits — both artfully rendered unrewarding:

> Six days of the week it soils
>> With its sickening poison —
> Just for paying a few bills! . . .
>
> Lots of folk live up lanes
>> With fires in a bucket,
> Eat windfalls and tinned sardines —
>> They seem to like it.

Instead of a resolution in some vision that harmonizes or transcends these tensions, the poem drops the reader back to the conclusion that there is no escape for the speaker, because there is something in him like the "toad work" that keeps him back:

> . . . something sufficiently toad-like
>> Squats in me, too . . .
>
> I don't say, one bodies the other
>> One's spiritual truth;

> But I do say it's hard to lose either,
>   When you have both.

The conclusion carefully guards against any poetic nonsense about the speaker's situation mirroring his inner condition; and the poem is a loaded put-down of poetic expectations, offering, as alternative to the humdrum work, the dream that he might "blarney/My way to getting/The fame and the girl and the money/All at one sitting" (a passage reminiscent of Amis's "A Dream of Fair Women"). The poem allows no place for the bogus high-mindedness that was a regular Movement target.

The essential light-heartedness of the poem should not be overlooked. It is emphasised by the crisp, jaunty movement and the very obvious alliterations. The wit is playful, as in the Shakespearean turn given to *"Stuff your pension"* (a phrase in 1953 only barely admissible in mixed company). Yet the poem talks about something that loomed large for everyone, and particularly for the educated but impoverished middle-class writer in the days before the economic boom of the late fifties, who sought some way to keep alive and yet find enough time to write.

If "Toads" was the most famous poem of the Movement, "Poetry of Departures" even more strongly typifies what would have been regarded as the Movement manner. Most obviously characteristic is the terse "We all hate home/And having to be there" — startlingly true for many, but deliberately shocking in its cool reversal of the revered commonplace "There's no place like home". "I detest my room,/Its specially-chosen junk,/The good books, the good bed,/ And my life, in perfect order" appears initially as a forthright amplification of "We all hate home", and makes the reader sympathetic to chucking *"up everything"*: there seems little enough to lose except staying "sober and industrious". Yet leaving is revealed to be merely a detour that leads back to "Books; china; a life/ Reprehensibly perfect." The poem traps the reader into this uncomfortable conclusion through his earlier assent.

"Poetry of Departures" is a translation of the phrase "poésie des départs" used to characterise a particular style of French nineteenth-century poem, such as Beaudelaire's "L'Invitation au Voyage", in which the poet contemplates leaving the everyday world for a more romantic setting. There is a light thumbing of the nose at foreign culture and cultural pretence on Larkin's part, though the main target is false expectations. Hard sense brings the discommoding reflection that we shall not escape ourselves by going away. However, for the readers of the fifties, the *pattern* of the poem may have been as disconcerting as anything else. Unlike so many poems of the forties, "Poetry of Departures" does not offer an unhappy situation that leads, via reflection, to an overcoming of the initial unhappiness. Instead, it offers a situation that leads, via reflection, back to the same disconcerting circumstances, and to the sense that you can do nothing about them: our romantic hopes are made to trick us into an admission that staying "sober and industrious" is what we are destined to do. The assertion of the ordinariness of the ordinary, and of how inescapable it is, brought a new note to poetry; particularly because, despite its paraded ironies, the poem is a work of controlled seriousness, without the exaggeration and distortion of satire.

Its stance is reinforced by the dramatized speech: "*He chucked up everything/And just cleared off*", with its suggestion of working class language and attitudes; while "*Then she undid her dress*" and "*Take that you bastard*" (phrases evocative of the hard-boiled crime novel) suggest cultural orientations at odds with the sensibility of many poetry readers of the day. Just to get these phrases into the poem with a controlled change of tone that did not destroy the decorum was an achievement of originality at the time.

The poem generates a particular speaking voice, low toned, diffident, which rises to slightly discreditable excitement in "flushed and stirred" or in phrases that display their own hollowness like "swagger the nut-strewn roads". The speaker is distant from the experiences he talks about — "Sometimes you hear, fifth-hand". The colourlessness of his environment is evoked by the generic naming of its few objects: "Books", "bed", "china". Indeed, the poem is aggressively un-imagistic: in contrast with the modernist ideal of recreating experience, it talks about it. Within its limited tonal range, the poem makes all its movements by changes in tone of voice; and through this "voice" the poet is dramatized as a particular type of speaker — someone who certainly resembles the real-life Larkin, but whose level of cultural nourishment has been rather depressed.

This use of a *persona*, often commented on in discussion of Larkin's poetry, is first encountered with an involved, ironic distancing in this poem and in "Reasons for Attendance" (though "Wedding-wind" is spoken by someone clearly other than the poet — a woman). In the poems that make up *In the Grip of Light*, the speaker is usually the poet after he has "limbered up" on Yeats. In "At Grass" and "Latest Face", it is the poet, un-self-consciously and unostentatiously himself, the man who "says" the poem. In the poems of 1954 and 1955, the speaker is more fully dramatized, to create a *persona* in which certain attitudes of the poet are given prominence, sometimes by guileful self-parody.

"I Remember, I Remember" is very much a constructed poem in this sense. Taking its title from Thomas Hood's famous anthology piece, it is aggressively deflative — so much so that Larkin later wrote an article, "Not the Place's Fault", to make it clear that Coventry, in which he grew up, was not being picked on. The target is the sentimentalization of childhood, particularly in the literature of the period, and this dimension makes it very much a Movement poem. Reviewing C. Day Lewis's autobiography, *The Buried Day*, in 1960, Larkin wrote: "This is the Forest-Reid-Walter-de-la-Mare view of life: nothing quite equals being a kid."[13] The friend in the train that stops at Coventry is given the commonplace question "Was that . . . where you 'have your roots'?"; and the last half of the poem consists of trotting out, with satirical rejection, the clichés of idealized autobiography: the garden where the poet "did not invent/Blinding theologies of flowers and fruits"; "that splendid family//I never ran to when I got depressed,/The boys all biceps and the girls all chest"; "The bracken where I never trembling sat,//Determined to go through with it." The forties had been a great period of turning back to childhood and youth as an earnest of potentialities lost through the corrupting inroads of experience. C. Day Lewis's "O Dreams, O Destinations" and Dylan Thomas's "Poem in October" had celebrated the wonder and innocence of childhood; while, on the other side of the Atlantic, Theodore Roethke had discovered transcendence in the potting shed. For Larkin's speaker, in contrast, "Nothing, like something, happens anywhere" — one of his lines most deflative of conventional attitudes.

"I Remember, I Remember" is only superficially autobiographical, consisting mainly of rejected stereotypes of biography. For Larkin such stereotypes constituted an important distortion within our culture; and this is the feeling from which the poem originates, rather than from a lurking resentment concerning the emptiness of his own childhood. Seen in this light, the poem involves a rather crude distortion of the "poet at the breakfast table" (the real-life Philip Larkin) — much cruder than in "Poetry of Departures", where the speaker remains puzzled and tentative.

"Mr. Bleaney" marks a new development in the use of the dramatized, reflexive speaker in Larkin's poetry. It appeared in *The Whitsun Weddings* in 1964, but was first published in *The Listener* of September 5th 1955, just ten days before the closing date for subscriptions for *The Less Deceived*. It is related in subject and attitude to "Poetry of Departures"; and, like that poem, must reflect Larkin's own experience of living in lodgings. The disturbing confrontation with the hum-drum, empty entrapment of everyday living explored in "Toads" and "Poetry of Departures", leads to the explicit and here devastating suggestion "That how we live measures our own nature".

The speaker of "Mr. Bleaney" is more decidedly a version of Larkin than is the speaker of "Poetry of Departures", and, as in "Reasons for Attendance", he is more fully dramatized. The speaker has taken a room previously occupied by Mr. Bleaney, whose range of tastes was limited to "preference for sauce to gravy" and "plugging at the four aways". The room has "Bed, upright chair, sixty-watt bulb, no hook//Behind the door" and is filled with the sound of the landlady's radio. The picture is of a life desperately bleak, lived in the unfulfilling "yearly frame: the Frinton folk/Who put him up for summer holidays,/And Christmas at his sister's house in Stoke" — a lodger in someone else's house even on holiday. Despite the fact that Mr. Bleaney seems to have enjoyed his life, the poem is a searing presentation of loneliness, compelling pity and despair at the possibilities that exist in our civilized human condition. Yet we miss an important dimension of the poem if we feel that we can stand back — or that the poet does — even in horror. For the speaker lies "Where Mr. Bleaney lay": he takes the room and looks out on the "strip of building land,/ Tussocky, littered" and the "bit of garden". The poem closes with the reflection

> But if he stood and watched the frigid wind
> Tousling the clouds, lay on the fusty bed
> Telling himself that this was home, and grinned,
> And shivered, without shaking off the dread
>
> That how we live measures our own nature,
> And at his age having no more to show
> Than one hired box should make him pretty sure
> He warranted no better, I don't know.

In "how we live measures our own nature", there lurks the fear that it measures that of the speaker — and of the reader, who has been led to make an identification with the speaker through a shared sense of difference from the landlady and Mr. Bleaney. Larkin himself said:

> The first two-thirds of the poem, down to 'But if', are concerned with my uneasy feeling that I'm becoming Mr. Bleaney, yes. The last third is reassuring myself that I'm not, because he was clearly quite content with his sauce instead of gravy and digging the garden and so on, and yet there's doubt lingering too, perhaps he hated it as much as I did.[14]

The statement was made in answer to a questioner who remarked that Larkin had "suffered from problems of identification with Mr.Bleaney", possibly because some readers were "missing the grammatical construction of the last two stanzas . . . which both ventures a judgement and refuses it at the same time".[15] The stanzas conclude in the characteristic disclaimer,"I don't know", which seems partially to disown what has gone before. The "grammatical construction" is easy enough to follow as one reads, but its direction is by no means clear when one has finished. In a poem of such accomplished artistry, one would suppose that, rhetorically, the confusing syntax mirrors the confusion of the speaker (though not that of the writer of the poem); and also that it hides a trap for the reader, requiring as it does reflective inspection for the realization that the statement applies as well to the speaker (and the reader) as it does to Mr. Bleaney.

Like "Poetry of Departures", "Mr. Bleaney" dramatizes a voice other than that of the speaker — in this case the landlady's — with which it opens, achieving surprise and temporary disorientation by not indicating immediately who is speaking. Here, as elsewhere, Larkin shows an acute sense of how people talk, particularly in ways that differentiate class: "the Bodies" for a motor car body works; or "took/My bit of garden properly in hand". The details provide a telling and assured evocation of a social ambience: "Flowered curtains, thin and frayed", "saucer-souvenir", "jabbering set". Within the sober diction of this serious poem are embedded phrases of working class slang appropriate to the situation: "stub my fags", "kept on plugging at the four aways". It is a measure of the range and originality of the idiom that the phrases do not obtrude but are part of the strength of the poem. In their day, they would have been conventionally expected only in satirical poems.

In "Church Going" we encounter a more complex self-dramatization of Larkin in a typical Movement role — unassuming, self-questioning, taking off his "cycle-clips in awkward reverence". Deeply serious both in apparent intent and actual impact, the poem conveys much that was important to Larkin at the time, and one has the sense of the poet speaking with unfiltered directness at the conclusion. It would be an absurd misreading of the poem to see its last lines as "qualified" by the social status of the speaker; and the temptation hardly arises, as what is offered is a self-portrait with only a mild touch of parody. It is true that the speaker tries a little hard in his agnostic role at the beginning, with "Up at the holy end" or the overloud "Here endeth" or donating "an Irish sixpence" (accepted currency in

Northern Ireland, where the poem was written, but not "coin of the realm").

The poem follows a pattern of situation, question, exploration and recognition. After the first two stanzas, which present the speaker and his situation, there is a contrast between the phrase that closes the second stanza and the one that opens the third: "Reflect the place was not worth stopping for.//Yet stop I did". The effect of balance and contrast is accentuated by the gap between the stanzas. The question of why he stops, "Wondering what to look for", leads into the question "When churches fall completely out of use/What shall we turn them into" — disarmingly matter of fact in its acceptance that churches will go out of use. This in turn leads to the speculations that are the heart of the poem, concerning what will happen to the needs and feelings to which religion has ministered in our lives — concerning "what remains when disbelief has gone?" With the question "I wonder who/Will be the last, the very last, to seek/This place for what it was", the poem is brought back to the speaker and his cultural situation: "will he be my representative,//Bored, uninformed, knowing the ghostly silt/ Dispersed" — so characteristic of the Movement in its "bored, uninformed" yet quite emphatic in its "knowing" that the imagined power of the past has become a detritus, a "silt". The final rallying consolation that the speaker offers himself is the recognition that we shall retain a need to see our lives as destiny — something meaningful that in some way *had* to be as it was.

> A serious house on serious earth it is,
> In whose blent air all our compulsions meet,
> Are recognised, and robed as destinies.
> And that much never can be obsolete,
> Since someone will forever be surprising
> A hunger in himself to be more serious.

That power to robe our compulsions as destinies is associated with the way in which the church "held unspilt/So long and equably what since is found/Only in separation — marriage, and birth,/And death, and thoughts of these". Though the poem might seem to have its later companion in "The Building", it reaches forward as well to the social rituals of "To the Sea" and "Show Saturday" and to the marriages of "The Whitsun Weddings" in its recognition that we derive a sense of our own being from these events that confer satisfactions and have an authority that goes beyond the immediate enjoyment and comfort we derive from them.

Stylistically the poem is characterized by oscillations of tone both within phrases and in contrast of phrases: "sprawlings of flowers"; "a tense, musty, unignorable silence,/Brewed God knows how long"; "if we shall keep/A few cathedrals chronically on show,/ Their parchment, plate and pyx in locked cases,/And let the rest rent-free to rain and sheep." The poem as a whole moves with controlled skill through a variety of tones that include the playful, the ironic and the unqualifiedly serious.

Much of the poem's character comes from the way in which positions are implied, or presented as accepted, by their inclusion in subordinate positions in statements or questions: "When churches fall completely out of use" takes for granted the disappearance of Christianity; while "superstition, like belief, must die/And what remains when disbelief has gone?" takes as the basis for its question agreement that belief will die. Nowhere is the strategy more unobtrusively employed than in the positioning of the phrases that pay homage to the church's immemorial function — "because it held unspilt/So long and equally what since is found/Only in separation". This passage is introduced with a tentative explanatory function in a question, so that the view it embodies is stated in passing rather than asserted. Controversy concerning belief or the decline of belief is sidestepped through astute manipulation of syntax and tone; though the speaker's position is everywhere quite clearly one of disbelief.

In the poem's progress from the presentation of the initial dramatized situation to its final unguarded statement, we encounter a pattern that Larkin was to employ in his most ambitious poems such as "The Whitsun Weddings", "Dockery and Son", "An Arundel Tomb", "The Building" and "The Old Fools". The power to carry an argument through a long poem with a complex form and with a subtle control of tone and movement is something that Larkin learned under the influence of Yeats: "Yeats and Auden, the management of lines, the formal distancing of emotion" he later said, recalling his debt ("An Interview with *Paris Review*", RW 67). Indeed, the poem of meditation that takes as its basis the experiences of suburban life and treats its details from a realist point of view, deriving its metaphorical resonances from the juxtaposition of its details, derives from Auden. "Church Going" is decidedly Audenesque in phrasing, as, towards its end, it moves, in a manner that was to become characteristic of Larkin, from tentativeness to unqualified assertion. The gift for sententious generalization, the firm assertive rhythms, the witty use of "surprising" when in fact it has been Larkin who has been surprised by his own "hunger . . . to be more serious" — all these features remind one of Auden.

The poem is a cultural milestone, marking a decisive change in poetic orientation to the question of belief. Yeats had stated the predicament and ambition of much modern poetry when he wrote: "I am very religious, and deprived by Huxley and Tyndall, whom I detested, of the simple-minded religion of my childhood, I had made a new religion, almost an infallible church of poetic tradition . . ."[16] Eliot's *Four Quartets* is a major religious poem that seeks self-transcendence without an overt ontological commitment to god. The careers of Yeats and Eliot can be seen as an attempt to retrieve through art what had been lost by religion, despite Eliot's critical rejection of such an ambition for art. Hardy, such an important example for Larkin, portrays a universe at the mercy of chance, abandoned by god: the perceived withdrawal of divine providence is the cause of immitigable agony for Hardy. For Dylan Thomas, only eight years older than Larkin, there is a nostalgia for the sanctification of experience that religion or a sense of the divine conferred. Larkin's speaker in "Church Going" has stepped beyond this, seeing himself as a precursor of the last visitor who will come to "seek/This place for what it was". The end of the process that began in the days of Matthew Arnold is summed up in the question "what remains when disbelief has gone?" — a question that is posed with detachment.

With Larkin's growing reputation, there came attempts to present the poem as a religious poem — attempts in keeping with the lingering sense in our culture that anything deeply serious must be religious. Much of this misreading of the poem came from a failure to respond to its tone and to observe its implied cultural ambience, which is an acceptance of the rational impossibility of belief in the divine. Larkin himself very forcefully remarked:

> It is of course an entirely secular poem. I was a bit irritated by an American who insisted to me it was a religious poem. It isn't religious at all. Religion surely means that the affairs of the world are under divine surveillance, and so on, and I go to some pains to point out that I don't bother about that kind of thing, that I'm deliberately ignorant of it — 'Up at the holy end', for instance. Ah no, it's a great religious poem; he knows better than me — trust the tale and not the teller, and all that stuff.
>
> Of course the poem is about going to church, not religion — I tried to suggest this by the title — and the union of the important stages of human life — birth, marriage and death — that going to church represents; and my own feeling that when they are dispersed into the

registry office and the crematorium chapel life will become thinner in consequence.[17]

The speakers of "Mr. Bleaney", "Church Going" and "Reasons for Attendance" might be described as "surprised by doubt" (to adapt Wordsworth's phrase). The process of discovering in an accidentally encountered and seemingly innocuous situation the cause for discomforting reflections concerning oneself is enacted in many of Larkin's poems — most notably in the later "Dockery and Son", where the speaker is surprised into a new perspective on his whole life. This is in keeping with the obvious theme of *The Less Deceived* (announced in its title) that our situation is frequently not what it seems to be and that experience constantly deceives us. In addition, we encounter Larkin's recurrent theme of the passage of time and the transience of experience. Yet embedded in so many of the poems is a related concern with identity — with what we are, how we are deceived in our perception of what we are, and how we come through time to be what we are. This concern is encountered in "At Grass", where the separation of the horses and their names is an important thread in the poem. The young lady's photograph album offers all her "ages" and "overwhelmingly persuades/That this is a real girl in a real place", yet leaves the poet and reader cut off from her many pasts. "Maiden Name", a companion poem, dwells more directly on the theme of identity, emphasizing the ironic gap between name and person that marriage has brought: "Now it's a phrase applicable to no one . . ./Or, since you're past and gone,//It means what we feel now about you then . . ."

The theme of identity is a rewarding one and is frequently treated rewardingly by Larkin. In the world of "Church Going", where we cannot appeal to beliefs that have a sanction beyond our own, the sense of what we are is all important and is a measure of what we should be and of what would be best for us to be. The search for one's identity is so common in modern literature as to require no further comment on its centrality as a theme. Yet for Larkin, as in "Reasons for Attendance", it is associated at times with a strain that comes close to overwhelming the poet and the poem; so that a longing for retreat from the concern is not surprising. In "At Grass", the fact that the horses in retirement "stand anonymous again" is a part of their idyll. In "Wants" the refrain of the first stanza "Beyond all this, the wish to be alone" modulates in the second stanza into "Beneath it all, desire of oblivion runs". The uncharacteristically symbolist poem "Absences" follows its rather vertiginous presentation of the sea with the exultant single line "Such attics cleared of me! Such absences."

Concern with identity remained with Larkin to the end. In "The Old Fools" death is seen as the moment when "the bits that were you/ Start speeding away from each other for ever"; while, in "Aubade", the last poem of any consequence to be published by him, there is the reflection that "An only life can take so long to climb/Clear of its wrong beginnings".

In 1954 Larkin started sending his poems to George Hartley's *Listen*; and later that year Hartley asked Larkin if he had enough poems for a book. Early in 1955 Larkin sent him a typescript entitled *Various Poems*, but Hartley did not like the title, and it was changed to *The Less Deceived*, the original title of the poem now called "Deceptions". The new book contained thirteen poems from *XX Poems*, the entire contents of the Fantasy Press pamphlet, and all the poems published in periodicals in 1953, 1954 and 1955, except for "Fiction and the Reading Public", "Mr. Bleaney" and "Reference Back", the last two of which just missed the book. Only "Wedding-wind" and "Going" survived from *In the Grip of Light*. *The Less Deceived* was published from the Marvell Press at Hessle, near Hull, and took most of what remained of 1955 to get into print. In the meantime, Larkin had moved to Hull to become head of the Brynmor Jones Library at the University there. The appointment was made on 23rd November 1954, and had nothing to do with Larkin's literary reputation, as he then had none. He took up the post on 21st March 1955, and thus found himself near to his publisher.

The Less Deceived first appeared in a subscription edition of 300 copies. It was mentioned in *The Times* in a review of the year's literature and sold out quickly. A further 400 copies were bound, and this set was exhausted by April 1956. Another printing of 1320 copies was made in August of that year.

XX Poems and the Fantasy Press pamphlet had each been the subject of only one review. In 1955 and 1956, *The Less Deceived* was reviewed sixteen times, with notices in most of the major weeklies that reviewed poetry. Anthony Hartley, in the *Spectator*, saw it "in the running for the best [book of poetry] published in this country since the war";[18] while for G.S. Fraser, in the *New Statesman & Nation*, Larkin seemed "to exemplify everything that is good in this 'new movement' and none of its faults".[19] *The Times Literary Supplement* felt that the book "should establish Mr. Philip Larkin as a poet of quite exceptional importance".[20] Older poets were less emphatic in their praise, or unwilling to praise at all. Roy Fuller, in the *London Magazine*, allowed that "the collection as a whole is most readable and enjoyable";[21] but David Wright in *Encounter* attacked the book and the Movement for "the palsy of playing safe".[22] Larkin's work was finally getting attention.

"Maiden Name" from January 1955 was the last poem to get into *The Less Deceived*. "Mr. Bleaney", written in May, and "The Importance of Elsewhere", written in June, clearly belong with that book. 1955 was not a prolific year, — only eight poems were written in all, two of which ("Long Sight in Age" and "Counting") were never published by Larkin and one of which, "Pigeons", was not collected in Larkin's lifetime. There are only two poems from 1956, "An Arundel Tomb" from February and "First Sight" from March. "An Arundel Tomb" marks a change in its undeflative treatment of the speaker of the poem and of the ironies it uncovered in experience.

In "Reference Back" (from August 1955), we have a transition to that undeflative presentation of the speaker and his experience. Larkin recalls an attempt by his mother to reach out to him emotionally in the "time at home" that she "Looked so much forward to".

> *That was a pretty one*, I heard you call
> From the unsatisfactory hall
> To the unsatisfactory room where I
> Played record after record, idly,
> Wasting my time at home, that you
> Looked so much forward to.

The inappropriateness of his mother's remark to the jazz record to which he is listening — King Oliver's "Riverside Blues" — evokes at once the emotional distance between them and the embarrassed attempts to bridge it. The word "unsatisfactory" is used four times in the poem; and, in tune with Larkin's other poems of the Movement period, the moment of closeness is itself "unsatisfactory". Yet it is the occasion for nostalgia; and, like the record made the "year after I was born", which will always recall this coming together, it links the speaker with the past.

The poem moves casually up to its concluding lines. It makes its turn on a sentence that is merely the name of the record: "Oliver's *Riverside Blues*." This has the feeling of bald, immutable fact, in contrast with the elusiveness of remembered emotion. The brevity shows up the long gangling sentence that follows and which seems to suggest the awkwardness of "this sudden bridge/From your unsatisfactory age/To my unsatisfactory prime". The naming of the record in so prominent a position and with so little ostentation gives the feeling that this is how it must have been; yet the recording is artfully chosen, having been made "The year after I was born". The primitive "pre-electric" sound seems as "antique" as the faded, posed photographs of the Oliver orchestra make them look, suggesting how distant Larkin's own beginnings seem to him, as does the closeness he once had with his mother.

Yet "our element is time", the cause of change and estrangement; it protects us from these "long perspectives /Open at each instant of our lives":

> They link us to our losses: worse,
> They show us what we have as it once was,
> Blindingly undiminished, just as though
> By acting differently we could have kept it so.

This potentiality, lurking in every moment, to show us how much time has taken away is a frightening one, bringing us round to Larkin's concern with time and the elusiveness of experience. The final hope, the sadness of which is established by the poem, is characteristically rejected as illusory.

"Reference Back" is a little heavy-handed in its opening and in the explicitness of its conclusion. In contrast with "Lines on a Young Lady's Photograph Album", where the poem concludes by placing its subject in a new focus, "Reference Back" enunciates what the poem is about, a practice to be increasingly encountered in Larkin's poems of the late fifties and early sixties. However, the poem lets its meaning fall out with the appearance of naturalness in its middle section, in contrast to the surprising twists of "Poetry of Departures" or "Mr. Bleaney" — or even "Church Going".

"An Arundel Tomb" is tentative in its disclosures and muted in its irony. It has no dramatized speaker, and, in this respect, is the descendant of "At Grass", as it is also in its lyrical nostalgia and its tone of ready acceptance. Its concern is with history — with the way in which it loads the present but is itself also changed over time. The poem marks the beginning for Larkin of a richer relationship with England and its past that was to flower in *The Whitsun Weddings*.

Coming to Hull had been a return to England from Northern Ireland. "Lonely in Ireland, since it was not home . . .// . . . went/To prove me separate, not unworkable", he wrote at this time in "The Importance of Elsewhere". However

> Living in England has no such excuse:
> These are my customs and establishments
> It would be much more serious to refuse.
> Here no elsewhere underwrites my existence.

"An Arundel Tomb" moves up quietly on the reader. It stays with the contemplation of its subject — the tomb of the Earl and Countess of Arundel in Chichester Cathedral — for four stanzas, the first three of which each end at the end of a sentence, giving the poem a measured movement in keeping with its air of considered and sometimes witty commentary. However, within this held back opening (which takes up nearly half of the poem) the important paradoxes are being developed through the central image, "His hand withdrawn, holding her hand". This touch — "A sculptor's sweet commissioned grace/Thrown off in helping to prolong/The Latin names around the base" — is seen, over time, as usurping the whole intent of the tomb, which was to eternalize the names of the occupants, not their love. "One sees" the hand "with a sharp tender shock"; and the poem reflects that it was "just a detail friends would see"; but with time "succeeding eyes begin/To look, not read", until "The stone fidelity/They hardly meant has come to be/Their final blazon": their love becomes their only heraldry for the modern visitor.

The contrast of seeing and reading is associated with a more pervasive contrast, that of truth and lies: "Time has transfigured them into/Untruth" — into an image of a faithfulness that was "hardly meant". This gives an unsuspected ambiguity to an earlier line "They would not think to lie so long", and even to the second line of the poem "The earl and countess lie in stone". These muted paradoxes, redolent of seventeenth-century poetry, may have been suggested by the subject; but they are in tune with the central paradox of the poem: the historical untruth that the modern visitor perceives *is* the important truth that the figures on the tomb have to show: "What will survive of us is love." Or rather, something slighter and more tentative: the figures on the tomb "prove/Our almost-instinct almost true".

As in "Reference Back", the poem concludes with an explicit statement of what the poem points to. However, here the conclusion is preceded by a characteristic gesture of withdrawal: logically, a qualification justified by experience; poetically, a gesture of sadness in the face of longing. It exemplifies Larkin's studiously devious handling of syntax: despite the disclaimer, the poem is made to conclude with the grand assertion whose "independence" is strengthened by the fact that the statement constitutes the complete last line. In the larger orchestration of the poem, it comes with the force of resolution, despite the preceding qualification. In 1980, Larkin called the poem "rather . . . romantic"; and said "I don't like it much"; but added "I think what survives of us is love, whether in the simple biological sense or just in terms of responding to life . . ."[23]

It is in the fifth stanza, where the syntax overflows the stanzaic form and the poem leaves the tighter limits of its ostensible subject, that we find the most memorable writing:

> Snow fell, undated. Light
> Each summer thronged the glass. A bright
> Litter of birdcalls strewed the same
> Bone-riddled ground. And up the paths
> The endless altered people came,
>
> Washing at their identity.

Here we encounter references to identity and to the passage of time, both of which involve enduring tensions for Larkin, in a context that is permeated by a feeling of ease and renewal. A freedom from the pressures of time is suggested by "undated", while the Audenesque "endless altered people" presents change as part of an unchanging procession. "Snow" falling suggests peace; "Light . . . thronged", a plenitude; and "A bright/Litter of bird calls", a careless joy. The sense of ease and stillness, for which there is such a powerful nostalgia in Larkin's poetry, is given an almost sacramental association in "Washing at their identity".

"An Arundel Tomb" gives an historical dimension to that pastoral vision of England that we encounter in "At Grass" and that was to be growingly important in Larkin's poetry. It marks, too, the decline of impulses associated with the Movement and the iconoclasm that seemed culturally appropriate at that important moment of artistic change.

During 1956, two important anthologies appeared: *Poets of the 1950's*, edited by D.J. Enright; and *New Lines*, edited by Robert Conquest. *Poets of the 1950's* was published in January in Tokyo. It contained poems by Enright, Larkin, Kingsley Amis, Robert Conquest, Donald Davie, John Holloway, Elizabeth Jennings and John Wain. *New Lines*, which appeared in June, contained contributions by the same poets, along with poems by Thom Gunn.

Poets of the 1950's, published outside England, had less impact than *New Lines*, even though it ran to a second edition by 1958. It seems to have found its way into only a very few libraries. Larkin was represented by "Skin", "Less Deceived" (later called "Deceptions"), "Wedding-wind", "At Grass", "Next Please", "If my darling" and "Going" — all from *XX Poems*, except for "Skin". This would suggest that Larkin's contribution had been compiled some time before the collection was published. The chief interest of *Poets of the 1950's* today lies in the "statements" by the poets that introduce the selections. Larkin's own "statement", evidently not intended for publication, became one of the most widely quoted examples of the Movement's "no nonsense" stance: "As a guiding principle I believe that every poem must be its own sole freshly created universe, and therefore have no belief in 'tradition' or a common myth-kitty or casual allusions in poems to other poems or poets, which last I find unpleasantly like the talk of literary understrappers letting you see they know the right people." ("Statement", *RW* 79) Despite the truculent tone and the glancing shot at Yeats and Eliot, Larkin seems never to have wavered from the main position stated here.

New Lines gained considerably more attention. In his introduction, Conquest expressed "the belief that a general tendency has once again set in, and that a genuine and healthy poetry . . . has established itself." He attacked the notion that "poetry *must* be metaphorical" and spoke up for "a rational structure and comprehensible language" and for the "intellectual component of poetry". He saw the poetry of the fifties as submitting "to no great systems of theoretical constructs nor agglomerations of unconscious commands . . . free from both mystical and logical compulsions . . . empirical in its attitude to all that comes." The collection did much to consolidate the reputations of the writers it included and to cause them to be seen as a group. Conquest's characterization of their work was, on the whole, just and accurate, and pointed to qualities they had in common and in terms of which they differed from writers of the forties. The notion that they constituted some sort of movement, intended or unintended, was justified, despite later denials (one of which, indeed, came from Conquest, who contended that, for him, the "Movement" was the group of young Empsonians whom he criticized in his Introduction).[24]

Larkin was represented in *New Lines* by "Maiden Name", "Church Going", "I Remember, I Remember", "Skin", "Latest Face", "Born Yesterday", "Triple Time", "Toads" and "Lines on a Young Lady's Photograph Album". "Church Going" and "Toads" became the best known poems from *New Lines*; and, with their tone of irreverence, seemed to typify Movement poetry for the reading public.

It is easy to underestimate Larkin's innovative contribution to the Movement tone in the light of the direction his poetry later took and his own later statements. His poems of the period do not have the surface toughness of contemporary poems by Wain and Amis. Nonetheless, following the example of Auden, they draw subtly and richly on the resources of colloquial speech to enhance the idiom of poetry in a way that occurs only once in a generation. In addition, poems like "Lines on a Young Lady's Photograph Album" or "Poetry of Departures" or "Toads" were much more lethal to received attitudes than most other writing of the period — and much more effective in the elusive complexity of their iconoclasm.

A parallel between *The Less Deceived* of 1955 and Lowell's *Life Studies* of 1959 serves to emphasise the radical innovativeness of Larkin's poetry at that time. The speaker of "Church Going", taking off his cycle-clips "in awkward reverence", has a similar function to the speaker of "Memories of West Street and Lepke", "book-worming/in pajamas . . ./ . . . on Boston's/ 'hardly passionate Marlborough Street'". Both poets seek to present a deflative persona, someone immersed in everyday experience and rather at its mercy — a persona at odds with the magisterial stance of the culturally ambitious poetry of high modernism. While *Life Studies* saw a turning away from the modernism of Eliot and Pound with its emphasis on the cultural duty of the poet, it stands in Lowell's work as a landmark of his continued engagement with poetic innovation that is part of the modernist heritage. Though Larkin never admired Eliot and Pound and was never drawn to their programme for poetry, his work in the nineteen-fifties brought about radical and innovative changes in English poetry.

Indeed, Larkin's ironic reversals that throw into doubt all that has gone before in a poem, can be seen as a manifestation of the questioning of the relation between writer and reader and writer and experience that has been a feature of so much late twentieth-century writing. His creation of ironically presented personae is in keeping with this sense of the questionable nature of any characterization of reality. In the ironic but fictive self-images of "Reasons for Attendance" and "Church Going", or of "Waking in the Blue" or "Skunk Hour" in *Life Studies*, and in the aggressive realism of "Poetry of Departures", "Reasons for Attendance" or "Memories of West Street and Lepke", there is the appearance, at least, of an attempt to head off any predilection the reader might have for putting either a grand or a definitive construction on the experiences embodied in the poems.

One of Larkin's few essays of this period, "The Pleasure Principle", published in *Listen* for Summer-Autumn 1957, may tend, in the perspective afforded by his whole career, to deflect attention from his innovative contribution to changes in poetry and the atmosphere in which it was received in the nineteen-fifties. The key statement that "if a poet loses his pleasure-seeking audience he has lost the only audience worth having" (*RW* 81–2) was one that Larkin stayed with throughout his life; but, embedded in this lively, polemical essay, it seems to involve a less simplistic rejection of modernism than it did when invoked at later stages of Larkin's career. Indeed, the essay is very much a Movement piece, with a title that involves a witty, anti-intellectual distortion of one of the central ideas of the twentieth-century, Freud's "pleasure-principle". Its target is another aspect of the intellectual establishment of the period, the criticism and exegesis of poetry, seen by Larkin as one of the outgrowths of modernism that has led to an undesirable change in the cultural role of poetry. The writing has a bantering Movement tone: let the reader "so much as breathe a word about not liking a poem, and he is in the dock before you can say Edwin Arlington Robinson." The "cash customers of poetry" have given it up, to be "replaced by a humbler squad, whose aim is not pleasure but self-improvement." (*RW* 81) The attitudes are very much in tune with the "Introduction" to *New Lines*.

However, as we have seen, Larkin had by 1956 begun to move away from the style of poetry represented by his Movement poems. Indeed, while *New Lines* may be seen as announcing a new tendency in English poetry, it was also its high-water mark. By 1958 the Movement impulse is still recognizable in books like Amis's *I Like It Here* or Wain's *The Contenders*, but these are the last stand of the compulsory iconoclasm of the Movement's early years.

Nonetheless, the Movement iconoclasm was crucial for Larkin. He said in *Poets of the 1950s* "I make a point of not knowing what poetry is or how to read a page or about the function of myth"; and he was saying something that was to remain vital to him. Equally important to him was to remain the justification he offered for those remarks: "I feel that my prime responsibility is to the experience itself". ("Statement", *RW* 79) He had started out (to adapt his own title) "in the grip of light", under the influence of the neo-romantic programme for poetry. The Movement's derision for anything bogusly high-toned must have provided an opportunity for an important clarification for him. Equally important were the associated ideals of diction and tone. 1953 to 1956 were key creative years for him in which he wrote a large number of the poems by which he seems destined to be remembered. Though he moved on to develop an idiom richer than that of any of the other poets associated with the Movement — including his own at the time — the association was a crucial one for him. Indeed, that later richness was implicit in the poems of the Movement years. The determination of Amis, Larkin and Wain to make poetry out of the experiences that figured importantly in their lives, rather than what was conventionally felt to be "important", was what many readers initially found smart, philistine and off-putting about the Movement. Yet that determination led to an acclimatisation of everyday things that was the basis of the power of later poems such as "The Whitsun Weddings", "Faith Healing", "Dockery and Son" and "To the Sea".

Chapter 6

THE CENTRAL VISION

After "An Arundel Tomb" in February 1956, Larkin completed only two poems in over two years — the uncharacteristically bland "First Sight" in March 1956 and "Love Songs in Age" in January 1957 — a poem originally drafted in July 1953. Such a break seems to have been quite usual for him. Following the compilation of *In the Grip of Light* in autumn of 1946, he wrote little until the end of 1947; *XX Poems* of 1951 was followed by a bleak period up to 1953; and, after the preparation of *The Whitsun Weddings*, which appeared in 1964, he produced only six poems in almost four years. However, as books went to press, there seems to have been a spill over of activity: in 1951, after the compilation of *XX Poems*, he wrote eight poems that he never collected; and the poems from 1955 and 1956 already discussed just missed *The Less Deceived* to appear in *The Whitsun Weddings*.

In 1957 and 1958, Larkin published only six short poems, three of which — "Pigeons", "Tops" and "Success Story", he chose never to collect. As in 1953, he drew on poems from an earlier time; but, on this occasion, the poems included ones that he had previously passed over for publication: "Tops" and "Days" were from 1953, "Success Story" from 1954, and "Pigeons" from December 1955. The omission of "Days" from *The Less Deceived* is, in retrospect, surprising: the reason may have been that it lacked the reflexive irony of many of Larkin's Movement poems. Its revival in 1957 is in keeping with the already noted turning away from the Movement's iconoclasm.

The return to writing came with the poem that was to be the title poem of Larkin's next volume, "The Whitsun Weddings", a highly orchestrated piece in the manner of "Church Going", where scene and incident are the vehicles for the complex movement of feeling and contemplation. Although it was first published in *Encounter* in June of 1959, it was begun in the summer of 1957: "After three pages, I dropped it for another poem that in fact was finished but never published. I picked it up again, in March 1958, and worked on it till October, when it was finished. But when I look at the diary I was keeping at the time, I see that the kind of incident it describes happened in July 1955." ("An Interview with *Paris Review*", *RW* 75) Larkin's remarks illustrate the sort of continuity that exists in his work — steady, but not inflexible; and allowing the development of a variety of styles of poem within his personal idiom.

The poem is not only the title poem of its volume, but, like "Church Going" in *The Less Deceived* and "The Building" in *High Windows*, it is the keynote poem of the book. It does not have the philosophical and cultural resonance of "Church Going", nor does it exploit so extensively the Larkinesque speaker as does that earlier poem. The "I" is clearly Larkin, the librarian, leaving Hull late on a Saturday afternoon for a week-end in London; and, apart from his initial obtuseness in thinking that the noise of the weddings was "porters larking with the mails", there is none of the self-deflation characteristic of the Movement poems. Nonetheless, the unassuming, initially puzzled speaker dramatized by the poem lends authenticity to the experiences and draws the reader in to share his attitudes. As in most of the non-satirical poems in *The Whitsun Weddings*, the poet seems unthreatened in his relationship with experience as a whole, relishing its details, so that it appears to surround him with a satisfying density.

The realistic rendering of detail could divert us from an awareness of the orchestration of the poem as a whole: indeed, its opening stanza portrays a scene immediately recognizable by anyone who had taken a train from Hull to London in those days. The first two stanzas place the speaker in a situation of isolated suspension in time that is frequently a desired good in Larkin's poetry. He is "late getting away", and finds himself alone in the "three-quarters-empty train" . . . "all sense/Of being in a hurry gone". The landscape has a sleepy stillness, never obtruding on his peace with anything like an "event":

> All afternoon, through the tall heat that slept
>   For miles inland,
> A slow and stopping curve southwards we kept.
> Wide farms went by, short-shadowed cattle, and
> Canals with floatings of industrial froth;
> A hothouse flashed uniquely: hedges dipped
> And rose: and now and then a smell of grass
> Displaced the reek of buttoned carriage-cloth
> Until the next town, new and nondescript,
> Approached with acres of dismantled cars.

He remains throughout the poem the observer, isolated in the slow and steady warmth of the afternoon: "sun destroys/The interest of what's happening in the shade"; and this isolation within his own life leads into the triumphant moment of the "frail/Travelling coincidence", as all the couples travel towards London and the lives they will separately make: "and none/Thought of the others they would never meet/Or how their lives would all contain this hour." Only he, the outsider, is aware of the sharing, which he celebrates in the concluding lines:

> what it held
> Stood ready to be loosed with all the power
> That being changed can give. We slowed again,
> And as the tightened brakes took hold, there swelled
> A sense of falling, like an arrow-shower
> Sent out of sight, somewhere becoming rain.

This coming together — both in the journey and the fact of marriage — constitutes a self-transcendence that is the obscured but half-understood significance in the awkwardness and vulgarity of the wedding "send-off's" that form the heart of the poem:

> Yes, from cafés
> And banquet-halls up yards, and bunting-dressed
> Coach-party annexes, the wedding-days
> Were coming to an end. All down the line
> Fresh couples climbed aboard: the rest stood round;
> The last confetti and advice were thrown,
> And, as we moved, each face seemed to define
> Just what it saw departing: children frowned
> At something dull; fathers had never known
>
> Success so huge and farcical;
>   The women shared
> The secret like a happy funeral;
> While girls, gripping their handbags tighter, stared
> At a religious wounding.

While there is community in the ceremony of marriage, each participant "defines" for himself the satisfaction the event brings.

In this section of the poem we sense most strongly Larkin's debt to Betjeman in the evocative rendering of detail, though with a critical and sympathetic focus on a class concerning which Betjeman would have tended to be satirical and dismissive:

> The fathers with broad belts under their suits
> And seamy foreheads; mothers loud and fat;
> An uncle shouting smut; and then the perms,
> The nylon gloves and jewellery-substitutes,
> The lemons, mauves, and olive-ochres that
>
> Marked off the girls unreally from the rest.

Later in the poem we encounter that peculiar power to evoke a landscape by the seemingly casual selection of a few key details — a gift that was very much Auden's at his best:

> An Odeon went past, a cooling tower,
> And someone running up to bowl . . ."

And finally there is that social placing through "voice" that only Larkin could do: "Some fifty minutes, that in time would seem// Just long enough to settle hats and say/ *I nearly died*".

In hardly any other poem of Larkin's is there such a clear feeling of transcending our everyday selves. It comes, not from any sense of something beyond the ordinary, but from one of those human ceremonies (marriage) "held so long unspilt" of "Church Going". That only the speaker is aware that "their lives would all contain this hour" may seem to qualify the feeling; but this may equally be seen as a sign that his discovered sense of community and renewal is contained within the bounds of the believable world of every day. As Larkin later said, "You couldn't be on that train without feeling the young lives all starting off, and that just for a moment you were touching them . . . It was a wonderful, a marvellous afternoon. It only needed writing down"[1]. The only blemish, if it is one, lies in the assumptions hidden in the phrase "writing down": the "We" with which the poem concludes comprises the speaker of the poem and the other occupants of the train; but the "we" implied by the valuations that are part of the "writing down", and which the poem depends upon for its reception, decidedly excludes tha newly-weds and their social group.

It is significant that "The Whitsun Weddings" marks not only a recommencement of writing after two years but also the beginning of an unironic, unprotected embracing of emotion that was a feature of Larkin's best work in those middle years. Over the next five years "The Whitsun Weddings" had companions in "Faith Healing" (May 1960), "Here" (October 1961) (another poem involving a railway journey — this time, *to* Hull), and "Dockery and Son" (March 1963), which are the most ambitious pieces in *The Whitsun Weddings* of 1964.

Few poems by Larkin seem to involve so little gap between speaker and author as does "Dockery and Son". The strategy is a familiar one with Larkin: a setting of apparent calm and inconsequence is found to contain the seeds of disturbance and leads to questioning and reorientation. The visit to Oxford suggests nothing more disquieting than that the speaker now feels out of place in his old haunts: "Death-suited, visitant, I nod". The talk with the dean seems a charade at odds with the reality of his college days, when "Black-gowned, unbreakfasted, and still half-tight/We used to stand before that desk, to give/ 'Our version' of 'these incidents last night'". He finds the door of his old room locked; and catches his train "ignored". Yet every detail reinforces a doubt about whether the speaker belongs — a doubt that will be so crucial to the development of the poem: his former life as undergraduate seems to elude him.

This poetic strategy of calculated indirection is one that Yeats developed in poems of meditation based on autobiographical incidents. "In Memory of Major Robert Gregory" begins with Yeats by the fire remembering old friends. He recalls Lionel Johnson, J.M. Synge, and his uncle, George Pollexfen; but, when he comes to Gregory, he declares that he is too upset to go further with his recollections. In fact, he has gone as far as he needs, and each figure recalled has his place in the pattern of contrasts that makes up the poem. The protestation is a device to hide the deliberateness of the poem and to give it the appearance of startling discovery for poet and reader. The structure of "Dockery and Son", like that of Yeats's poems, is ostensibly associational, and the speaker appears to search for his meaning: "Of . . . No, that's not the difference: rather . . ." Even the length of the poem and the use of an eight line rhyming stanza (with variations) reinforces the sense of debt to Yeats.

As in "Mr. Bleaney", the opening is in the form of direct speech by someone who has not yet been named, and reference is made to a person whose identity we have yet to discover: "Dockery" — the seed of the poem is the first word. As the poem opens out for us, a variety of devices is used to give the feeling of the speaker groping for understanding of his experiences: he falls asleep; he tries out an explanation and then rejects it. As in "Church Going", assertion becomes more definite as the poem moves towards its close. The pivotal question is "Where do these/Innate assumptions come from?". After that, there are no more questions. The assumptions that differentiate Dockery's life from that of the speaker lead to considerations of the role of choice and individual control in the shaping of life — one of Larkin's haunting and most significant themes:

They're more a style
Our lives bring with them: habit for a while
Suddenly they harden into all we've got

And how we got it. . .

The word "harden" suggests not only destiny taking a decided form,
but also a "hardening" in obduracy, and with a sense of denial and
limitation — "all we've got". What we become does not spring from
"what/We think truest, or most want to do:/Those warp tight-shut,
like doors" — an observation not of pessimism, but of psychological
profundity: life is finding out what you can do, not implementing
what you think you want. "Nothing with all a son's harsh patronage"
may seem a frightening recognition; yet the speaker is equally shocked
at the thought that Dockery tied his life up by begetting a son at the
age of nineteen or twenty. If Dockery's certainty does anything in the
poem, it is to highlight how time takes away while we are discovering
what it is we are and want — a common tragic theme in Western
literature. When we come to see this, the way in which the speaker's
past eluded him at the beginning of the poem falls into place.

The central scene of the poem is one where the speaker wakes to the
lurid and slightly unreal "fumes/And furnace-glares of Sheffield" to
change trains and wait on a platform surrounded by "ranged/Joining
and parting lines", suggestive of how his life has passed so "widely
from the others". It is a moment of isolation, in the middle of a journey, illuminated by "a strong//Unhindered moon". The separation of
"strong" and "Unhindered" by the break between stanzas gives them
surprising emphasis; and, indeed, the words almost seem to function
separately from what they describe, naming the qualities that the
speaker may feel were absent from his handling of his own destiny.

The locked door of the speaker's old rooms — seeming to suggest
exclusion from re-entry to his past — links with the doors that "warp
tight-shut" as images of our exclusion from "what/We think truest,
or most want to do". The use of "warp" implies a distortion that
develops unnoticed over time, and seems to refer (at one remove) to
the speaker's destiny as well as to his hopes.

Indeed, there is a firm orchestration of imagery of disappointment,
deflection from purpose, and elusiveness: the locked door; the "known
bell", heard but neither seen nor visited; the departure from Oxford
"ignored"; the "awful pie"; the warped doors; even the maze of crossing lines. They constitute not only an enactment of the speaker's
predicament, but a powerful unitary aspect of the experience of the

poem — an assertion that life has a particular quality of bewilderment and disappointment. This is resumed explicitly in the final lines:

> Whether or not we use it, it goes,
> And leaves what something hidden from us chose,
> And age, and then the only end of age.

These lines come fittingly after the experience of the poem; and the oblique reference to death shows Larkin's masterly handling of tone. But what of the previous line — "Life is first boredom, then fear"? It may be true; and it is consonant with the poem as a whole; but is it the conclusion towards which the poem inevitably pushes us? It seems to evince a bent of sensibility not clearly recognised for what it is. The central recognition of the poem is that living reveals the direction of our lives, in contrast with the more comforting notion that we choose our destinies. The sense that there lurks within experience the potentiality for such revelations is an abiding and disturbing theme of Larkin's poetry.

In the poems where the speaker is a dramatized version of the poet, some sort of autobiographical involvement is implied. Larkin seems close to the experience of his poems, in this sense, in *The Less Deceived* and in the poems from *The Whitsun Weddings* so far discussed. However, in his later work we find more and more poems in which the concerns are dramatized in a situation in which the speaker is no more than an anonymous commentator; while there is less reliance on the manipulation of the relationship of poet, speaker and reader to get the shifting stances of self-doubt characteristic of *The Less Deceived*.

Among the most moving poems of this new type is "Faith Healing". Like "At Grass", it arose from seeing a documentary rather than from a personal experience, Larkin's usual starting point. Here, more than anywhere else, we feel how wrong it is to speak of Larkin selling life short, on the basis of the aspects to which he gives attention. The poem is about those whom life *has* sold short; and Larkin's concern merges with a contemplation of how life fails to live up to what we can imagine it might be — fails sometimes tragically. The power of his frequent negatives to imply what they negate has been a noted feature of the rhetoric of his poetry. Here, what is lamented as unattained becomes the measure for the poem.

The movement of feeling is superbly controlled by changes in writing. The opening is transparently declarative, setting the scene: "Slowly the women file to where he stands". A change of tone comes in

"Stewards tirelessly/Persuade them onwards", where "persuade" introduces a sense of manipulation, of exploitation of feelings, enforced startlingly by "Within whose warm spring rain of loving care/Each dwells twenty seconds". The focus is strongly deflating by the end of the stanza — "scarcely pausing, goes into a prayer/Directing God about this eye, that knee".

There is a tidy consonance of form and sentence structure up to this point; but the next sentence breaks over the stanza end, as its rambling movement (running on into the third stanza) mirrors the bewilderment of those who came to believe and be cured:

> some
> Sheepishly stray, not back into their lives
> Just yet; but some stay stiff, twitching and loud
> With deep hoarse tears, as if a kind of dumb
> And idiot child within them still survives
> To re-awake at kindness . . .

"Their thick tongues blort" — where the invented word "blort", evoking "blurt" and "blot", suggests (in its failure to be a known word) an incoherence, an inability to bring feeling to a satisfying resolution; and this is made explicit in "unheard answers jam and rejoice", where the clash between "jam" and "rejoice" gives a sense of things brought to a halt and hints at the major absence in these lives — the absence of something about which to rejoice.

After the pathetically grotesque image "Moustached in flowered frocks they shake", the movement of the poem becomes more orderly and assured in the series of comments that generalize the feelings of the poem:

> In everyone there sleeps
> A sense of life lived according to love.
> To some it means the difference they could make
> By loving others, but across most it sweeps
> As all they might have done had they been loved.
> That nothing cures.

The loss and pain attendant on the absence of love — "An immense slackening ache" — is a feeling deeply present in Larkin's poetry — a more heartfelt tribute to the power of love than much that passes for "deeply human" poetry. It goes along with a keen sense of what it is like to be someone whom others don't particularly want — an awareness, as Kingsley Amis put it, that "the division between the attractive and the unattractive is a decisive one".[2] These feelings come to bear, in "Faith Healing", in a sense of the pathetic vulnerability of human hope. It offers an extreme example of all our attempts to make something of what we are given, to redeem the shortcomings of our lives, however deludedly. With characteristic poetic tact, Larkin closes, not with another generalization, but with an unresolved reference to the despairing side of experience: "and all time has disproved."

The sense of defeat, of the elusiveness of hope and of the selves we felt we were or might have been, is presented again with touching and direct humanity in "Afternoons":

> In the hollows of afternoons
> Young mothers assemble
> At swing and sandpit
> Setting free their children.
>
> Behind them, at intervals,
> Stand husbands in skilled trades,
> An estateful of washing,
> And the albums, lettered
> *Our Wedding*, lying
> Near the television:
> Before them, the wind
> Is ruining their courting-places . . .

The Betjemanesque detail of the wedding albums enters the poem with exactly the "placing" it would have achieved in cultural satire, yet without condescension: it is an epitome of the limited hope of most lives. The conclusion reiterates the sense given by "Dockery and Son" that we cannot make our destinies conform to our hopes:

> Their beauty has thickened.
> Something is pushing them
> To the side of their own lives.

The contrast between what we are and how we aspire to see ourselves is at the heart of another "Hull" poem, "The Large Cool Store", where the "weekday world of those//Who leave at dawn low terraced houses/Timed for factory, yard and site" is contrasted with the "Modes for Night" that they purchse:

> To suppose
> They share that world, to think this sort is
> Matched by something in it, shows
> How separate and unearthly love is . . .

That "much mentioned brilliance, love" is also the theme of "Love Songs in Age", where the music, marked and worn, becomes an emblem of the preservation of the past, bringing back, when it is played, that "certainty of time laid up in store", and "love . . . /Still promising to solve, and satisfy,/And set unchangeably in order" — as "It had not done . . . then, and could not now". Both the power of music and the contrasting artificiality and smallness of art in the face of life are evoked:

> . . . how each frank submissive chord
> Had ushered in
> Word after sprawling hyphenated word,
> And the unfailing sense of being young
> Spread out like a spring-woken tree . . .

Contrivance and strain are suggested by the image of the broken arrangement of the words of the song over the music. While the poem ends acknowledging the need to admit that love was not the panacea in the past and could not be now, it is permeated by that longing for transcendence characteristic of Larkin's poetry of all periods.

"Broadcast" Larkin said "seems to be about as near as I get in this collection to a love poem. It's not, I'm afraid, very near."[3] The speaker of the poem is evidently listening on the radio to a concert at which he knows a woman he loves is present. It has been a somewhat misread poem, one critic even imagining that " 'The Queen', and a huge resettling" indicated that the Queen had attended the concert and that the poem treated her disrespectfully. After capturing very well the type of sound that used to precede concerts on the radio, the poem goes on (in the old Movement manner) to treat the music disrespectfully — "A snivel on the violins", "Cascades of monumental slithering", "rabid storms of chording"; and for some readers this seems to have rubbed off on everything else in the poem. Perhaps this denigration served psychologically as a protection in what is, for Larkin, a very openly emotional poem. The sense of intimacy is conveyed subtly by a detail that the speaker imagines: "One of your gloves unnoticed on the floor/Beside those new, slightly-outmoded shoes"; and, as his room darkens, he has the sense of being very much alone in his world: "I lose/All but the outline of the still and withering//Leaves on half-emptied trees". The music ends in the darkness it has filled, and he is left "desperate to pick out/Your hands, tiny in all that air, applauding." The poem's power comes from the way in which it finds so natural an image for the vulnerability and the power of love in the "hands" whose sound is lost in the disembodied

applause heard at such a distance by the speaker in the darkness of
his room. Love is celebrated in an image from the commonplace world
that it redeems for us.

"Talking in Bed", another poem about love, is, in contrast, rather
frightening. Closeness here is at first equated with honesty and openness:

> Talking in bed ought to be easiest,
> Lying together there goes back so far,
> An emblem of two people being honest.

Yet, it concludes

> At this unique distance from isolation
>
> It becomes still more difficult to find
> Words at once true and kind,
> Or not untrue and not unkind.

The concluding line, in its paraphrase of the previous line, suggests a
kind of second best that also eludes. The world outside the room is
disturbed, but indifferent:

> Outside, the wind's incomplete unrest
> Builds and disperses clouds about the sky,
>
> And dark towns heap up on the horizon.
> None of this cares for us.

There is not even the consolation of insight: "Nothing shows why"
these things are as they are; while "more and more time passes
silently". The full irony of the poem is realized only when we look
back into it: nobody says anything in "Talking in Bed". The loneliness is frightening; but the redeeming power of the poem lies in
its quietly underplayed sense of the conflict that true closeness must
bring — between being "honest" and being "kind". Its measure is a
high one.

Loneliness emerges in a different perspective in "Here", a poem
that seems to arise from the experience of travelling back to Hull
from London, arriving in the morning. The places passed through,
as the train swings east around the Humber in the dawn, have a
ghostly quality, as if awaiting habitation. The train sets the speaker
down in Hull, where the working day is beginning and life is a matter
of "Cheap suits, red kitchen-ware, sharp shoes, iced lollies,/Electric
mixers, toasters, washers, driers"; yet the mind continues the jour-

ney beyond the urban terminus, out into the countryside of "Isolate villages", and, finally, to where the land falls away to the sea. The austerity of impulse and experience at the conclusion contrasts with the suggestive potentiality of the opening, yet seems also to be its fulfilment. Between lies the "cut-price crowd". The poem evokes the quality of life in Hull with the poetic force and affection that the younger Auden brought to the urban landscape. However, the town, to which the train has been journeying all night, comes as a "surprise" in the golden landscape of morning, and the speaker has a wistful longing for the country beyond, with "Fast-shadowed wheat-fields . . . /Isolate villages, where removed lives//Loneliness clarifies". Beyond this lies "unfenced existence . . . untalkative, out of reach", reminiscent of the idyll of anonymity that the horses enjoy in "At Grass". Loneliness emerges frequently in Larkin's work as a deeply depriving condition; but here, as in several poems, it is associated with stillness, with an absence of pressures concerning what one is, and with an attendant clarity and ease.

The sense of a possible condition of being — in this case "inno-cence" — having its locus in a particular time and place is again communicated in "MCMXIV". Seen otherwise, the poem might ap-pear false in its apparently simplistic final assertion "Never such in-nocence,/Never before or since,/As changed itself to past/Without a word"; whereas this is one of Larkin's most perfectly achieved poems in its sensitive rendering of evocative detail:

> the shut shops, the bleached
> Established names on the sunblinds,
> The farthings and sovereigns,
> And dark-clothed children at play
> Called after kings and queens
> The tin advertisements
> For cocoa and twist

The poem is drenched in a particular type of nostaligia; and its appar-ently simplistic conclusion might seem an assertion flatly at variance with historical truth; but it is evidently in the lack of awareness of incipient catastrophe that Larkin perceives the enviable innocence that contrasts with the knowledge that the Great War was to bring. Larkin remarked, concerning the Roman numerals of the title, that "the emotional impact of nineteen-fourteen in Arabic numerals was too great for anything I could possibly write myself";[4] and the his-torical awareness of the change in British sensibility brought about by the first World War gives the poem a powerful cultural resonance.

This is reinforced by the intense love of England that is felt in the details of the poem. Yet there is another resonance set up within the body of Larkin's poetry as a whole;

> The place-names all hazed over
> With flowering grasses, and fields
> Shadowing Domesday lines
> Under wheat's restless silence

suggests a relation to "Here". The lost pre-1914 world becomes a place of stillness, clarity, silence, where everything is at rest or moving slowly and patiently forward; and we have another English idyll whose companionship with "At Grass" needs no emphasis. There is a sense of permanence — "Established names on the sunblinds", "Domesday lines"; and the details come with a clarity that suggests an absence of change. Syntactically the poem is a list without a verb, broken only by the verbless interjection "Never such innocence"; so that in terms of its structure, too, the poem creates a feeling of scarcely moving forward.

The opening line of "MCMXIV" seems to be echoed in the "Introduction" that Larkin wrote for an American edition of Betjeman's poems, "It Could Only Happen in England": "the 'long- dead generations' going back beyond Ypres and the Somme to the golden summers of Edward and Victoria" (*RW* 212). In that same essay he quotes, from *Notes Towards a Definition of Culture*, Eliot's sense of the "way of life" that constitutes "culture" in England: "Derby Day, Henley Regatta, Cowes, the twelfth of August, a cup final, the dog races, the pin table, the dart board, Wensleydale cheese, boiled cabbage cut in sections, beetroot in vinegar, nineteenth-century gothic churches, and the music of Elgar." (*RW* 218) Larkin goes on to remark that "if this passage reminds us of anyone's poetry, it is Betjeman's rather than Eliot's or anyone else's." (*RW* 212) It could also remind us of Larkin's own poetry and point to his debt to Betjeman. This debt is especially felt in *The Whitsun Weddings* — in "MCMXIV", "Here", "The Large Cool Store", "Ambulances", "Afternoons", and in the title poem. What is rejected culturally by Betjeman is often accepted half-lovingly by Larkin; but there is the same "eager pleasure in recreating incidents and circumstances", the same "astonishing command of detail" ("The Blending of Betjeman" *RW* 130 & 132); and this command is controlled by the same concern with "relation to human use, to human scale and size" ("It Could Only Happen in England" *RW* 208). The line of inheritance is made partially explicit by Larkin:

"Betjeman is the true heir of Thomas Hardy, who found clouds, mists and mountains 'unimportant beside the wear on the threshold, or the print of a hand': his poems are about the threshold, but it and they would be nothing without the wear." ("It Could Only Happen in England" *RW* 211) That same command of detail and the power to evoke it in its human dimension and in all its Englishness is found in Larkin's work, and was also a feature of Auden's poetry in the thirties.

A recognition of the importance of Betjeman is found in a key essay that Larkin contributed to the *Spectator* at about this time, "The Blending of Betjeman", published in 1960, where he sees Betjeman as "registering 'dear old, bloody old England'" (*RW* 129). He couples Betjeman, approvingly, with Auden (*RW* 129), concerning whom he wrote another key essay that year, "What's Become of Wystan?". Both essays are lively and polemical. He sees the later Auden as having become "an engaging,bookish, American talent, too verbose to be memorable and too intellectual to be moving" (*RW* 123); and he finds the source of Auden's decline in his departure from England. Auden's early poetry is marked by its tremendous feeling for its English setting; and Larkin's essay underlines how important his old admiration, the Auden of *Poems* (1930) and *Look, Stranger!* (1936), was for him in these days of his greatest creativity.

Larkin's poetry has frequently been characterized as self-questioning, self-deprecatory; and his most noted strategy has been the creation of *personae* who are not only the object of self-doubt, but who, as speakers of his poems, are deflated through their own speech. We first encounter such a speaker in "Reasons for Attendance", and he is the central figure in "I Remember, I Remember", "Poetry of Departures", "Mr. Bleaney" and (with less self-deflation) "Church Going". All these poems were written in the eighteen months between December 1953 and May 1955, the period when the "Movement" was, if ever, a conscious coming together of like-minded writers intent on unmasking established attitudes. These poems have successors in *The Whitsun Weddings* and *High Windows* — most notably "Wild Oats" of 1962 or "Sad Steps" of 1968; but in his later poems Larkin's self-dramatization was more successful where he offered a straighter presentation of the autobiographical figure, as in "Dockery and Son".

Some of the poems with satirized personae in *The Whitsun Weddings* have given problems concerning how they are to be taken — problems involving the attitude to the poem or to the speaker generated by the poem. In "Mr. Bleaney" there seems to be a conscious and clear control of tone, however complex the interplay of attitudes;

whereas in "Self's the Man" or "A Study of Reading Habits", readers have felt unsure about the degree of identification that the poet
makes with the speaker of the poem and his attitudes. Larkin said
of "A Study of Reading Habits": "I was trying to provide an account
of how for the ordinary man reading slowly loses its emotional satisfaction. In childhood one identifies oneself with the hero and in
adolesence one identifies oneself with the villain; but when one grows
up one sees that one isn't really the hero or the villain. One is a very
unimportant character and perhaps even a rather contemptible one,
and one throws the whole thing aside in favour of something that
gives more immediate returns."[5] He reads the poem immediately after giving the explanation, and everything seems to fall in place. Yet,
even in the explanation, there is something gratuitously Larkinesque
in the phrase "a rather contemptible one"; and almost everything
that makes the poem funny is in tune with this, and gives rise to
humour at the speaker's expense that is in the main not required by
the account of the poem given by Larkin. The scenario of the poem
involves the speaker revealing how funny and false his past attitudes
seem now, and how he himself really doesn't amount to much. This is
brought together with the "study of reading habits" in the dismissive
last line, "Books are a load of crap." As with other poems of this
type, there seems to be a hidden poem lurking behind the ostensible one — a poem that involves the poet's own insecurity concerning
himself.

In the case of some of the other poems of this type, there are misunderstandings, which, when cleared up, remove the apparent barriers
to acceptance. Of no poem is this more true than "Naturally the
Foundation Will Bear Your Expenses". Larkin told Ian Hamilton in
1964 that "It came from having been to London and having heard
that A had gone to India and B had just come back from India; then
when I got back home, happening unexpectedly across the memorial
service at the Cenotaph on the wireless, on what used to be called
Armistice Day, and the two things got mixed up together . . . Actually,
it's as serious as anything I have written . . . Certainly it was a dig at
the middleman who gives a lot of talks to America and then brushes
them up and does them on the Third and then brushes them up again
and puts them out as a book with Chatto. Why he should be blamed
for not sympathising with the crowds on Armistice Day, I don't quite
know . . . I've never written a poem that has been less understood;
one editor refused it on the grounds . . . that it was 'rather hard on
the Queen' . . . There is nothing like writing poems for realizing how
low the level of critical understanding is; maybe the average reader

can understand what I say, but the above-average often can't."[6] The
Armistice Day ceremonies may have been the cause of the trouble:
Armistice Day was an "Establishment" event; and, in 1961, a feeling
of traditional reverence for it was probably not shared by admirers
of *Lucky Jim* and *Hurry On Down*, so that the first stanza steered
them into identification with the speaker. Once one grasps that every
attitude is being satirized, the poem has a coherence that otherwise
seems lacking.

Nonetheless, one can remain uncomfortable with a poem that does
not seem readily to declare itself to its readers — that depends so
much on our right sense of tone and our attitude to detail at every point. Indeed, it points to a problem that arises from a mode
of procedure that gives Larkin's poetry much of its characteristic
power. Details are presented with startling particularity, but with
the assumption that the reader will respond in a particular way. The
response frequently depends on the reader sharing certain cultural
attitudes with the poet. Where he does, the effect is one of intimacy
and immediacy; where he does not, misunderstanding can arise.

Another poem that seems to have troubled some readers is "Wild
Oats". "Anyone obsessed with a girl he did not take out twenty years
ago deserves our pity" wrote Simon Petch, who concluded that "the
poem's pained bewilderment marshals the feelings of a man who is
permanently out of date".[7] Others have found the speaker pusillani-
mous to the point that they can only despise him. Yet the poem seems
poised and delicately tactful as, with un-self-important humour, it
deals with one of Larkin's recurrent themes — the way in which we
find ourselves doing something quite other than what we imagined
we wanted to do; so that, as in "Dockery and Son", life is seen as
a process of recognizing what we are. The stereotyped contrast of
"bosomy English rose/And her friend in specs I could talk to" sets
a light, derisory tone, sustained by the "seven years" and "four hundred letters", the "ten-guinea ring" and the meetings in "numerous
cathedral cities/ Unknown to the clergy". The tone seems to change
in the final stanza:

> Parting, after about five
> Rehearsals, was an agreement
> That I was too selfish, withdrawn,
> And easily bored to love.
> Well, useful to get that learnt.
> In my wallet are still two snaps
> Of bosomy rose with fur gloves on.
> Unlucky charms, perhaps.

The banter is still there; and the unflattering view of the speaker as "too selfish" is clearly neither his nor one that we are pressed to agree with. Although one has the feeling that what lies behind the poem is rather close to the bone for the poet, and that the banter could hence be protective, the speaker does not seem sorry for himself. The stance he accepts is that of one not too handy in these matters; and the snaps are used whimsically to clinch this — "Unlucky charms". The poem is entirely true to the common experience of being led into relationships we do not seem to want; while not going for "bosomy rose", who "was trying/ . . . not to laugh" both times he met her, seems to show that the speaker sensed he was not in her league. If one is left with any unease, it is because of an underlying passivity regarding experience already noted in the character of John Kemp in *Jill* — the recurrent stance of someone to whom things puzzlingly *happen*, which is encountered in several poems by Larkin concerning relations with women.

"Sunny Prestatyn" has been the subject of some misguided "close commentary". Larkin's feeling for the language and imagery of sexual wall-scoring has been admired; yet it is in this area that at least one commentator has gone astray. "Titch Thomas" is an established character from British sexual folk-lore — "titch" meaning "little"; while the "tuberous cock and balls//Autographed *Titch Thomas*" are not a sign of the exhibitionist tendencies of some small man who drew them, but a demotic extension of the old bit of folk humour — "little man, big cock". The conclusion of the poem is surely its "conclusion": "She was too good for this life" and hence invited the abuse. "Now *Fight Cancer* is there", replacing the once cheering if false image. This presents a sobering reality, taking us back into the poem with the suggestion that the need to deface and unload all this sexual disgustingness is a cancer itself. This is in keeping with the progress of defacement, with which the poem makes considerable play: from "snaggle-toothed and boss-eyed" through the "tuberous cock and balls" to the "stab right through/The moustached lips" and the final "tear" that left "only a hand", it goes from the merely crude to the potentially viscous. The poem captures brilliantly the "feel" and social connotations of what it portrays, but allows a darker sense of things to fall out in its last line.

Seeking *personae* for this type of poem and then making them the subject of serious criticism could be somewhat akin to reading the lyrics of drinking songs as though they were a serious defence of beer by inebriated and degenerate morons. The poems, it might be argued, are to be treated in terms of their particular mode or idiom

— sometimes only realized in a reading aloud, where the attitudes are "placed" by the gross and simplified forms in which the poems are written. The element of caricature is certainly appropriate to light poetry.

Yet these observations do not entirely save all the poems. As Dan Jacobson said of the "satirical poems", they are in a "mode in which Larkin's touch is liable to falter more often than in any other . . . the object of their satire . . . is so often not the world, not the reader, but himself . . . some critics have accepted the picture . . . as a truthful self-portrait . . . the spokesman in such poems is almost always denounced, shown to be a self-deceiver". He goes on to talk of "flippant or self-wounding impulses";[8] and the disgust one senses in "What does it prove? Sod all" (from "Send No Money") involves a self-doubt from which the poet seems to find it hard to disengage himself — though Larkin remarked that "Send No Money" was, of his poems, "the one I repeat to myself."[9]

The flippant and self-wounding impulses are most evident in poems concerning women and sex — or in those parts of poems pertaining to these topics. They are impulses that suggest doubt and a need for protection against the exposure of other impulses. While these poems might seem to imply a difficulty that the writer has in relating to the subjects involved, the uncertainty of control of tone could spring from a difficulty that he has in relating to his own feelings and ultimately to himself. Larkin's fruitful preoccupation with identity must have been associated with a vulnerability that manifests itself in this sensitive area of feeling. This seems abundantly clear in a poem Larkin chose not to collect, "Breadfruit" (November 1961), where sexual dreams are seen as leading to "A mortgaged semi-with a silver birch;/Nippers; the widowed mum". "Self's the Man" is more disturbing in this way. The title points to a satirizing of the very unpleasant speaker, who shares with Larkin his unmarried state. The married life of the contrasted "Arnold" is portrayed in terms of music-hall stereotypes of the nagging wife and the visiting mother-in-law; yet, at the same time, it is all much too funny for the reader to disengage himself from "Self's" view of Arnold.

As Janice Rossen has pointed out, poems like "Wild Oats" and "Self's the Man" are structured as arguments concerning contrasting stereotyped possibilities, implying that these are the only choices in these matters.[10] As neither choice seems acceptable, the reader and the speaker are left in the air. One has the sense that the poems are as much structured to avoid a conclusion as to arrive at one. As with some of Larkin's "Movement" poems, we are reminded of the poetry of Kingsley Amis. In two of Amis's poems from this period, we encounter laconic, aphoristic conclusions such as Larkin employs in "A Study of Reading Habits", "Sunny Prestatyn" and "Wild Oats": "Sex is a momentary itch,/Love never lets you go." ("An Ever-Fixed Mark"); "Change is for kids." ("Out-Patient"). As in the earlier period, Amis's poems have a less equivocal tone than do Larkin's and the conclusions do not leave us puzzled in the way Larkin's do.

A poem, brilliant in detail, that Larkin did not publish, "Letter to a Friend about Girls" (December 1959) attempts to explain his "mortification" at his friend's "pushovers" by explaining that "all the while/I've met a different gauge of girl from yours" — girls who "put off men/By being unattractive, or too shy,/Or having morals"; girls with whom "you mine away/For months, both of you, till the collapse comes/Into remorse, tears and wondering why . . ." This world is contrasted with "that world/Described on Sundays only, where to want/Is straightway to be wanted" — the world that John Kemp sought to enter in *Jill*. The speaker concludes, "It's strange we never meet each other's sort", expressing a natural enough feeling of frustrations at a lack of sexual success; but he seems, as does the speaker of many of Larkin's poems, unable to distinguish between being unable to succeed because he doesn't know how or is not attractive enough, and being unable to succeed because, in the world in which he finds himself, to do so might require him to take unfair advantage of somebody else.

The concerns of the poem are mirrored in an account given by Jean Hartley:

> Most weeks Philip would have a good moan about the aridity of his sex life and would perhaps mention, enviously, how he had seen so-and-so (a university colleague) coming out of a tutorial room with his arm round some toothsome undergraduate. 'He's no doubt having it off with her. Lucky sod.' But I think he was too polite, diffident and 'gentlemanly' to have the sort of rakish success he thought he wanted, and also, I imagine, too fastidious.[11]

One suspects that the girls that the speaker of the poem met better represented the type of girl that Larkin found congenial than did the girls the speaker wished he could meet.

A more mature attempt to grapple dramatically with this quandary is "The Dance", an unfinished and clearly autobiographical poem. It recounts attending a dance in a university hall at which someone to whom the speaker is evidently attracted is present. The physical details and the feel of the event are tellingly evoked:

                    The light has almost failed,
And the faint thudding stridency
Some band we have been 'fortunate to secure'
Proclaims from lit-up windows comes to me
More as a final warning than a lure . . .

The same intimate awareness is felt in the descriptions of the speaker's
reactions:

            . . . your eyes greet me over commonplaces,
And your arms are bare,
And I wish desperately for qualities

Moments like this demand, and which I lack.
I face you on the floor, clumsily, as
Something starts up . . .

                    In the slug
And snarl of music, under cover of
A few permitted movements, you suggest
A whole consenting language, that my chest
Quickens and tightens at, descrying love . . .

   The speaker is ashamed at having attended the dance; and the
question of why he is there, compromising his sense of himself, is
what the poem opens with. In a characteristic manner, the speaker
proceeds to discuss the situation with himself: "How useless to invite
/The sickended breathlessness of being young//Into my life again!"
This is the mode of "Church Going", "The Whitsun Weddings" and
"Dockery and Son", where argument and incident interact to lead the
speaker (and the poem) to a conclusion in which thought and feeling
are importantly resolved. Yet the question of whether the speaker
is being unworthy of himself in attending the dance merges into the
question of whether he was foolish or not to come seeking the response
he looks for. One senses that Larkin was too intimately involved with
the success or unsuccess of the speaker, an involvement betrayed in
places by the poem's stridency — "I am caught/By some shoptalking
shit". There seems nowhere poetically satisfactory for the poem to
go; and it is not surprising that it was not finished. As so frequently
when the theme of sexual success emerges, Larkin seems unable to
attain a steady focus.
   In "Annus Mirabilis" (June 1967) there would seem to be a recognition that the state of affairs that gave rise to some of Larkin's
problems has gone:

Up till then there'd only been
A sort of bargaining,
A wrangle for a ring,
A shame that started at sixteen
And spread to everything.

Then all at once the quarrel sank . . .

However, the inhibitions he felt had more to do with his concerns about "selfishness" and "unselfishness", which were often interpreted in terms of shyness and a denigrative view of his own sexual prowess, to the confusion of the poet and the detriment of the poems.

The disatisfaction to be felt concerning the satirical poems in *The Whitsun Weddings* goes along with a related change in Larkin's idiom. An often delicate and complex play of wit accompanied the lyricism of "Lines on a Young Lady's Photograph Album", "Maiden Name" (both poems about the opposite sex) and was a feature of "Church Going"; and the use of a self-parody as narrator in "Church Going" and "Poetry of Departures" gave a subtle irony to these essentially serious poems. "Lines on a Young Lady's Photograph Album" and "Maiden Name" both conclude in a manner that depends on their pervasive wit, which contrives an ending in which the subject is brought into a new focus. This contrasts with the mode of proceeding in "Dockery and Son" and "Faith Healing", where the speaker concludes by extracting a message from the experience of the poem. Despite the resonance and power of the best poems in *The Whitsun Weddings*, a certain simplification of idiom has taken place: the play of wit is less present in the serious poems; while the witty poems display a coarsening of characterization such as one associates with "light verse".

In "Dockery and Son", the speaker is surprised by the perception of his own life that events force upon him; yet he takes a quite unequivocal stance in relation to his experiences and to the very decided conclusions to which they lead. Both closure and reification of detail are very pronounced in this poem, as in so many others that Larkin wrote after 1956; while the self-doubting speaker who pulls the carpet from under his own feet is now encountered mainly in ostensibly comic poems. The valuations implied by the best poems, or expected of their readers, have a centrality and certainty at odds with the aggressive reversals of common sentiments encountered in *The Less Deceived*.

In an interview with Ian Hamilton published at about the same time as *The Whitsun Weddings*, Larkin gave voice to characteristic literary views: an admiration for poets "to whom technique seems to matter less than content";[12] criticism of Eliot and Pound and their concern with "culture in the abstract";[13] a distaste for foreign poetry. These views had always been his and were to stay with him. In the years of the Movement, they seemed — and were — radical. In retrospect, they appear conservative, and are consonant with the conservatism so notable in Larkin's later work. In 1964 they were presented with only the defensiveness always encountered when Larkin talked about literary matters that really concerned him. However, Larkin's asseveration that his positions were commonsense and unchanging should not be allowed to obscure the fact that very decided changes in his idiom were constantly taking place. Indeed, in the interview with Hamilton we see a firming up of an "official" no-nonsense Larkin that later came to be a defence behind which the real Larkin made poetry out of his concerns and experience.

The Whitsun Weddings, which appeared in 1964, nonetheless constitutes a plateau of artistic attainment in Larkin's work. In the non-satirical poems there is a security and stability of idiom. It is also the volume in which Larkin makes his richest response to the world, and in which he seems most open to the often tragic shortfalls in the lives of others. It is not merely a change of poetic strategy that makes the ironically viewed "Larkin figure" less frequent in the poems of this book. There is less concern with his own situation in life and more with that of others. In "Toads Revisited" Larkin makes fun of his own earlier irony by a playful comparison with the way in which he presented himself in "Toads". In the new poem, the life of those who exist outside the world of work is pictured with a haunting sense of the insecurity concerning identity that idleness brings; and it is contrasted, with a humour that is at Larkin's expense, with the world of his "in-tray" and "loaf-haired secretary", and concludes with the plea for work to "Help me down cemetery road".

In the best poems in *The Whitsun Weddings* experience surrounds the poet unthreateningly, without the tincture of self-doubt or the sense that time is closing in. The stillness, the suspension in time that is a hidden good in Larkin's poetry, seems a condition more readily encountered, as in "MCMXIV" or "An Arundel Tomb" or the opening of "The Whitsun Weddings". The fragile vulnerability of happiness is still felt, in "Broadcast", for instance; but he seems able to reach out from his own preoccupations to a concern with "all that time has disproved" in the lives of others. The England of his everyday experience — Hull with its fish-dock and cut-price stores and estates full of washing — seems, without forcing, the natural ambience and exemplar for his vision of life; while words and attitudes unexpected in the poetry of the day are no longer thrust under the reader's nose, as they sometimes were in *The Less Deceived*, but have taken their place in an idiom flexible, evocative and unforcedly contemporary. *The Whitsun Weddings* gives us Larkin's England in all its rich humanity.

Chapter 7

DARKER PERSPECTIVES

The Whitsun Weddings appeared in February 1964, and must have gone to press some time before that. In the interview published in November 1964, Larkin told Ian Hamilton that he had not written a poem for eighteen months.[1] Indeed, the middle and late sixties seem to have been a rather fallow time: Barbara Pym, in December 1967, referred to the fact that Larkin had said that he was not writing anything at that time.[2] Between the compilation of *The Whitsun Weddings* and the end of 1969 only ten poems appeared in periodicals, and only fifteen were written. Indeed, in the four year between March 1963 and February 1967 he began seven poems and completed five, only three of which he collected.

The period from June 1963 to May 1964 produced only the long, unfinished poem "The Dance" — a poem of realistically evoked incidents such as is found in *The Less Deceived* and *The Whitsun Weddings*. "Solar", the first poem to be completed after the publication of *The Whitsun Weddings*, seems an attempt to move away from Larkin's established manner. A "Hymn" to the sun, it embeds in its conclusion an archetypal image, that of Jacob's Ladder:

> Coined there among
> Lonely horizontals
> You exist openly.
> Our needs hourly
> Climb and return like angels.
> Unclosing like a hand,
> You give for ever.

A poem of unqualified emotion, it appeared to be a direct attempt at a symbolist mode of poetry, which some saw as an enrichment of Larkin's work. Sentences like "Heat is the echo of your/Gold" gave a new tone; and here the associations of words resonate fruitfully with one another, as they do in Larkin's best poetry. However, phrases such as "Single stalkless flower" and "Your petalled head of flames" are not merely conventional: they have a linguistic inertness not normally encountered in Larkin's work.

A hint of the symbolist background to the poem is perhaps given in the title of one of the poems from 1967 — the humorous "Sympathy in White Major", whose title parodies that of "Symphonie en Blanc Majeur" by one of the leading French Parnassians, Théophile Gautier. The vein of unironic lyricism encountered in "Solar" is continued in "Trees" (also from 1967) and in "Cut Grass" (from 1971). These cannot be counted among Larkin's more powerful poems; and certain lines seem rather close to the type of Georgian poetry that Larkin represented so strongly in the *Oxford Book of Twentieth-Century English Verse* (1973), which he was compiling around this time:

> Lost lanes of Queen Anne's lace,
> And that high-builded cloud
> Moving at summer's pace.   ("Cut Grass")

"High Windows", the title poem of Larkin's next volume, seems on the other hand an attempt to marry the new symbolistic manner with Larkin's earlier style. It opens with his old panache, even if the parading of the word "fucking" (almost compulsory for 1968) makes the characteristic combination of the formal and colloquial a little strained here. The rambling, seemingly endless, first sentence, spilling into the third stanza, rehearses perfectly the unconstrained freedom of "everyone young going down the long slide" that rather appals the speaker, even as he envies it. Against it are set the words of someone who looked at the speaker when he was a boy and envied him because there would be "*No God anymore, or sweating in the dark//About hell . . . /. . . his lot will all go down the long slide/Like free bloody birds.*" The imagined alternative may seem a bit of a paper tiger; and, in contrast with the procedures of the earlier poems, the tensions set up are not resolved by argument, but by an image:

> Rather than words comes the thought of high windows:
> The sun-comprehending glass,
> And beyond it, the deep blue air, that shows
> Nothing, and is nowhere, and is endless.

The image is one of great beauty, evoking a freedom and openness quite other than that suggested by "going down the long slide": it is an image, perhaps, of an ideal freedom and happiness. Yet its relationship to the remainder of the poem remains elusive, even though the ecclesiastical associations of "high windows" reach back to the reference to "*sweating in the dark/About hell*". The experience of the poem, for some readers at least, is not effectively brought into focus.

"Friday Night at the Royal Station Hotel" (from 1966) has a similar structure. The main body of the poem is vintage Larkin:

> Through open doors, the dining-room declares
> A larger loneliness of knives and glass
> And silence laid like carpet.

Yet this typical setting of loneliness and exile, with its abandoned objects, ends abruptly and elliptically with a glimpse of a much more primitive and threatening loneliness: *"Now/Night comes on. Waves fold behind villages"*, taking the poem out of the ambience of the socially redemptive gestures that offer emotional security in so much of Larkin's work.

Indeed, at this time Larkin seems to have been drawn to attempting poems in modes different from those previously encountered in his poetry. In 1972 he said, "What I should like to do is write different kinds of poem that might be by different people. Someone said once that the great thing is not to be different from other people, but to be different from yourself. That's why I've chosen to read now a poem that isn't especially "like" me, or like what I fancy I'm supposed to be like."[3] He then read "The Explosion".

"The Explosion" (from 1970) is the most moving of several poems about death in *High Windows*. It presents the terror of sudden bereavement as few modern English poems do. It opens with a picture, cool and clear, of miners going to work, turning aside to play in the early morning sunlight:

> One chased after rabbits; lost them;
> Came back with a nest of lark's eggs;
> Showed them; lodged them in the grasses.
>
> So they passed in beards and moleskins,
> Fathers, brothers, nicknames, laughter,
> Through the tall gates standing open.

Then comes the tremor of the explosion, followed immediately by the words from the chapel:

> At noon, there came the tremor; cows
> Stopped chewing for a second; sun,
> Scarfed as in a heat-haze, dimmed.
>
> *The dead go on before us, they*
> *Are sitting in God's house in comfort,*
> *We shall see them face to face —*

Plain as lettering in the chapels
It was said, and for a second
Wives saw men of the explosion

Larger than in life they managed —
Gold as on a coin, or walking
Somewhere from the sun toward them,

One showing the eggs unbroken.

The surprising leap from the event to the words of consolation gives
that sense of perceiving everything at once that comes in moments of
great emotional shock.

Images are revealed in their full implication only on completion
of the poem. None is more powerful that that of the eggs in the
nest, suggesting fertility and fragility — the fragility of life, and the
fragility of hope — as well as the beauty of love, the tenderness of
concern. The eggs become, at the conclusion, an image of both hope
and loss, as though the man were showing them across a barrier from
another world.

Other images too are illuminated by the juxtaposition of the tremor
and the words in the chapel. The "tall gates" take on the suggestion
of the gates to the world of the dead; while the sunlight, suggesting
innocence and the ease of happiness in the opening, becomes a light of
transfiguration at the end. Whether or not the apparent dimming of
the sun is an effect observed with earth tremors, it certainly suggests
the darkening of the sun at the death of Christ, and, if nothing else,
a pathetic sense of a reverent harmony in nature — also hinted at by
"cows/Stopped chewing".

The poem achieves its unforced tone through the natural syntax
and rhythms of the speaking voice; so that it comes as a surprise
to realise that the metre is the trochaic of Longfellow's "The Song
of Hiawatha". Yet, though the syntax is relaxed and undistorted,
the poem is not structured around an argument or the play of the
discursive mind, as is "The Building", for instance, or "Dockery and
Son" or "Church Going". It works by a juxtaposition of images —
startling at the centre of the poem, but muted and hidden within its
narrative for the most part.

There are poems in *High Windows* where this type of structure is
more obvious. Nothing in *The Whitsun Weddings* would prepare us
for "Solar" or for the second section of "Livings" (seemingly a poem
spoken by a lighthouse keeper); if the latter recalls anything from
Larkin's earlier work, it is "Absences", a poem that seemed out of
place in *The Less Deceived*:

Seventy feet down
The sea explodes upwards,
Relapsing, to slaver
Off landing-stage steps —
Running suds, rejoice!

Rocks writhe back to sight.
Mussels, limpets,
Husband their tenacity
In the freezing slither —
Creatures, I cherish you!

While the syntax is not irregular, it has a minor function in the impact of the poem, hardly muting the effect of the disjunctive presentation of the images. The final lines "Lit shelved liners/ Grope like mad worlds westward" emphasise the threatening nature of all the images of natural violence and storm. The speaker sets "plate and spoon/And after, divining-cards", suggesting a desire to control by knowledge — though knowledge irrationally attained. In contrast to most of Larkin's mature poems, "Livings II" is notably undiscursive. The gesture of setting the cards, and the injunctions "rejoice", "Keep it all off" and "Creatures, I cherish you", are the only overt suggestions of a stance concerning the violent images of the poem, which, like "Solar" and "Cut Grass", works by an imagistic evocation of a generalized sense of things rather than through the exploration of specific detail.

An interesting, almost hybrid poem is "Sad Steps" (from April 1968) which takes its title from the celebrated sonnet by Sir Philip Sidney. It opens with a typical Larkin situation that comes close to self-parody: "Groping back to bed after a piss". Watching the moon among the clouds, he comes out with images that would have been in place in *The North Ship*: "a cavernous, a wind-picked sky", "clouds that blow/Loosely as cannon-smoke". This leads him to invoke the moon, with ironic self-deflation, in terms that are intended, one feels, to recall nineteenth-century French symbolist poetry — as though the rhetoric constituted, for a moment, a literary temptation: "Lozenge of love! Medallion of art!/O wolves of memory! Immensements!" But "No": he "shivers slightly" and turns to reflect (in a conclusion at once stark and tender in the manner of his finest poetry):

The hardness and the brightness and the plain
Far-reaching singleness of that wide stare

Is a reminder of the strength and pain
Of being young; that it can't come again,
But is for others undiminished somewhere.

It would be wrong to regard these changes in manner as purely stylistic. Just as they involve some return to images and strategies of Larkin's earliest poetry, so they also mark a re-emergence of concerns found in that work. "Livings II", in its evocation of the violence of nature, stands far apart from the rationally distanced and accepted everyday world of *The Whitsun Weddings*. It is not so far, perhaps, from *The North Ship*, whose pervasive wind images are associated with destruction, and, in "Climbing the hill" (IX), suggest features of behaviour that break the bounds of control. Knowledge and control are modes of coming to terms with experience in much of Larkin's work; and the ordered forms of Larkin's mature poetry are gestures of control. In *High Windows* we encounter poems, such as "The Building" or "The Old Fools", that confront, in the same rational and ordering manner, the one experience that we must accept but cannot ultimately control or comprehend — the cessation of our own existence. It is not surprising that we also encounter poems and images that attempt to dramatize those elements of existence that resist control.

"The Card-Players", which may appear at first reading to be a satirical poem, in fact is very central to this vision of the book. It is, undoubtedly a study of the disgusting — and one that delves deep. Without its last line, it might be nothing but that. However, those final phrases, standing apart from the remainder of the poem, must be intended to change our orientation to what has gone before: "Rain, wind and fire! The secret, bestial peace!" "Rain" and "wind" recall the imagery of *The North Ship*, of ravagement and disorder. "Rain, wind and fire" are three of the ancient elements: earth, the fourth, is clearly the composition of the human beings in the poem. Every human action depicted is disgusting; yet what we have is a scene of human contentment — "The secret, bestial peace" that is the basis of contentment in living, in contrast with the other ultimately bestial impulse, the fear of death.

It would be ridiculous to attempt to underplay the extent to which "The Card Players" is concerned with the disgusting and the primitive. The poem closest to it in tone is "Living III":

> Tonight we dine without the Master
> (Nocturnal vapours do not please);
> The port goes round so much the faster,
> Topics are raised with no less ease —
> Which advowson looks the fairest,
> What wood from Snape will fetch,

> Names for *pudendum mulieris*,
> Why is Judas like Jack Ketch?

Its concerns seem reduced to self-satisfied and petty rapacity and preoccupation with personal comfort. "Livings I" is spoken by someone caught in a way of life that is reduced to the cut and dried and the matter of fact:

> One beer, and then 'the dinner', at which I read
> The——*shire Times* from soup to stewed pears.
> Births, deaths. For sale. Police Court. Motor spares.

Though the poem resembles several in *The Whitsun Weddings* in its feeling for evocative detail, it is quite different in that there is none of the complex manipulation of the sociological implications of the details encountered in the earlier poems. Nor is there any inner drama; but rather the poem seems an extended attempt to project imagistically a sense of a quality, trivial and inert, that a life might possess. In a contrasting poem, "The Trees", the primitive aspects of life emerge more positively:

> Yet still the unresting castles thresh
> In fullgrown thickness every May.
> Last year is dead, they seem to say,
> Begin afresh, afresh, asfresh.

Again, the imagery is utilised independently of any historical or sociological connotations.

The poem "Forget What Did" (August 1971) seems, obliquely, to discuss the change of poetic stance. Its opening phrase "Stopping the diary" denotes an action that would be of significance to someone like Larkin, who kept a diary and whose notebooks meticulously recorded dates of completion and revision. Larkin later said it was "about getting away from the miseries of life . . . It's about a time when I stopped keeping a diary because I couldn't bear to record what was going on."[4] The noting of the underlying patterns of nature is to replace the recording of personal events, which the speaker "wanted . . . over/ Hurried to burial." Suggested is a relinquishing of the attempt to take hold of experience and, by doing so, preserve it — something that Larkin had earlier said was at the root of his impulse to write poetry.

The poem that most recalls *The Whitsun Weddings* and the earlier poetry is "To the Sea" (October 1969), which opens *High Windows*. It is a celebration of visiting the seaside "half an annual pleasure, half a rite". It is the most Audenesque poem in the book, discovering in the scene itself an exemplification of everything the poem has to say, orchestrating the details of the scene to project its vision, so that the vision seems elucidated rather than imposed. In its perfect evocation of an English seaside scene, it recalls Auden's "August and the people for their favourite islands".

The perspective of the poem is established in the first words:

> To step over the low wall that divides
> Road from concrete walk above the shore
> Brings back something known long before —
> The miniature gaiety of seasides.

We step into a separate world, known from the past, though the speaker is "Strange to it now". It is a coming back for him; and authentic fragments of autobiography are woven into the poem: "happy at being on my own,/I searched the sand for Famous Cricketers" — the cigarette cards spoken of in "Not the Places Fault".[5] This miniature world represents the larger one, with "the uncertain children, frilled in White" or "The rigid old", wheeled along "to feel/A final summer". It reaches back not merely to the speaker's youth but to the days when his "parents, listeners/To the same seaside quack, first became known." The only point of change in the poem is when the day moves (like life, perhaps) towards its end and we find that "Like breathed-on glass/The sunlight has turned milky": the clarity with which everything was seen in its significance in the early part of the poem is clouding. This leads into the culminating reflection:

> If the worst
> Of flawless weather is our falling short,
> It may be that through habit these do best,
> Coming to water clumsily undressed
> Yearly; teaching their children by a sort
> Of clowning; helping the old, too, as they ought.

The phrase "clumsily undressed" takes up the note sounded in the description of the children "grasping at enormous air". The day at the sea, "teaching the children" and "helping the old" becomes a "rite" in which we awkwardly make the best of "our falling short" — and, in doing so, redeem it.

"To the Sea" has a remarkable serenity — a serenity mirrored in the very slight changes in perspective that make up the only "action" of the poem: it triumphs by conveying a deeply felt sense of things while seeming to be no more than description. It is much less heavily "plotted" than earlier poems like "Dockery and Son" or than the other more ambitious poems in *High Windows*, "The Building" and "The Old Fools" — both poems about death. Of these, "The Building" is most similar in character to Larkin's earlier work, and may be seen as paralleling "Church Going" and "The Whitsun Weddings" as the central philosophical poem of its volume. Like them, it is constructed about a particular event or scene that leads into the book's most important meditations on life and its continuities — and on death. In 1970 Larkin had written a poem that began "How high they build hospitals", which was not republished in *High Windows*. "The Building", completed almost two years later, in February 1972, nowhere uses the word "hospital"; and, while we are meant to recognize what the "building" is, the vocabulary of hospitals is subdued to mentions of "nurse" and "ward". Sickness itself is not directly mentioned: "something has gone wrong./It must be error of a serious sort".

This obliqueness functions not merely to surprise or add mystery: it emphasizes the perspective of the poem, in which the building emerges not as a place of cure, but as a reminder of the final end of life and how inescapable it is:

> All know they are going to die.
> Not yet, perhaps not here, but in the end,
> And somewhere like this. That is what it means,
> This clean-sliced cliff . . .

The building presents itself as a hygenic warren of rooms beyond rooms, "each one further off//And harder to return from". It has the aspect of a prison to which all must come: the most touching image is of "someone walking . . . /Out to the car park, free". It is set in the world of everyday living, which is tantalizingly close — "A touching dream to which we all are lulled/But wake from separately" — a world evoked with the same affection as in *The Whitsun Weddings*:

> Traffic; a locked church; short terraced streets
> Where kids chalk games, and girls in hair-dos fetch
> Their separates from the cleaners . . .

It rises from the "close-ribbed streets" as a church might; and the image of the "locked church" sets us in tune for the conclusion:

for unless its powers
Outbuild cathedrals nothing contravenes
The coming dark, though crowds each evening try

With wasteful, weak, propitiatory flowers.

The final image is strikingly pathetic; and there is no sense in which "unless its powers/Outbuild cathedrals" is entertained as more than a forlorn wish — a lost hope that religion once brought. Indeed, hidden in the word "Outbuild" is the implication that not even cathedrals succeeded in contravening the "coming dark". Religion, as in "Church Going", is taken as something whose consolations are no longer available because no longer to be believed in. Yet religion's institutionalized framework of interpretation and hope is used powerfully in the poem, where the parallels between the mysterious, unnamed "building" and the church as places of mediation between the living and their unavoidable death are structurally important. "It must be error of a serious sort" suggests original sin — the emblem of our irremediable shortcomings; and death, in the poem, has this same irremediable quality.

While "The Building" resembles "The Whitsun Weddings" in finding the locus for its central apprehension in a situation that is prominent in all our environments, the touch of mystery concerning what the building is — the holding off from calling it a hospital — gives the poem an avowedly symbolic quality not present in "The Whitsun Weddings", where the significance of the images seems no more than the unforced elucidation of what is to be found in the actual and where "things" are very much what they always seem to be. In this respect, "The Building" is in keeping with new tendencies already noted in poems from *High Windows*.

"The Old Fools" is an ostensibly shocking poem about old age; yet its strategies had been characteristic of Larkin since the fifties. Earlier statements, such as "We all hate home/And having to be there" or "Home is so sad", gave a similar deliberate affront to conventional pieties, despite the essential decency of Larkin's stance.

What do they think has happened, the old fools,
To make them like this? Do they somehow suppose
It's more grown-up when your mouth hangs open and drools,
And you keep on pissing yourself, and can't remember
Who called this morning?

The "old fools" are characterized in these first few lines without our being quite sure who they are; so that, as quite frequently in Larkin's

poems, the surprise of slow recognition reinforces the shock of the
perspective.

This is the first of Larkin's poems in which death is perceived, not
only as physical loss, but in terms of the dissolution of self:

> At death you break up: the bits that were you
> Start speeding away from each other for ever
> With no one to see.

Written in long-lined, complex stanzas, each with a short concluding
line, the poem asserts its structure firmly, shocking us in the first
stanza with a series of questions that conclude "Why aren't they
screaming?", and giving the facts of extinction in the next stanza,
which ends with the further question "How can they ignore it?" The
poem then seems to let up a little with the allowance that "Perhaps
being old is having lighted rooms/Inside your head" — though here
the yearning for the past is as disturbing as anything in the poem. The
concluding stanza brings a series of further questions, as apparently
disrespectful and devastating as those of the opening:

>   Can they never tell
> What is dragging them back, and how it will end? Not at night?
> Not when the strangers come? Never, throughout
> The whole hideous inverted childhood?

The pattern of thought is tightly fitted to the stanza pattern:
only between the third and fourth is there any running over; and
this tight consonance of form and sentence structure reinforces the
almost desperate assertiveness of the poem, which thrusts its picture of old age before the reader with very little of the tentativeness
and self-deprecation found in Larkin's earlier poetry. Within three
lines we twice encounter a favourite word: "from known doors turning,/Setting down a lamp, smiling from a stair, extracting/A known
book" — surely not a blemish but an intended emphasis of what for
Larkin constitutes our hold on life, "knowledge" — along with the
ability to choose, the loss of which is also lamented: "Not knowing
how, not hearing who, the power/Of choosing gone". One of the supposed illusions of the "old fools" is "that if they only chose,/They
could alter things back" — a hope frequently encountered in Larkin's
work, as in "Myxomatosis", "Love Songs in Age", "Reference Back"
or "Faith Healing".

The devastating and uncompassionate stance assumed in the poem
is part of a long looping swing whereby the speaker (very much the

poet) hits himself and the reader in the reversal of the final line — "We shall find out". The grip on us is enforced by images startling in their psychological acumen: "days of thin continuous dreaming/Watching light move", or by others of physical bluntness: "Ash hair, toad hands, prune face dried into lines"; and one horror of the poem becomes our recognition that this is in store for us. For Larkin there can be no consolation in telling himself that death might not be an end, or that it is in some way a form of self-transcendence, a final source of human dignity. Indeed, the often truculent tone surely reflects the fact that the poem is really an assertion that such modes of cheering oneself up will not wash. "Once you realise you're going to die, you can't see anything else again except in that context", he once remarked.[6] Similarly, the way in which the tone seems nearly out of control in the first stanza, so that the poem itself almost "screams", is symptomatic of how close to the bone the subject was for Larkin.

"Heads in the Women's Wards", possibly occasioned by his mother's old age and written in March 1972, six months before "The Old Fools", offers the same vision in little:

> On pillow after pillow lies
> The wild white hair and staring eyes;
> Jaws stand open; necks are stretched
> With every tendon sharply sketched;
> A bearded mouth talks silently
> To someone no one else can see.
>
> Sixty years ago they smiled
> At lover, husband, first-born child.
>
> Smiles are for youth. For old age come
> Death's terror and delirium.

It may have seemed to have been made redundant by the more developed "The Old Fools" and was not included in *High Windows*.

"The Old Fools" and "Heads in the Women's Wards" are unusual in their unconsoled and starkly physical presentation of death. There are few poems, if any, like them in English. Structurally, "The Old Fools" is an extreme extension of the form of certain poems in *The Less Deceived* and *The Whitsun Weddings*, where asserted generalizations have an important role in the economy of the poems.

If *High Windows* seems bleaker and less engaging than *The Whitsun Weddings*, it is not merely because it confronts with such starkness the physical aspects of aging and death, with little sense of any compensating consolation or of any rewarding peace in the wisdom of old age. The bleakness comes in part from a diminution in that cherishing of experience that had marked the earlier poetry — something found strongly only in "To the Sea", "Show Saturday" and "Dublinesque" from *High Windows*. A chill seems to have settled on Larkin's apprehension of the once loved details of life. In addition, the "cut-price crowd", perceived as culturally and economically disadvantaged in *The Whitsun Weddings*, appear to have overtaken Larkin somewhat as America overtook Sinclair Lewis. As Alfred Kazin put it, Lewis's "jokes against the old American ways became new American ways themselves";[7] and Larkin's "cut-price crowd" are no longer pushed to "the side of their own lives", but seem to own their world and be a threat to the poet who was once saddened by their lot:

> The crowd
> Is young in the MI café;
> Their kids are screaming for more —
> More houses, more parking allowed,
> More caravan sites, more pay.   ("Going, Going")

It is the speaker who feels threatened: "For the first time I feel somehow/That it isn't going to last".

High Windows contains other poems that adopt simple positions: "Homage to a Government", concerning the reduction of British garrisons abroad for financial reasons, is only an extreme example. The volume as a whole is assertive rather than exploratory, in comparison with earlier ones. The play of questioning wit in *The Less Deceived* had been succeeded by a firm and resonant assurance in *The Whitsun Weddings*; which, if it involved a simplification of idiom in this respect, went along with a broadening and sensitivity of response. One feels at times that the poems in *High Windows* are the work of someone who has too much made up his mind about things. This is particularly true of "This Be the Verse" ("They fuck you up, your mum and dad"), which, for all its protective humour, is starkly assertive — even in comparison with another humorous poem from the volume, the playful "Annus Mirabilis" ("Sexual intercourse began/In nineteen sixty-three/(Which was rather late for me)"). "Vers de Société" oscillates between shrill statements ("I could spend half my evenings, if I wanted,/Holding a glass of washing sherry, canted/Over to catch the drivel of some bitch/Who's read nothing but *Which*") and profound, psychological observations in the best Larkin manner ("Only the young can be alone freely."). He said himself, "I almost never go out. I suppose everyone tries to ignore the passing of time: some people by doing a lot . . . or there's my way — making every day and

every year exactly the same." ("An Interview with *Paris Review*",
RW 57–58) One of the considerations confronted in this poem is the
slow disappearance of one's life: "Just think of all the spare time that
has flown//Straight into nothingness by being filled/With forks and
faces". The speaker pulls the mat from under himself at the end of the
poem, just as did the speaker of "Reasons for Attendance"; yet, after
the somewhat bitter and unqualified characterizations of social life
earlier in the poem, the concluding *"Dear Warlock-Williams: Why,
of course"* is a bit hard to swallow.

"Posterity" is one of Larkin's most popular satirical poems, with
its "Jake Balokowsky", Larkin's imaginary biographer, in his "air-
conditioned cell at Kennedy". "It's stinking dead, the research line"
he says, and longs to "teach school in Tel Aviv" or "work on Protest
Theater". The poem's humour is slightly marred by the fact that, in
the North American culture that it satirizes, the penultimate syllable
of Jake's surname would be pronounced to rhyme with "cow" rather
than "cough". However, behind the poem about Jake Balokowsky is
a poem about Philip Larkin; and the two poems come together in
the last line, "One of those old-type *natural* fouled-up guys." Jake
Balokowsky is a bit of a cardboard figure, and a satire on his activities
would be neither new nor funny. It is the satirical application of
elements of the poem to Larkin himself that hits home; and there
is much of the harshness here that we encounter in his self-satirical
poems.

"Show Saturday" is one of the last poems in *High Windows* to be
written, and it is one of the most ambitious in the book. It is on
a theme that seems to have been increasingly important to Larkin
in this late period: that these annual ceremonies have an immense
importance for the cohesion of society and for our regeneration:

> Let it stay hidden there like strength, below
> Sale-bills and swindling; something people do,
> Not noticing how time's rolling smithy-smoke
> Shadows much greater gestures; something they share
> That breaks ancestrally each year into
> Regenerate union. Let it always be there.

The preceding, impeccably realized eight stanzas amply support this
sense of things:

> Broad beans (one split open), dark shining-leafed cabbages — rows
> Of single supreme versions, followed (on laced
> Paper mats) by dairy and kitchen; four brown eggs, four white eggs,

Four plain scones, four dropped scones, pure excellences that enclose
A recession of skills.

Yet the scene does not come to life with the power of "Church Going"
or the immediacy of "The Whitsun Weddings". This could, of course,
be seen as an important aspect of the impact of the poem: that
this focusing, annual event itself does not transcend the ordinariness
of our everyday existence. It is only in the wistful passage about
the breaking up of the fair that the details seem to reach beyond
themselves in their significance, as they do in Larkin's greatest poems:

Back now to private addresses, gates and lamps
In high stone one-street villages, empty at dusk,
And side roads of small towns (sports finals stuck
In front doors, allotments reaching down to the railway) . . .

Indeed, there is little resonance between the details of the poem, perhaps because the poem has so little inner drama. The description of
the show is done with ample virtuosity in the first five of the eight
stanzas; and the only event in the poem is its break-up. The discovery of the meaning of the show does not come as something we feel
has been incipient in the handling of detail in the early part of the
poem; nor is there the drama of discovery that provides the structure
of many of Larkin's best poems. Despite the sustained power of observation, one is not surprised to find that "Show Saturday", written
in December 1973, was one of Larkin's last poems of any size. It has a
static quality that contrasts with the lively intellectual and emotional
movement of the earlier poetry.

The two most moving poems in *High Windows* are "The Explosion" and "Dublinesque". In "Dublinesque", the details seem to carry
suggestions that go beyond themselves:

Down stucco sidestreets,
Where light is pewter
And afternoon mist
Brings lights on in shops
Above race-guides and rosaries,
A funeral passes.

In these poems there is not the stark assertion we encounter in places
in *High Windows*: we are left to find the "poems" in the poems. Nor
is there that monotony of tone that characterizes certain poems in
the book. "The Explosion" and "Dublinesque" do not have the air of
being written by someone who has made his mind up about the world;

whereas some of the other poems force one to recall Robert Frost's adage: "No surprise for the writer, no surprise for the reader."[8]

Indeed, *High Windows* seems to show an emotional hardening. It is not merely that death is a more central and pressing concern than in *The Less Deceived* or *The Whitsun Weddings*, or that it is more directly confronted than in the two earlier books. There is a change of tone. The unconsoled look at life becomes the unconsoled look at death; and the sense of things is starker, even when death is not the theme. In *The Whitsun Weddings*, "Days" and "Nothing To Be Said" confront the fact that "Life is slow dying" with an unevasive directness. Yet there is an unhurriedness, a "stillness" about the movement of these poems that countervails the urgency of the theme. Such a stillness is felt in "Dublinesque" and "The Explosion"; but, in "The Old Fools", there is an edginess that is mirrored in the movement of the poem. A bitterness and an abruptness is felt in the reversals and terse summary positions of poems like "Friday Night in the Royal Station Hotel", "The Card Players" and "Vers de Société"; while "Going, Going" and "Homage to a Government" offer an all too decided and emotionally hollow look at a world that the speaker no longer seems to have any sympathy with. That rich, empathetic interplay with the everyday world around him, so much a mark of Larkin's poetry in *The Whitsun Weddings* — and still there in such poems as "To the Sea" — seems less in evidence in *High Windows*. One has the sense of life closing in, that the world is usurping his "proper ground".

A feeling that experience offers not a reassuring reflection of the observer's sense of the world and of himself, but rather threatens it, can be seen as the source of changes in manner that have been observed in the poetry of *High Windows*. "The Building" and "The Old Fools" (like the later "Aubade") evince the strategies of "Church Going" and "Dockery and Son", where the experience of the poem is held tightly within the structure of an argument that the speaker conducts with himself (though we no longer encounter that dramatization of the speaker that gave such a feeling of authenticity to the earlier poems). The experience is "contained" within the unimpeded flow of syntax; and the sense of things communicated by the poem is ennunciated by the speaker rather than focused imagistically. In "High Windows", "Livings II", "The Card-players", "Friday Night in the Royal Station Hotel" and "The Explosion" we encounter more abrupt transitions and the use of images to focus experience. The containing, explanatory power of discursive syntax seems to be foregone as inappropriate to the aspects of experience explored in the poems.

It would be wrong to speak of a new manner or a "final phase", for the old manner exists side by side with the new and seems to have been returned to in the final poems; while Larkin's poetry as a whole evinced a greater variety of manners than has been allowed. Nonetheless, a different mode of encountering experience is seen in some of these poems, and it seems symptomatic of a less secure relationship to experience than we find in *The Whitsun Weddings*.

After the appearance of *High Windows* there were only seventeen poems from the remaining ten years of Larkin's life. Eight of these were occasional, including celebratory offerings for Gavin Ewart and Charles Causley, a poem for the Queen's Silver Jubilee and a poem about drinking for the *Poetry Review*. "Bridge for the Living" — "Words of a cantata by Anthony Hedges to celebrate the opening of the Humber Bridge" — in its first part endearingly evokes Hull and its surroundings through details that recall the earlier "Here". The second part illustrates the difficulty that poetry of public celebration presents in our age. The whole is as well-mannered as Larkin's essay on Hull's other major poet, Andrew Marvell (*RW* 245–53).

The non-occasional poems include three spoken by the self-deflating Larkin person. One, "The Winter Palace", about getting old and forgetting things, is touchingly affecting in its self-deprecating tone (though Larkin was only 56 when he wrote it). The same cannot be said for "The Life with a Hole in it", about getting "your own way" — the theme of the earlier and equally disturbing "Self's the Man". The subject of selfishness, which haunted *A Girl in Winter* in 1945, seems still to have been one that Larkin could not approach with equanimity. Most of the poem is conducted in a humorous manner in terms of a contrast between "the shit in the shuttered château/Who does his five hundred words/Then parts out the rest of the day/Between bathing and booze and birds" and the "spectacled schoolteaching sod/(Six kids, and the wife in pod,/And her parents coming to stay)". These caricatures — the second from the music-hall view of marriage — are surely not what Larkin would have had us see as the Scylla and Charybdis of the literary life; yet, at the end, the poem shifts gear into what is evidently a tone of deadly earnest:

> Life is an immobile, locked,
> Three-handed struggle between
> Your wants, the world's for you, and (worse)
> The unbeatable slow machine
> That brings what you'll get.

There is nothing flippant in the bitterness here; and once again we are left with that uncertainty concerning tone that Larkin's satirical poems seem to induce.

More disturbing still is "Love Again" from 1979, a poem that seems to go along with three poems of 1975 about the coming of love. All three earlier poems are delicately restrained; and the question of their biographical origin is irrelevant to their power to move us and to take us into their world:

> The decades of a different life
> That opened past your inch-close eyes
> Belonged to others, lavished, lost;
> Nor could I hold you hard enough
> To call my years of hunger-strife
> Back from your mouth to colonise.

In contrast, "Love Again" concludes with a bitter, Hardyesque reflection:

> Isolate rather this element
>
> That spreads through other lives like a tree
> And sways them in a sort of sense
> And say why it never worked for me.
> Something to do with violence
> A long way back, and wrong rewards,
> And arrogant eternity.

Taken alone, this bitter ending seems to sum up much that Larkin at times felt about life. However, the poem begins:

> Love again: wanking at ten past three
> (Surely he's taken her home by now?),
> The bedroom hot as bakery,
> The drink gone dead . . .
>
> Someone else feeling her breasts and cunt,
> Someone else drowned in that lash-wide stare . . .

This may reflect accurately the interior language of jealousy; but neither the diction nor the unhesitant rhythms of the poem do anything to focus the experience, which appears to overwhelm the speaker in a raw prelude to the seemingly considered judgement of the last lines.

The attractively nostalgic "Poem about Oxford" , for Monica Jones, from 1970, never printed in Larkin's lifetime, suffers a similar lapse of tone:

City we shared without knowing
In blacked-out and butterless days,
Till we left, and were glad to be going
(Unlike the arselicker who stays) . . .

Why the sudden, interpolated blanket dismissal? The "arselicker" has
nothing to do with the rest of the poem; and were they all arselickers
who stayed — as did his friend, John Wain, for instance? The need
for the gratuitous put-down eludes one.

If "The Life with a Hole in it" stands as a summary shot in a long
line of satirical poems, "Aubade" of 1977 stands in relation to Larkin's
life and work and major themes as a sort of "final word". Written
three years after *High Windows* appeared, it takes up again the theme
of "the total emptiness for ever,/The sure extinction that we travel
to/And shall be lost in always" when we leave this "uncaring/Intricate
rented world". "Aubade" — the song before morning of lovers who
must part at first light — becomes the meditation in the early hours
of one who fears separation from what he most loves — life itself:
"Not in remorse/ . . . nor wretchedly because/An only life can take
so long to climb/Clear of its wrong beginnings . . . /But at the total
emptiness for ever." Neither religion ("That vast moth-eaten musical
brocade/Created to pretend we never die") nor rational reflection
can set aside this coming emptiness: "Courage is no good:/ . . . Being
brave/Let no one off the grave."

There is some attempt at ironic self-dramatization at the beginning: "I work all day, and get half-drunk at night"; and there is a
defeated gesture at accepting the world at the conclusion, as daylight
brings it into view:

Slowly light strengthens, and the room takes shape.
It stands as plain as a wardrobe, what we know . . .
The sky is white as clay, with no sun.
Work has to be done.
Postmen like doctors go from house to house.

In these final lines, "plain as a wardrobe" and "The sky is white
as clay" are among the few attempts to manipulate the setting into
metaphor. There is a paucity of startling tropes, of which the most
notable is "The anaesthetic from which none come round". The poem
is resolutely declarative, unwavering in its intent, with none of the
hesitation of discovery imitated in "Dockery and Son" — none of
the self-doubt of the earlier poetry. Indeed, it offers no counterpoise
to the starkness of its vision except the steady clarity and lack of

sentimentality with which it is presented. Its stylistic bleakness has
the forthrightness of a slightly earlier riposte by Larkin concerning his
preoccupation with death: "If you were sentenced to death by firing
squad, but were told that you would not be shot today, nor tomorrow,
but eventually, would you not think about your predicament a great
deal."[9]

Larkin's three mature books of poetry had been carefully structured, each with a thematically central poem and each with related
opening and closing poems; and "Aubade", published in the prominent *Times Literary Supplement* just before Christmas 1977, had the
air of being placed in his life as its concluding poem — the farewell
to poetry and to life. In 1982 he remarked that he did not think
that there would be any more poems. ("An Interview with *Paris Review*", *RW* 75) Seventeen poems in his last ten years was slow even
for Larkin, though the ten years from *The Whitsun Weddings* to *High
Windows* produced only twice that number. By the time he died in
December 1985, he seemed largely to have stopped writing, except
for the occasional book review.

Chapter 8

ALL WHAT JAZZ?

Writers about Larkin have tended to give very little attention to his book of jazz criticism, *All What Jazz?*. Yet Larkin said: "I think to me and to other members of my generation, the great jazz players had the same emotional effect as perhaps a hundred years ago the great poets had";[1] and he claimed elsewhere, "I can live a week without poetry but not a day without jazz."[2] The retrospective introduction to *All What Jazz?* has become celebrated for its forceful rejection of modernism in the arts generally; but it has seldom been discussed with reference to the text that follows it. No doubt it might be argued that neither the readers nor the critics have the special knowledge needed to make a detailed judgement of what Larkin wrote about jazz; yet were he, like Betjeman, to have written about architecture, his views would be discussed without any condescension to the reader, whose lack of knowledge would be regarded as ignorance. Indeed the continued insistence of Larkin's writings about jazz — an insistence of main importance, coming from a writer of his stature — is that jazz is not only a major cultural phenomenon of our time, but an art that is to be taken as seriously as any other.

A devotion to jazz had been with him since his youth; and it was as much a ground of his friendship with Kingsley Amis as was their devotion to writing. Of their days at Oxford Larkin said: "I suppose we devoted to some hundred records that early anatomizing passion normally reserved for the more established arts." ("Introduction to *Jill*", *RW* 23) Classical music was the music of what was later to be called "The Establishment" — a music of high-toned pleasure, of people who had the sense that they were doing something important in listening to it. Jazz was a music that spoke with immediacy and to feelings not always spoken to by the official music — and certainly, not in its idiom. A taste for jazz was iconoclastic, if for no other reason than that it was seen that way by most educated people. In this area of experience, it was a small step for Amis and Larkin to the attitudes that characterized the Movement. As Amis's hero in *Lucky Jim* (1953) says in contemplating an invitation from the madrigal-loving Professor Welch: "you know as well as I do that I can't sing, I can't act, I can hardly read, and thank God I can't read music."[3]

Amis recalled: "our heroes were the white Chicagoans, Count Basie's band, Bix Beiderbecke, Sidney Bechet, Henry Allen, Muggsy Spanier, Fats Waller, early Armstrong and early Ellington . . . and our heroines Bessie Smith, Billy Holiday, Rosetta Howard . . . and Cleo Brown."[4] These included the recognized "greats" of jazz at that time — but something more than that. Among them were the players who, in a certain sense, invented the music, transforming it from a popular idiom based on ragtime and the blues into an improvised music of great artistic stature. The transformation they effected was, in its time, almost unbelievable. They had the good fortune to come along when the music was new and ready to be shaped. There was no sense for them of looking over their shoulders at what had been done before, at previous achievements whose character had to be avoided or improved upon. Theirs was an art that spoke with directness and seemed to require no sense of its "significance" to justify it. It was to become for Larkin an epitome of the accessible, unself-conscious art that the modern world seemed to have turned away from.

All What Jazz? is made up of the reviews Larkin wrote for the *Daily Telegraph* from 1961 to 1971 during the years when he was writing some of his greatest poetry. Though Larkin was confined to the records sent to him in the "exciting square packages" (*AWJ* 19), almost every jazz artist of consequence came by in the plethora of issues and reissues of the sixties. After a time, it became his custom, when he had a record by an artist he admired, to begin his brief review with an even briefer essay on that artist; and those so treated give us the spectrum of Larkin's tastes: Pee-Wee Russell; Bix Beiderbecke; Billy Holiday; Bubber Miley; Fats Waller; Sidney Bechet; Bessie Smith; Duke Ellington; Wild Bill Davison; Luis Russell; Count Basie; Charlie Christian; Jimmy Yancey; Louis Armstrong. In 1968 he asks "when are we going to get some really *original* reissues? Bob Howard, say? Prima with Russell? Billy Banks and the Rhythmakers?" (*AWJ* 203); and in a personal plea, "Whose Flaming Youth?", asks "Isn't it about time they started recapturing *my* youth, the golden hours of the thirties? . . . what about Artie Shaw? . . . the rest of the Commodore catalogue, and the early Blue Notes? And think of all those 78s that formed us, the Wilson-James 'Blue Mood', Johnny Hodges on Hampton's 'Sunny Side of the Street', even Hawkins' 'Body and Soul' — where are they?" (*AWJ* 206) He never tired of campaigning for the reissue of the "Billy Banks sides" — remarkable early mixed group recordings from 1932 with a personnel that included such of his heroes as Henry Allen, Pee-Wee Russell and Eddie Condon, and whose manner was never duplicated.

Wherever Larkin writes about music sympathetic to him, he shows an unerring balance in bringing out what is important, even in the small space he has, as in "The Bubbles Waller Blew":

> Nobody, not even Armstrong, Bechet, or Bessie Smith, left a more characteristic opus, nor perhaps one based on a more limited formula: a commercial tune, first played on the piano, then sung by Waller with varying degrees of respect, then a chorus split between trumpet and tenor, and a final, much less respectful vocal with the band playing hell-for-leather behind. Interspersed with the solos was a great deal of stylised jiving from Waller to his sidemen, often based mockingly on the lyrics he had just sung. What was so good about these performances was not so much the music, which could be threadbare (Waller was a king of cliché), nor the Waller humour (for Fats, like most famous humorists, was desperately unfunny two-thirds of the time), but the irresistible drive and bouncing jubilation that pervaded them.
>
> (*AWJ* 163–4)

Concerning Billy Holiday, he reverses the conventional judgement that "'using her voice like a horn' produced her best work", and asserts "she is best when singing a tune because she likes it and words because she believes them" (*AWJ* 148); while in another context, he observes that "her taut, vibrant voice expresses all the human feeling of the words while modifying both rhythm and melody in accord with altoist Johnny Hodges' superb accompaniment." (*AWJ* 72)

Some of Larkin's summary discussions, such as his opening paragraph on some reissues of Ellington's music, give evidence of a power to project a new conception of an artist and to sustain it through a reordering of our perception of the whole body of his work:

> There are times when one wants to attack the whole Ellington mystique, to expose him as an indifferent pianist whose orchestral tastes lie in the direction of alternate vapidity and pretension and who has been carried along since the twenties by a succession of magnificent soloists and his own charm, intelligence and energy. True, this would mean ignoring the famous Ellington band ethos — a mixture of the Athenaeum and A.S. Neill — and discounting the creativity which keeps him (at an age when professors are forcibly retired) scribbling new works that edge old favourites out of the band book . . . But when did he last make a record as good as, say, 'Harlem Airshaft'?

The second three-disc instalment of 'The Ellington Era, 1927–1940' (CBS), however, stresses, if it does nothing else, that the second fifty Ellington records have more personality, variety and historical interest than anyone else of the period could muster for their first choices. (*AWJ* 176–7)

This capacity to epitomize briefly, to capture the essence in a few words, has been characterized by Clive James as a manifestation of Larkin's wit — the steady play of mind on everything he writes about.[5] We encounter an intensely conscious use of evocative language when he describes the cornet playing of Wild Bill Davison:

> . . . a player of notable energy, he uses a wide range of conscious tonal distortions, heavy vibrato, and an urgent, bustling attack. At slow tempos he is melting, almost articulate . . . the deep hoarse blurrings, the athletic in-front-of-the-beat timing, the flaring shakes . . . imposed as they are on a conventional Armstrong basis, make Davison one of the most exciting of white small-band trumpeters. (*AWJ* 182–3)

His most brilliant passage concerns the Chicago clarinetist Pee-Wee Russell ("our Swinburne and our Byron" of his undergraduate days with Kingsley Amis): "the characteristic excitement of his solos, their lurid snuffling, asthmatic voicelessness, notes leant on till they split, and the sudden passionate intensities . . ." (*AWJ* 47) The phrase ". . . notes leant on till they split . . ." calls to mind Whitney Balliett, the *New Yorker* jazz critic whom Larkin admired, and whose writings are studded with descriptive cadenzas; though Larkin's writing is always the product of careful, perceptive, engaged listening.

It is in his dismissals that Larkin's wit, in the conventional sense, is most felt. John Coltrane, the tenor saxophone player whose work dominated the new jazz of the sixties, might be described as the anti-hero of *All What Jazz?*. The first column of 1964 is devoted entirely to a plea that the record companies reissue the Billy Banks sides, "instead of one of the six John Coltrane records no doubt already in production." (*AWJ* 104) Yet Larkin never misses a Coltrane record: in 1962, he sits on the fence, listening to Coltrane "in preference to many a less adventurous set", but noting his "drizzling, snake-charmer tone." (*AWJ* 65) (Coltrane began the fashion of playing the soprano saxophone with a tone like that of the oboe.) By February 1963 Coltrane's tenor saxophone is an "individual amalgam of bagpipe and squeaker" (*AWJ* 80); "a solo of characteristic dreariness" (*AWJ* 86) is remarked upon in May 1963; he is "earnest, humourless" (*AWJ* 96) in October; and in December "the master of the thinly disagreeable . . . sounds as if he is playing for an audience of cobras." (*AWJ* 102) In the following August Larkin found himself liking *Coltrane Live at Birdland*; but by July 1965, "Coltrane sounds like nothing so much as a club bore who has been metamorphosed by a fellow-member of magical powers into a pair of bagpipes" (*AWJ* 141); "screeching dreariness" (*AWJ* 150) in November 1965 is succeeded by the "double-sided carpet of bellowing and screeching" in which "Soloists appear and submerge like Titanic passengers" (*AWJ* 166) in July 1966; while in November Larkin encounters "the most astounding piece of ugliness I have ever heard" (*AWJ* 172), and in March 1967 "blended insolence and ugliness." (*AWJ* 177) This culminated in a retrospect at the time of Coltrane's death: "That reedy, catarrhal tone, . . . that insolent egotism . . . that latter day religiosity . . . that set up pretension as a way of life; that wilful and hideous distortion of tone . . . If he was boring, he was enormously boring. If he was ugly, he was massively ugly. To squeak and gibber for 16 bars is nothing; Coltrane could do it for 16 minutes, stunning the listener into a kind of hypnotic state in which he read and re-read the sleeve-note and believed, not of course that he was enjoying himself, but that he was hearing something significant. Perhaps he was. Time will tell." (*AWJ* 187–8) The *Telegraph* did not print this — possibly, one feels, because its tone was felt to be out of harmony with the obituary period, though they did publish a final post-mortem: "Time was, when a man had snuffed it, you heard no more of him . . . but 'Selflessness' . . . has Coltrane in his habit as he lived, or rather two habits, bad and worse . . . ." (*AWJ* 254) One cannot say that time has told: nearly two decades later, Coltrane is still regarded as a major instrumentalist and one of the leaders of post-modernist jazz. Only if one agrees with Larkin's dismissal of modern jazz, so forcefully enunciated in the "Introduction" to *All What Jazz?*, can one say "How right he was." For Larkin, "Coltrane was simply part of the melancholy tendency since 1945 to remove jazz from our pleasures and place it, with all the other 'modern' arts, among our duties" (*AWJ* 187); though today the average buyer of a Coltrane record like *Crescent* (from 1963 and now more than twenty-five years old) will never have encountered the critical bally-hoo of the sixties: he taps his feet and smiles.

The music of John Coltrane (and of the other innovators of a freer jazz, Ornette Coleman and Cecil Taylor) was just beginning to establish itself when Larkin started reviewing; and Larkin was forced to articulate his response to what might be described as the encounter of jazz with modern music. In so doing, he found himself defining his own attitude to modernist art in general. Larkin recalls that he felt ill-equipped in the face of it, as most reviewers did at the outset; and, in looking back on those early days, he felt like someone who "had confidently gone into an examination hall only to find I couldn't make head or tail of the questions". (*AWJ* 19) The only strategy was "undiscriminating praise". (*AWJ* 21) Coltrane's music seemed to mark the point to which this strategy could not reach, and the growing openness of ridicule shows the limits of Larkin's patience or his growing readiness to let "truthfulness break in, despite my initial resolve". (*AWJ* 25) Yet Larkin writes with unusual perceptiveness about early modern jazz. In November 1963 Larkin reviewed two concert recordings by Dizzy Gillespie and Charlie Parker, the Massey Hall Concert of 1963 and the Carnegie Hall concert of 1947. The 1947 concert was badly recorded on acetates, so that some performances fade or are incomplete. The Massey Hall Concert, on the other hand, was already a legend by 1965; yet Larkin perceives how superior the music was at Carnegie Hall: "The four pieces . . . show Parker at his most incandescently complex, on 'Dizzy Atmosphere' jetting flurries of perfectly articulated notes, and on 'Confirmation' achieving one of his most warmly beautiful solos . . . The Massey Hall Night was different . . . despite Parker's still-formidable contributions, . . . in 1953 Dizzy was five years stronger . . . while the Bird [Parker] was five years deeper into self-immolation." (*AWJ* 100) Those familiar with the music might say that one had to be writing with engagement and perception to offer so discriminating a critique. These are certainly not the comments of a baffled, dismayed reviewer.

It is Parker, the founding father of modern jazz in the mid-forties, to whom Larkin links his rejection of modern jazz and modern art generally. Boning up on newer developments as he began reviewing, he found:

> "there was something about the books I was now reading that seemed oddly familiar. This *development* . . . that required you *to work hard at appreciating it* . . . this *revolutionary explosion* that *spoke for our time* while at the same time being *traditional* in the *fullest*, the *deepest* . . . Of course! This was the language of criticism of modern painting, modern poetry, modern music . . . Parker was a modern jazz player just as Picasso was a modern painter and Pound a modern poet. I hadn't realised that jazz had gone from Lascaux to Jackson Pollock in fifty years . . . 'After Parker, you had to be something of a musician to follow the best jazz of the day.' Of course! After Picasso! After Pound! There could hardly be a conciser summary of what I don't believe about art." (*AWJ* 22–3)

Larkin makes it quite clear that he is not ignorant of the supposed background of these changes — "the post-war Negro was better educated, more politically conscious and culturally aware . . . more musically sophisticated". (*AWJ* 22) He knows that jazz is viewed as "catching up with the rest of the music, becoming chromatic instead of diatonic" (*AWJ* 22); though the distance covered harmonically was more like that from Mozart to Debussy than from "Lascaux to Jackson Pollock", even if Buddy Bolden (the late nineteenth century founder of New Orleans jazz who never recorded) seemed as legendary as the cave painters. Larkin invokes the "pleasure principle" that he had enunciated years before ("The Pleasure Principle", *RW* 80–82), and offers his "essential criticism of modernism, whether perpetrated by Parker, Pound or Picasso: it helps us neither to enjoy nor endure." (*AWJ* 27) He concludes with a characterization of his ideal readers — those with whom he makes an identification — that everyone will recognise as vintage Larkin:

> My readers . . . sometimes I wonder whether they really exist . . . Sometimes I imagine them, sullen fleshy inarticulate men, stockbrokers, sellers of goods, living in 30-year-old detached houses among the golf courses of Outer London, husbands of aging and bitter wives they first seduced to Artie Shaw's 'Begin the Beguine' or The Squadronaires' 'The Nearness of You'; fathers of cold-eyed lascivious daughters on the pill, to whom Ramsay Macdonald is coeval with Rameses II, and cannabis-smoking jeans-and-bearded Stuart-haired sons whose oriental contempt for 'bread' is equalled only by their insatiable demand for it; men in whom a pile of scratched coverless 78's in the attic can awaken memories of vomiting blindly from small Tudor windows to Muggsy Spanier's 'Sister Kate', or winding up a gramophone in a punt to play Armstrong's 'Body and Soul'; men whose first coronary is coming like Christmas; who drift, loaded helplessly with commitments and obligations and necessary observances, into the darkening avenues of age and incapacity, deserted by everything that once made life sweet. These I have tried to remind of the excitement of jazz, and tell where it may still be found. (*AWJ* 28–9)

This is a bravura performance — one in which we can sense the writer relishing his effects, reminiscent in its lighter way of the conclusion of *The Dunciad*. A tone of mock seriousness or of Larkinesque self-deflation is frequent throughout most of the "Introduction" to *All What Jazz?*, especially when Larkin presents himself as the embarrassed new reviewer. There is no questioning the factual truth of what he says; it is the tone to which we should be alert: led along by his somewhat playful self-deprecation, we are drawn to conclusions of seemingly devastating seriousness concerning music and the other arts.

There are some puzzling indirections in Larkin's attitudes to jazz. How did someone who hated Parker's music so much write so perceptively about his concert recordings? It is said that, as late as 1984, Larkin gave a friend a list of his favourite trumpeters, the last of whom was Miles Davis, Parker's protégé and a major innovator in modern jazz.[6] Did Larkin really believe that he wrote for an audience of over-burdened stockbrokers? Isn't the basis of his attitudes to be detected in the reference to the "jeans-and-bearded Stuart-haired sons", who represented a threat to Larkin's relation to jazz and to his sense of life? The intense sniping at Coltrane is a mark of a hardening defensiveness, as was his remark "I love jazz . . . To have it all destroyed by a paranoiac drug-addict made me furious." ("An Interview with *Paris Review*", *RW* 72) Was the reference to Parker's drug addiction an added criticism or an explanation of why Parker had ruined jazz? Larkin's great admiration, Billie Holiday, was as notorious an addict as Parker.

The reviews exist to speak for themselves and be judged by what they say about the music they address; but the linkage that Larkin makes between his tastes in jazz and his tastes in art generally, like his characterization of modernism and its origins, raises more complex questions and points to connections not immediately obvious. The bracketing of Parker with the inveterately "difficult" Pound seems the Achilles heel of Larkin's "Introduction". The rhythms and harmonies that Parker introduced are now the language of more conservative popular music; while, to jazz collectors forty-five or younger, Parker's records present no impediment: they are as old as was the legendary King Oliver record of "Reference Back" when Larkin was a boy (as indeed Larkin was aware (*AWJ* 21)). Larkin's wish to see the music he liked as exemplifying his own views concerning the relationship between art and pleasure led him later to write, when Louis Armstrong died, that he was "an artist of world stature . . . At the same time he was a humble, hard-working man who night after night set out to do no more than 'please people' to earn his fee . . . He was never original in the sense that Parker was original: he simply did what everyone else was doing twenty times better." (*AWJ* 282–3) The last sentence is quite stunning in what it asks one to believe. No jazz musician was more original than Armstrong, who transformed jazz, making it something that nobody could have imagined it would be until he had done it. It is like saying that Leonardo was not original because his pictures seem so natural. Both he and Armstrong had the fortune to come to the medium when its central possibilities had not been pre-empted or exhausted — something, one senses, Larkin wished had been his fate.

Larkin's tastes in jazz should be seen, too, in their historical perspective. Interest in jazz in England began with the collecting of the hotter dance music records of the twenties. The existence of a distinct jazz public seems first to have been recognised by the Parlophone Record Company's "New Rhythm Style" series in 1928; and from then until the beginning of World War II it issued recordings from the Okeh catalogue of the late twenties and early thirties. This series, with similar issues by Brunswick and H.M.V., did much to focus British tastes. The new "swing" music that emerged in America with the triumph of Benny Goodman's Orchestra in 1935 was not as well received by many British jazz collectors as it was by the young Larkin, some of whom regarded it as a commercialization of jazz. By the beginning of the war positions had hardened; so that, when "modern" jazz emerged in the playing of Charlie Parker and Dizzy Gillespie in the mid-forties, it was regarded by many as a perversion. The public for this new music was initially small, being strongest among professional musicians. Under the influence of recordings of some of the earlier New Orleans players, the position of traditionalists became more extreme, and the hostility between the two camps was ferocious by the early fifties. Eventually success obliterated the hostility: the purist traditional music became lost in the "trad fad" to which it gave rise — a characteristically "decent" British cultural phenomenon; while the world-wide success of modern jazz made it a part of the semi-popular, semi-highbrow cultural scene. Finally, when the "new wave" associated with John Coltrane, Ornette Coleman and Cecil Taylor emerged in the nineteen-sixties, it was popularly viewed as part of the "new freedom" of the era; while, in intellectual circles, it was seen as the coming-of-age of jazz as a twentieth-century art form.

This "contemporary jazz" was too much for many devotees to take; and it was to these developments that Larkin reacted so violently. For Larkin, in his youth, jazz had provided a focus of individuation and identity — something that belonged to his generation and set it apart. It had provided the ambience of his friendship with Kingsley Amis; and there can be no question that it epitomized for them an art vital and immediate in its appeal, in contrast to the established "classical" music, with its philosophical underpinnings, its high-toned sense of beauty and the assumption that one needed to have "studied" music to respond to it properly. The no-nonsense relationship to the arts that jazz seemed to encourage was one that Larkin and Amis desired for all the arts at the time of Movement. Ten years later, in the late sixties, the voice of change was that of the "hip", with an emphasis on the strange, the new — what was "far out". Jazz had joined this; and, in so doing, had embraced modernism and departed from its conventional harmonies. Larkin found himself on the other side of the fence, as did many other jazz devotees of his generation.

It was as an example of an art at once powerful and popular that Larkin in his later years looked nostalgically back on jazz; yet it remains to be asked to what extent and for whom the music was ever popular. It was popular with lower class urban negroes in some parts of the United States from 1900 to 1945. During the thirties it merged with the music of the big swing bands that were among the innumerable orchestras that catered to the popularity of ballroom dancing in that era. This was the period in which Larkin discovered it, and in which the cultural position of jazz was most nearly the one that he ascribes to it. It was a minority music of sophisticated drinkers in the bars of the late thirties, forties and early fifties. In a deboshed form, as the "trad fad", it was the dance music of the young in the late fifties in England; and, in its "modern" form, it had a semi-highbrow concert audience in America and Europe in the same period.

Yet, in the thirties and early forties, when Larkin collected his Parlophones and Vocalions, they sounded to most people like a prelude to the Battle of Omdurman. Those who listened to them were regarded as eccentric and were a much smaller minority than the devotees of modern poetry (or than present-day followers of even the most exotic avante-garde jazz). Pressings of 300 copies were usual for jazz records in England in the thirties. Similarly, there was no time at which Muggsy Spanier and his Ragtimers (heroes of Larkin at Oxford) were ever *popular* in America or England: as Larkin himself pointed out, the band folded for financial reasons within a year. Yet their records epitomize for Larkin the days of a lost accessible art. This sense of things seems to have been prompted by (or at least to have been in tune with) two books by Henry Pleasants that Larkin reviewed, *Death of a Music* (1961) and *Serious Music and All That Jazz* (1969).[7] These present the widely accepted thesis that modern "serious" music has lost contact with its concert-going public, and look back to the days when there was no distinction drawn between "serious" and "popular" music. In jazz the books find a music that is at once "serious" and "popular" — yet without the self-consciousness of modern serious music. Pleasants offers an aphorism that must have recommended itself to Larkin: "When a music becomes self-conscious it has lost its innocence."[8]

Larkin used his discussion of the development of jazz in the sixties to characterize what he felt to be the cultural malaise of his time; and his characterization of that malaise is often acute. It embodies that sense of a lost rapport between artist and discriminating audience that haunts the work of F.R. and Q.D. Leavis. Yet the periods in which the enduring art of the time was also a popular one, in the sense of being culturally accessible, recede further the more we examine the question; or they are revealed to be moments of classical felicity, often with ironies of their own. Tennyson's large following emerged just as he abandoned the doubts that made him such a powerful poet up to *In Memoriam*; the masterpieces of nineteenth-century music, which today command an audience larger and socially more heterogeneous than existed in the days of their provenance, often puzzled contemporary listeners and were dismissed in favour of works now forgotten. Nor is the popular and accesssible today always economically self-supporting: reissues of King Oliver's accoustical recordings of 1923 still pay for themselves; but only in a few places can a ballet so popular as "Swan Lake" be put on without subsidy. The problems broached are complex ones; and it is questionable whether we can with any candour set over against them the ideal of an art unself-conscious, happy with the medium as it finds it, and widely and readily accepted. That was certainly not what the contributors to *New Lines* saw themselves as offering, even if they spoke up for common sense. Yet it seems to be what Larkin was searching for in some of his literary essays, such as "The Pleasure Principle", and in the "Introduction" to *All What Jazz?*.

These criticisms in no way fault *All What Jazz?* as a book of jazz criticism. Compellingly readable, acute and perceptive in judgement, it stands out in the vast literature of jazz, where wit and critical acumen are not the rule. Its main drawback derives from its origin in newspaper reviews: some of the comments on records are too brief to be interesting in themselves; and many of the records to which they refer are now known only to dedicated collectors. As for Larkin's high estimation of jazz, one need only quote a passage where he writes with the directness he longs for in the music: "How dreadful to have lived in the twentieth century, but died before King Oliver led his men into the Gennett studio at Richmond, Indiana . . . ." (*AWJ* 28)

Chapter 9

PREFERENCES

Larkin's very large body of occasional writing includes even more literary reviews than jazz reviews. The most substantial of these were contained in *Required Writing* (1983), whose title implies a typically Larkinesque disclaiming of any larger authorial intent for the collection. The success of the book, which went into a fourth printing in twelve months, emphasizes how illuminating and readable the pieces are in their own right; and to pore over these mainly commissioned articles for a "poetic" would run contrary to Larkin's own sense of the very direct relationship of literature to experience. Nonetheless, certain attitudes and preferences emerge from Larkin's critical writings, and these illuminate his whole achievement as a writer.

Required Writing reprinted the "Introduction" to *All What Jazz?*, whose real subject was Larkin's attitude to modernism in the arts:

> My own theory is that it is related to an imbalance between the two tensions from which art springs: these are the tension between the artist and his material, and between the artist and his audience, and that in the last seventy-five years or so the second of these has slackened or even perished. In consequence the artist has become over-concerned with his material (hence an age of technical experiment), and, in isolation, has busied himself with the two principal themes of modernism, mystification and outrage. Piqued at being neglected, he has painted portraits with both eyes on the same side of the nose, or smothered a model with paint and rolled her over a blank canvas. He has designed a dwelling-house to be built underground. He has written poems resembling the kind of pictures typists make with their machines during the coffee break, or a novel in gibberish, or a play in which the characters sit in dustbins . . . And parallel to this activity . . . there has grown up a kind of critical journalism designed to put it over. The terms and the arguments vary with circumstances, but basically the message is: Don't trust your eyes, or ears, or understanding. They'll tell you this is ridiculous, or ugly, or meaningless. Don't believe them. You've got to work at this: after all, you don't expect to understand anything as important as art straight off, do you?   (*RW* 293)

This situation gave rise to Larkin's deepest criticism of modernism, that "it helps us neither to enjoy nor endure":

> . . . as long as it was only Parker I didn't like, I might believe that my ears had shut up about the age of twenty-five and that jazz had left me behind. My dislike of Pound and Picasso, both of whom pre-date me by a considerable margin, can't be explained in this way. The same can be said of Henry Moore and James Joyce (a textbook case of declension from talent to absurdity). No, I dislike such things not because they are new, but because they are irresponsible exploitations of technique in contradiction of human life as we know it. This is my essential criticism of modernism, whether perpetrated by Parker, Pound or Picasso: it helps us neither to enjoy nor endure. It will divert us as long as we are prepared to be mystified or outraged, but maintains its hold only by being more mystifying and more outrageous: it has no lasting power. (*RW* 297)

This exposition isolates certain well-defined features of modernism that Larkin found objectionable: the emphasis on technique and the associated distorted presentation of reality to mirror "vision"; a consequent obscurity and ugliness; and a concern with what is culturally significant rather than with an immediate commerce with experience. The position is a fiercer extension of what Larkin had to say in Enright's *Poets of the 1950s* (1956), and is in keeping with the Movement position, as enunciated in the introduction to *New Lines* (1956).

One of the prime modernist techniques was the distortion of conventional features of the medium in order to mirror "vision". *The Waste Land* offers a signal example in its deliberate fragmentation of "narrative line" and syntax in the service of its vision of cultural fragmentation. In this instance, we can see how the distortion leads to another feature of modernism that Larkin found disturbing — obscurity, in that the uninitiated reader is not provided with clues concerning the connections he should make between the various elements of the poem. Obscurity is also the product of obliqueness — the working through unexplained images that is the method of both symbolist and imagist art. Obscurity, Larkin came to feel, was for modernist poetry "its definitive characteristic, an obscurity unlike previous types in being deliberate and unnecessary."[1] Nothing better exemplifies what Larkin was against than Eliot's celebrated statement in his essay "The Metaphysical Poets": "We can only say that it appears likely that poets in our civilisation, as it exists at present, must be *difficult*. Our civilisation comprehends great variety and complexity, and this variety and complexity, playing upon a refined sensibility, must produce various and complex results."[2] Larkin

cited this passage with disapproval, setting over against it the example of Betjeman, who proved that "a direct relation with the reading
public could be established by anyone prepared to be moving and
memorable." ("The Blending of Betjeman", *RW* 129)

The Waste Land also provides an example of the cultivation of
ugliness that Larkin objected to: Eliot's handling of conventionally
non-poetic subjects would no longer be found ugly (as Larkin would
have recognized); but the fragmentation of form and narrative line,
denying a wish for an overall harmony and cohesion, might be. The
visual arts and music, from which Larkin cites instances in the "Introduction" to *All What Jazz?*, offer countless examples in the twentieth
century of effects that seem ugly to the conventionally attuned eye or
ear.

These aspects of modernism decried by Larkin were never features
of his art. However, there were aspects of modernism which, when
they first emerged, were quite as offensive to popular poetic tastes as
those so far described. These were things that modernist art had in
common with realist art: irony; the serious treatment of seemingly
trivial or sordid subjects; and the use of the language of everyday
speech, frequently with a demotic flavour, in writing about "serious"
subjects. To take *The Waste Land* again as example, these were the
aspects that the readers of 1922 perhaps found most inimical to their
sense of what poetry should be.

All these stylistic features are to be found in Larkin's poetry; and
it is indeed in terms of them that he expanded the scope of English
poetry, showing his greatest originality, and taking a central place
in the development of poetry in his day. In his celebrated review,
"What's Become of Wystan?" (*Spectator* July 15, 1960) Larkin remarked: "We need not remind ourselves of his virtues . . . He was . . .
the first 'modern' poet, in that he could employ modern properties
unself-consciously." (*RW* 123) Larkin's own poetry does not lead us
to feel that he relented concerning this gift for bringing contemporary
life into poetry; and it is the aspect of Betjeman's poetry that he most
praises.

Irony was a pervasive feature of Anglo-American modernist poetry;
and the deployment of irony, both satirically and non-satirically, was,
if anything, over-worked by the poets associated with the Movement.
It was certainly an unforced feature of the sensibility of the period.
A favourite figure with Larkin was that of ironic self-contradiction,
as in such phrases as "awkward reverence". In poems such as "Lines
on a Young Lady's Photograph Album", there is a pervasive play of
ironic wit that is crucial to the manner of the poem.

However, it was in the continuation of the use of a natural language for poetry, begun by the modernists and developed by Auden and MacNeice and their contemporaries, that Larkin showed his great originality, expanding the linguistic range of British poetry. The use of slang and colloquialism with a subtle (and serious) control of tone in poems like "Poetry of Departures"; the combination of demotic speech with lyricism in "Places, Loved Ones"; the masterly modulations of linguistic tone in "Church Going"; the careful use of fashion terms and other "in" phrases of everyday speech in "The Large Cool Store" or "Mr. Bleaney": these were the marks of Larkin's style — the Larkin "voice" — that gave his work such freshness and immediacy; and they constitute a continuation of the revolution in the language of poetry inaugurated by the great modernists.

There is no question that the basis of Larkin's objection to modernism was that it is alienated and inaccessible: "at bottom poetry, like all art, is inextricably bound up with giving pleasure, and if a poet loses his pleasure-seeking audience he has lost the only audience worth having." ("The Pleasure Principle", RW 81–82) This, coupled with the wish that "readers . . . carry away from the poem . . . not the poem, but the experience", points to a deeply and directly humanistic conception of the arts that was very basic for Larkin. Larkin himself was drawn to symbolism in his early following of Yeats, and he was later to say: "Yeats came to seem so artificial — all that crap about masks and Crazy Jane . . ."[3] The discovery of Hardy was a revelation and a relief because, unlike Yeats, "He's not a transcendental writer" ("The Poetry of Hardy", RW 175); though, even in this seemingly commonsense break with symbolism and the emphasis on metaphor as a key figure in modernist poetics, Larkin was more innovative than he later liked to allow. As David Lodge has pointed out: "Poetry, especially lyric poetry, is an inherently metaphoric mode, and to displace it towards the metonymic pole is (whether Larkin likes it or not) an 'experimental' literary gesture."[4]

For Eliot the business of the poet was to create "*significant* emotion"[5] and the intent of the writers of *The Waste Land* and *The Cantos* was clearly the creation of culturally significant artifacts. With this sense of artistic mission Larkin had no sympathy. In praising Betjeman, he wrote: "For him there has been no symbolism, no objective correlative, no T.S. Eliot or Ezra Pound, no reinvestment in myth or casting of language as gesture, no *Seven Types* or *Some Versions*, no works of criticism with titles such as *Communication as Discipline* or *Implicit and Explicit Image-Obliquity in Sir Lewis Morris*". ("It Could Happen Only in England", RW 209) For Larkin poetry seemed to "have got into the hands of a critical industry which is concerned with culture in the abstract, and this I do rather lay at the door of Eliot and Pound".[6] Yet the sureness of touch in his criticism points to considerable familiarity with that "industry"; and it would be wrong, as always, to see Larkin turning away in baffled disgust from a sophistication whose methods and purposes he chose to ignore for a less reflective view of the arts. He admired in Betjeman the ability to "bypass the whole light industry of exegesis" ("The Blending of Betjeman", *RW* 129) that he felt had come to usurp the true function of art. Larkin particularly disliked the "kind of critic who denies the poet supreme authority regarding his work". ("Masters' Voices", *RW* 137) He speaks for a direct relationship between reader and work, unmediated by cultural explanation. This direct relationship with the reader arises from Larkin's relationship to his material and to experience as a whole. His generation was not involved in the modernist preoccupation with a culture in which the shared symbolism of Christianity, along with its world-explaining power, was no longer valid. "Church Going", with its unagonized question "what remains when disbelief has gone?", reflects this change of attitude. Larkin does not find himself, like Yeats and Eliot, seeking to order things through an obscure and invented personal symbolism. The order that he finds is the momentary order that reveals itself in our everyday commerce with experience, and the objects of that everyday experience provide the readily apprehended images of his poetry.

There was a time when Larkin's most quoted remark was one he contributed to D.J. Enright's collection *Poets of the 1950s*: "I believe that every poem must be its own sole fresh created universe, and therefore have no belief in 'tradition' or a common myth-kitty or casual allusions in poems to other poems or poets, which last I find unpleasantly like the talk of literary understrappers letting you see they know the right people." ("Statement", *RW* 79) This is in line with his views on the direct relationship of poet to reader; but it also reminds one of Amis's "Something Nasty in the Bookshop" or of Robert Conquest's introduction to *New Lines*. In that introduction the break with the poetry of the forties involved a turning from the irrational to stances which were clear and commonsensically rational. Larkin's remarks are in keeping with this, and characteristic of the speaker of the most substantial poem in *New Lines*, "Church Going": for one who believed that the "ghostly silt" was dispersed, there could be no belief in myths, and to work in terms of what he did not believe was anathema to Larkin. Equally, it is clear that, for the author of

The Less Deceived, this sceptical, rational stance was crucial in a way that it may not have been for him later.

Nonetheless, behind Larkin's opinions there seem to have been inclinations that went beyond artistic considerations. In reviewing the poems of John Heath-Stubbs (which he evidently did not find particularly congenial) Larkin was happy to suggest that it was "their refusal to be self-important or self-righteous, that wins the reader's goodwill".[7] In his review of John Coltrane's *A Love Supreme* he wrote: "there is a lot of pretentious guff on the sleeve . . . a signed statement by Coltrane that this album is 'an attempt to say "THANK YOU, GOD" through our work'. Let us hope this is the whim of the A. & R. man, for otherwise it would point to a degree of self-seriousness most inimical to an artist." (*AWJ* 142) The self-importance of modernist art was evidently very off-putting to Larkin; and there is a corresponding reductive pressure behind much of his writing about literature.

Larkin's preferences are in tune with the attitudes so far examined. Asked what new poets he admired, he reflected that in "an age that sees poetry as syllabus rather than menu" it was a luxury not to have to worry "about poetry in the abstract". For the mature poet "experience makes literature look insignificant beside life . . . Such reasons may contribute to the growing disinclination . . . to keep up with poetry. Within reach at the moment are collections by Hopkins, Whitman, Wordsworth, Frost, Barnes, Praed, Betjeman, Edward Thomas, Hardy, Christina Rossetti, Sassoon and Auden".[8] No doubt much more was in reach: it is quite clear from Larkin's reviewing that his reading of English poetry of any era was extremely extensive. Later he was to remark that this collection of books was placed near to him as "exemplars" ("Books", *RW* 86) — his considered admirations. With the exception of Whitman and Wordsworth, it could be said that none of the poets named had grand philosophical ambitions for their art, and all favoured poetry of direct human concern. Except for Hopkins, all wrote in a manner easily accessible to the untutored reader; though the work of Whitman, Wordsworth and Hopkins was initially found ugly or banal by their contemporaries.

Some of these preferences are reflected in the choice of poems for *The Oxford Book of Twentieth Century English Verse* (1973). The book met with a great deal of criticism, and was seen by some as being as perverse as the book it replaced, W.B. Yeats's *Oxford Book of Modern Verse* of 1936, in which Yeats included so many of his friends and also showed his distaste for modernism. Donald Davie saw "the clock put back to the languid all-too-English amateurism which two Americans and an Irishman bullied us out of 60 years ago."[9] Another reviewer, Peter Scupham, felt that Larkin had "an unhappy knack of representing good poets by their more occasional or frivolous poems"; and that the selection was marked by a "lack of verve, vitality, risk-taking, which Larkin can turn to such wonderful advantage in his own work . . ."[10] The book reminds one, by contrast, of Geoffrey Grigson's remark about Michael Roberts's selection for *The Faber Book of Modern Verse* in 1936 — "that nauseating concern for *poetry*."[11] For Grigson, Roberts had ignored good poetry for the sake of offering an anthology of poets important to the development of poetry; Larkin, in contrast, seemed to show a deliberate lack of any such literary-historical concern.

If we take Larkin's selection period by period, it is clear that few would argue with the choice for poets born between 1900 and 1930; and for poets born later, there is a recognition that choice is problematical as one comes close to the present. It was concerning the selection of poets born between the birth of Yeats in 1865 and the birth of Lawrence in 1885 that there was the greatest surprise. It occupies 92 of the anthology's 625 pages of poetry, and includes poems by Arnold Bennett, Charlotte Mew, Laurence Binyon, T. Sturge Moore, Hilaire Belloc, W.H. Davies, Ralph Hodgson, G.K. Chesterton, Oliver St.J. Gogerty, Wilfred Gibson, John Masefield, Harold Munro, Alfred Noyes, Herbert Palmer, James Stephens, John Drinkwater, James Elroy Flecker, and J.C. Squire. There are only two poets of the period who would be found outstanding by most present-day readers: Edward Thomas (b. 1878) and Walter de la Mare (b. 1873). Of course, these writers do "represent" English poetry of that time, because they dominated it until 1922; and these poets provided much of the contents of Yeats's anthology. Many were Georgians; and Larkin himself said, in commenting on his choice, that "the worst thing about the Georgians as a class was . . . that their language was stale".[12] Yet he showed a disturbing readiness to represent such poetry where it appeared later by the inclusion of such poets as Richard Church (b. 1893), L.A.G. Strong (b. 1896), Ruth Pitter (b. 1897) or A.L. Rowse (b. 1903).

According to Larkin's Preface, the poems chosen belong to "three groups: poems representing aspects of the talents of poets judged either by the age or by myself to be worthy of inclusion, poems judged by me to be worthy of inclusion without reference to their authors, and poems judged by me to carry with them something of the century in which they were written."[13] One senses that it is the application of the second criterion that has caused the most unease. There are just over two hundred poets in a little over six hundred pages: poets like Herbert Asquith, Gilbert Frankau, G.D.H. Cole, Stella Benson and J.B.S. Haldane do not seem to many to belong in a representation of the treasures of English poetry of this century. Yet what Anthony Thwaite called "A Great Parade of Single Poems" must reflect Larkin's dislike of concern with "poetry in the abstract" and his sense that a poem is the product of the direct response of the writer to experience, and that it becomes the subject of the unmediated response of the reader. This, coupled with Larkin's aversion for "modernism", goes a long way towards explaining the bent of the anthology. While Eliot is adequately represented, Pound is omitted as an American, and the Imagist movement makes a small splash, as it did, quantitatively, in British poetry. Larkin said, "I had in mind a notion that there might have been what I'll call, for want of a better phrase, an English tradition coming from the 19th century with people like Hardy, which was interrupted partly by the Great War, when many English poets were killed off, and partly by the really tremendous impact of Yeats, whom I think of as Celtic, and Eliot, whom I think of as American."[14]

Within the preferences Larkin enunciated and that were exemplified in the anthology, there is embedded this line of inheritance, going from Hardy to Auden and Betjeman — and on to Larkin himself. If his choices seem provincial, it is with the provinciality that has characterized British literature and been, in part, one of its strengths. Larkin was as provincial as Auden, who disliked French culture, admired Hardy, brought back the traditional English verse forms in the thirties, and made a home for the modern industrial landscape in English poetry. Like Auden, Larkin was an innovator in language, drawing into serious poetry the resources that lay outside literature in common speech. The poetry he admired was characterised by a direct handling of experience — it was not made the stalking horse for some larger philosophical or artistic concern. Here too Larkin, like Auden, opts for virtues that have marked English poetry since the mid-eighteenth century, in contrast with grander conceptions encountered in continental (and American) literature. Nonetheless, the very conservative nature of Larkin's selection for his anthology cannot be ignored; and this conservatism, despite his protestations, became more marked as he got older.

While Larkin's reviews were, as he called them when collected, "Required Writing", he seems (except for briefer notices in the *Telegraph* and the *Guardian*) not to have taken anything that was uncongenial. Through a long career of reviewing, he wrote respectfully about the poets one would expect him to admire: Hardy, Barnes, Owen, Auden, Betjeman, Watkins. His dislikes were not confined to doctrinaire modernists. They included Robert Graves, who, he felt, did not write the utterly compelling poem "amply demonstrated by his inability to leave a poem alone when he has finished it";[15] Edwin Muir — "not to my mind an individual poet";[16] Roy Campbell; and R.S. Thomas, whose readers were "mistaking sympathetic subject matter and good intentions for evidence of real poetic talent".[17] Yet, while his critical essays are all judicious discussions of their subject, they do not seem to embody a powerfully held point of view. The second essay on Owen offers a superbly judicious and perceptive discussion of Owen's life in the light of the very large amount of new material that became available in the 1960's and 1970's; but it is only the occasional passage that might make the uninformed reader think that the writer was a poet himself, as when Larkin says of "Strange Meeting": " 'It seemed that out of battle I escaped . . .' It was less an escape than a contrived withdrawal into mythopoeic impersonality that so far from muffling his words lent them extraordinary resonance." ("The War Poet", *RW* 162) One may, indeed, say of most of the essays that he does not offer us challenging readings or unexpected perceptions: the virtues of the reviews — and they are very considerable — are sanity and balance.

Clive James said of *All What Jazz?* that "no wittier book of criticism has ever been written".[18] It is hard to imagine anyone saying that of *Required Writing*. In *All What Jazz?* Larkin was ready to spring out in defence of what he felt music should or should not be. Some of the literary topics on which Larkin was asked to write, such as Ogden Nash or Gladys Mitchell, hardly give opportunity for promulgating a broad or polemical sense of what is to be valued in literature. Nonetheless, in *Required Writing* we seem frequently to encounter Larkin on his best behaviour, particularly in the later essays. "The Changing Face of Andrew Marvell", about the great poet of his adopted city, Hull, shows scholarship, breadth of reading, attention to detail, and balance. It contrasts with the famous essay by T.S. Eliot that Larkin mentions in his first paragraph. Eliot's essay was also judicial, perceptive, scholarly; but it embodied his sense of what poetry should be, and it affected the course of poetry and criticism in its day.

"Wanted: Good Hardy Critic" is the title of one of the longer critical pieces; and its effect is not to convince us that Larkin has shown what should be done by filling the role himself. Despite his attestation of the great influence that Hardy had on him, Larkin does not articulate, with compelling insight, a sense of what it is that makes Hardy so powerful. This is true of almost all his writing about other writers. If we look for the exceptions, where he evinces that enthusiastic inwardness with his subject that we find throughout *All What Jazz?*, we will come up perhaps with only four examples: Auden, Betjeman, Barbara Pym and Stevie Smith.

His essays on Auden and Stevie Smith, and the initial essay on Betjeman, are all early ones, written when Larkin was making his own contribution to changing the face of English poetry. They provide, along with "Statement" of 1955, "The Pleasure Principle" of 1957 and the interview of 1964 with Ian Hamilton (which Larkin did not collect) a synopsis of his views on poetry.

In "What's Become of Wystan?" (written in 1960) there is a concern with a quality that is brilliantly pin-pointed and whose disappearance from Auden's work is felt as an irreparable loss: "this dominant and ubiquitous unease that lay at the centre of Auden's verse and which he was so apt to express." (*RW* 124) It is this concerned perceptiveness that makes the review one of the liveliest and funniest, as when he describes Auden's later dialect as "a wilful jumble of Age-of-Plastic nursery rhyme, ballet folklore, and Hollywood Lemprière served up with a lisping archness that sets the teeth on edge" (*RW* 127), and goes on to ask "Are there people who talk this dialect, or is it how Auden talks to himself?" (*RW* 128) The early Auden was Larkin's first model; the later Auden exemplified for him some of the pitfalls that poetry could face.

Betjeman's gifts he summarized perceptively in a review of *Collected Poems* in 1958:

> Betjeman goes further than anyone else towards summarising "Dear old, bloody old England. Of telegraph poles and tin" simply because no one else has his breadth of poetic reception. Betjeman picks it all up: the decay of surviving nineteenth-century institutions, the decline of the Church, the altered countryside and ways of living, subtopia and socialism, and all the tiny vivid little manifestations of snobbery and silliness, and with his simply loving enthusiasm transmutes it into poetry . . . he is in the best sense a committed writer, whose poems spring from what he really feels about real life, and as a result he brings back to poetry a sense of dramatic urgency and a jumble of properties it had all but lost.[19]

Larkin writes here with the insight that comes from affinity. Indeed, substitute "Larkin" for "Betjeman", and the remarks would be almost as appropriate.

Auden and Betjeman were important influences on Larkin's own poetry. The articles quoted from were written in the years when Larkin was still in close touch with the revitalising changes that he had made in his own idiom — and in that of English poetry as a whole. His criticism is still informed by the concerns that brought about those changes. Those concerns do not make themselves felt in the later literary essays. He seems unduly judicious. In his response to Barbara Pym and Stevie Smith we sense a recognition of a relationship to what is old and seemingly out-moded that, in its public aspect, may appear as idiosyncratic as his own. Barbara Pym he got to know in 1961, when he wrote to her, suggesting that he might review her next novel; and the friendship grew in years of correspondence when she found herself without a publisher because her modest, sensitive — if polite — celebration of English middle-class life and its decencies was out of tune with more strident tastes in fiction prevailing in the 'sixties. In Larkin's article of 1977, "The World of Barbara Pym", the feeling of affinity is related to this: "the underlying loneliness of life, the sense of *vulnerant omnes*, whatever one thinks of when turning out the light in bed." (*RW* 243) Her return to fame was in considerable measure due to Larkin, by then famous himself, when he picked her "six novels" as the underrated books of the last 75 years in a *Times Literary Supplement* symposium, "Reputations Revisited", in January 1977. (Characteristically he picked as overrated "*Women in Love* . . . boring, turgid, mechanical, ugly, and dominated by the kind of deathly will-power that elsewhere Lawrence always attacked."[20]

As with Betjeman, and to a marked degree with Stevie Smith, Barbara Pym's achievement is associated with an incapacity to give up being herself or to modify her idiom in deference to any sense of what literature ought to be. Yet this individuality, this truth to what one is and to the world in which one has lived, is accompanied in all three writers by limitations that are associated with a provincialism and a degree of idiosyncrasy not found in Larkin's own writing. In the case of Stevie Smith, Larkin acknowledged this oddity, but praised her for "uttering the unexpected that once expressed is never forgotten" (*RW* 156), and said of her poems "they are completely original and now and again they are moving" (*RW* 153) — an epitome of his highest praise. In the case of Betjeman, Larkin's failure to see his limitations has been remarked on by his critics; and reservations concerning his admiration for Betjeman are in tune with the protests concerning some of the poetry he found it worthwhile to enshrine in his *Oxford Book of Twentieth-Century English Verse*, where, for some, he manifests a resolutely unambitious provincialism, rooted in his respect for the personal and the local.

A refusal to acknowledge any interest in foreign literature was a related and seemingly limiting feature of Larkin's preferences. *"Foreign* poetry? *No!"* he retorted in 1964 when Ian Hamilton asked whether he read "much foreign poetry";[21] and in the *Paris Review* interview in 1982 he explained: "I don't see how one can ever know a foreign language well enough to make reading poems in it worthwhile" (*RW* 69); though as a young man he had produced a creditable version of Baudelaire's "Femmes Damnées". As with his strongly held opinions about modern jazz, his attitude to foreign literature was typical of his generation, and especially his immediate group. Kingsley Amis's *I Like It Here* (1958) was the product of a Somerset Maugham award that took its author to Portugal, which his hero did not like. The Movement's "no nonsense" stance concerning literature was in part a reaction to the Francophile connoisseurship that dominated the British Sunday papers and the British cultural scene in the days of Harold Nicholson and Cyril Connolly. George Orwell, mentioned with admiration in the Introduction to *New Lines*, was aggressively English in his praise of unsophisticated pleasures like fish and chips; while F.R. Leavis, who had such an influence on the cultural views of Larkin's generation, seldom had a good word to say about a foreign work of literature. Writing with "a feeling that the whole of the literature of Europe from Homer . . . has a simultaneous existence"[22] was what Eliot and Pound, the American modernists, advocated. In contrast, the pressure to which Larkin, Amis and Wain had responded was that important experiences should be presented in terms of the everyday events that loom so large in our individual worlds. Larkin, who "didn't eat any Brie"[23] when he had lunch with Barbara Pym, was in tune with a main drift of English sensibility in his generation, so far as things foreign were concerned.

The explanation Larkin offered later in life for his attitude to things un-English was, however, a personal one: "My father liked going to Germany, and took me twice, when I was 14 or so. I found it petrifying, not being able to speak to anyone or read anything . . . My father liked the jolly singing in the beercellars . . . think of that for someone who was just buying the first Count Basie records! . . . It's a language thing with me: I can't learn foreign languages, I just don't believe in them."[24] No doubt this kind of feeling was a very strong one for him. It is said that he had the opportunity to go to New Orleans, the home of his favourite music, but changed his mind about it, though no language problem could have been involved. One senses that something deeply personal and not articulated was involved in his stay-at-home insularity — something that went beyond the residual dislike left by boyhood visits to Germany with his family; something associated with his concern with identity and its vulnerability.

If one observes that some of Larkin's attitudes, such as his dislike of children or his need to be alone, are — for all his clear sightedness concerning them — attitudes not shared by most people; one has to go on to declare that his poetry, while embodying these attitudes, triumphs over them in the centrality it attains. The same cannot be said of some of his critical stances. To see, for instance, what there was to be learned from Betjeman was a poetic and critical triumph; not to have seen Betjeman's limitations points to limitations in Larkin himself — the concomitant, one might say, of one of his most noted strengths: his unwillingness to tailor what he was as a poet to what he thought he ought to be. He showed a readiness to give strong praise to minor and sometimes idiosyncratic writers in his later writing; while the discussion of major writers whom he admired has a certain seamless blandness, offering no articulation of what literature should or should not be, yet never letting us feel the absence of such an articulation. It is perhaps quite usual that criticism that discriminates passionately should come from a poet in his formative years: this was the case with Eliot. Yet, with Larkin, we encounter the strident passion of the introduction to *All What Jazz?* (and of some of his jazz reviews) in the years that gave us many of the more sedate literary essays in *Required Writing*. This could reflect the fact that for Larkin the important artistic positions were taken early and at a very fundamental emotional level: the devotion to jazz; the rejection of foreign culture; turning his back on the larger cultural ambitions for literature associated with Yeats and modernism. They were part of the "philistinism" that Barbara Everett saw as one of Larkin's most important contributions to British culture;[25] and when issues related to these attitudes emerged, Larkin reacted with force. Whatever the reason, one could have wished for critically more adventurous assessments in *Required Writing*.

Larkin and the Movement had made a conservative reaction to modernism; yet Larkin had at the same time changed the face of English poetry. Indeed, changes that in retrospect seem conservative were in those days radical, because they involved a confrontation with the sense of what the arts should be that modernism had established. It is largely true that Larkin's basic positions concerning poetry changed very little during his lifetime; but attitudes and opinions that seemed radical in the days of the Movement became central and accepted, as the work of those associated with the Movement moved to cultural dominance. It then became easy to see the rejection of aspects of modernism as a purely conservative reaction and to ignore the changes brought about in British poetry; and Larkin, in his later years, seemed pleased to accept such a characterization. Indeed, his dislike of the new in his later years was a manifestation of a growing and uncomfortable conservatism that one cannot feel was entirely the fault of the age into which he had lived. In his later vociferous rejection of modernism, he seemed to draw back from a recognition of how powerfully innovative his own work had been.

Viewed as a whole, Larkin's critical work has paradoxical features; and the most paradoxical, perhaps, is that this poet, who did so much to change the manner of British poetry and the sensibility of its readers, should insist so strongly in later years that his aim was merely to please the ordinary reader and that he had no time for opinions on what poetry should be. This was the stance implied by his later reviews; and along with it went a sense that his readers would share such views. There was no need to probe the nature of poetry or to question what poetry should be, except to emphasize, in an increasingly simplistic way, "the pleasure principle".

A return to the lively essay that first enunciated that principle in 1957 highlights the later shift in attitude, if not in explicit opinion, on Larkin's part. The essay positions itself polemically in relation to an emerging but widely accepted cultural situation in which the encounter with poetry was more and more mediated by criticism and a derived sense of what ought to be liked. Larkin's opening position, that the poet seeks to "construct a verbal device that will reproduce [his] emotional concept in anyone who cares to read it" (*RW* 80), is, ironically, very similar in phrasing to Eliot's definition of the "objective correlative" in his essay on *Hamlet*.[26] The tone of the essay is aggressively down-to-earth in a charcteristic Movement manner, with phrases such as the"cash customers of poetry." (*RW* 81) In Larkin's later writing, the "pleasure principle" — in its day part of a radical attack on the critical establishment — seems to stand clear of its origins, to emerge as a blandly commonsense, simplistic position.

Indeed, enormous questions are by implication set aside in some of Larkin's later writing, such as why the harmonies of nineteenth-century music should seem "natural"; or why, for that matter, the use of traditional forms in poetry, which involves (as Larkin recognised) a complex game with rhyme and metre, should have validity. There came to be what one might term an "official" set of Larkin attitudes — a "no-nonsense" position; and later interviews, such as "An Interview with *Paris Review*" (*RW*), succeed largely in eliciting these "official" responses. No doubt Larkin believed what he said (or wished to); and no doubt he was sincere in the impression he conveyed that he had not changed in his attitudes. Yet he must have been aware of how polemical his stance was, as in the selection he made for his *Oxford Book of Twentieth-Century English Verse*. The blandness of many of his later reviews, in comparison with the biting criticism of "What's Become of Wystan?", reflected a wish not to bring in question the "official" Larkin position. Yet, when something came along to threaten that position, as did post-modern art and post-modern jazz in the late sixties, the result was a vituperative explosion.

The aggressive/defensive nature of these outbursts is obvious and suggests that Larkin felt insecure in the face of these new developments in the arts. Though he liked the Beats and the Liverpool poets, he evidently felt threatened by the cultural changes of the nineteen-sixties that seemed to carry to extreme certain tendencies implicit in modernism — tendencies that manifested themselves in his beloved jazz. These feelings went along with a defensive hardening of attitude encountered in some of his poetry, as in "Homage to a Government" and "Going, Going", and in his admiration for Mrs. Thatcher — manifestations of a conservatism that came to permeate his work.

Chapter 10

THE MAKING OF THE POEMS

Some of the most powerful insights into the character of a poet's work can come through a knowledge of his mode of composition, as revealed in manuscripts or notebooks. Strangely enough, there are very few great poetry workbooks. Emily Dickinson and the young Dylan Thomas compiled celebrated manuscript books, but these were in fact "good copy" books in which finished versions were brought together. Larkin's own school period notebooks are just such compilations. There are only a few work books, such as Stephen Spender's "Sketch Book III" in the Lockwood Memorial Library at the University of New York at Buffalo, and Roy Fuller's notebooks in the Brotherton Collection at the University of Leeds, that show us the whole process of composition of individual poems, and also allow us to see the creative process in its completeness over an extensive period. Among these are Philip Larkin's notebooks.

Larkin probably began using the books around December 1943, about a year before the compilation of *The North Ship* (published 1945), though the sequence of entries begins in October 1944. The books were used in a methodical way from the beginning to the end, and there is very little interlocking of drafts of different poems, and few blank spaces. Poems are regularly dated, mainly only on completion; and discarded material is regularly crossed out. The entries were evidently written with what Larkin once facetiously called "a succession of Royal Sovereign 2B pencils". ("Writing Poems", *RW* 83)

While the notebooks give a very detailed picture of the development of Larkin's idiom, they also give example after example of his mode of composition. Throughout the books, poems seem to be worked on one at a time, though poems are quite often set aside after considerable work has been done on them, and are then returned to, sometimes considerably later. This was true of two central masterpieces, "Church Going" and "The Whitsun Weddings". Sometimes a draft of a part of a poem will be made, to be followed by a second attempt that usually runs further than the first. This may be repeated until the whole poem is there; or a section of the poem may be drafted to completion, after which a further section is attempted. Up to 1946, quite frequently the whole poem appears in the first draft. This was the case with "Wedding-wind". Alterations were then made, until it seemed appropriate to make a further draft or a good (and possibly final) copy. However, after 1950 we find extensive drafting, redrafting and alteration. The change occurs with "At Grass" (drafted at the end of 1949), which occupies twelve pages. The poem marks a decided change in the poetry, and with this change seems to have come a much more intense working and reworking of detail.

"Going" is an example of an earlier poem that came in very much its final shape. The following reproduces the complete working of the poem in the notebook:

> There
> ~~Here~~ is an evening coming in
>   one never seen before
> Across the fields, ~~now—?—in—its—path~~
> That lights
> ~~It—has—~~[indecipherable] no lamps.
> Silken it seems at distance; when
>   up   breast
> It is drawn / over the knees and [indecipherable]
>   brings no comfort
> It ~~is—harsh—as—sacking~~.
> Where has the tree gone, that locks
> Earth to the sky? What is under my hands
> That I cannot feel ~~it~~?
> What loads my hands down?

As will be seen, the corrected version is almost the published one. The alterations do not change the impact of the poem, merely strengthen it, as with "That lights no lamps" for the less sensuous "It has no lamps". The replacement of "harsh as sacking" by "brings no comfort" does not alter the basic tenor of the line but prevents the over-realization of the cloth image implicit in "drawn up over the knees". "There" for "Here" enhances the feeling of distance and elusiveness important to the poem.

"Wedding-wind" occupies one page in the notebook, and the version, as corrected there, is the same as in *XX Poems* and *The Less Deceived*, except for one word and some punctuation. There are considerable alterations to the original draft, but twelve lines of this twenty-three line poem stand unamended. Even in the case of "Deceptions", subject to far more reworking, we can see in the first page

of drafting that a great deal of the final shape is there in the initial
writing:

> ~~Now it's so long ago~~
> ~~Where they ca~~
> ~~Where can they be found,~~
> ~~Even from such a distance I can feel~~
> Even so distant I can taste the grief,
>   sharp   made
> Bitter and [~~indecipherable~~] with stalks, he ~~forced~~ you gulp:
>
>   sun
> The heartless patterns of [~~indecipherable~~], the brisk, brief
> ~~Jingle~~ Passing   along
> Rasping ~~Trotting~~ of ~~horses in~~ the street outside
>   ~~was~~ striding
> All London/ ~~walking~~ quickly the other way
> ~~That~~   And the daylight   greedy
> ~~And the day~~   [~~indecipherable~~] and unanswerable and wide
>
> Even so distant I can taste the grief,
>   [~~indecipherable~~]
>   ~~stalk~~ sharp with stalks
> Bitter and ~~sharp with stalks~~, he made you gulp:
>   occasional print
>   ~~sun's oold patterns~~   and
> The ~~heartless patterns of sun~~, the brisk brief
> Worry of wheels along the street outside —
> All London walking quickly the other way;
>   [~~indecipherable~~]   tall
> And light unanswerable and   [~~indecipherable~~] / and wide
>   shame
> With nowhere to secrete the scar, no [~~indecipherable~~]

Of special note is the second line in the second version, where "sharp
with stalks", a phrase from the first version that found its way into
the printed poem, is deleted, only to be replaced before emendation
can take written form. It was not infrequent for Larkin to work
on a phrase, only to return finally to its original. This, and the
way in which so much of "Deceptions" is present in its first drafting,
demonstrates how coherently Larkin's poems presented themselves to
him when he began to write. Larkin quickly reaches a striking first
line that remains unaltered. His distance from the event, the grief —
and the reference to tasting (that is used again) are all in this first
line. The images of dazzling light and moving traffic are also there:

characteristically, they arise from a psychological *observation* — that for those in pain, light seems harsh and the world callously concerned with its own business.

"At Grass" provides an illuminating example of extensive drafting. On this occasion, there is no final "good version" in the notebook; but the following is a reconstruction of what seems to have been the poem as drafted there.

"At Grass"

(Draft version from Notebook — BM Ad MS 52619)

[The stanzas of the published version are indicated by numbers in the left-hand margin. Changes (other than of punctuation) made in the published version are shown in the right-hand margin.]

1. The eye can hardly pick them out
  From the cold shade they shelter in,
  Till the wind distresses tail and mane;
  Then one crops grass, and moves about,
  The other seeming to look on.
  The sky blows dark with new Spring rain.   /And stands anonymous
                                                  again/

  And now no London newspaper
  Pries round their paddock solitude.
  They are as other horses are.
  Yet, fifteen years ago, both were
  More famous than most men, pursued
  By camera, field-glasses and car.

  In City dining-rooms in clubs
  And barbers'-shops and billiard halls,
  Their flippant names were burrs that stuck
  To gossip; and in back-street pubs
  Their tinted pictures on the walls
  Embodied every earthly luck.

2. Through thirty-three and-four, perhaps   /Yet fifteen years ago,
  perhaps/ Two dozen distances sufficed
  To fable them, far afternoon   /faint afternoons/
  Of Cups and Stakes and Handicaps,
  Whereby their names were artificed
  To inlay faded, classic Junes.

3. Silks at the start: against the sky
  Numbers and parasols: outside,
  Squadrons of empty cars, and heat,
  And littered grass; then the long cry

That hangs unhushed till it subside
To sports editions in the street.   /To stop press columns/

But money rode them, led them in,
Curry-combed their croups and flanks;
Every canter, swerve or sweat
Money measured; every win
Was endorsed at different banks.
Guiltlessly they galloped, yet

Broke three people in one day,
The two of them, and every race
They ran brought small disturbances —
One pawns his coat, one cannot pay:
(Strange such seediness to trace)   (Not drafted to completion)
Back to such splendid energies.

4. Do memories plague their ears like flies?
They shake their heads. Dusk brims the shadows.
Summer by summer all ebbed away.   /all stole away/
— The starting-gates, the crowds and cries
All but the unmolesting meadows.
Almanacked, their names live; they

5. Have slipped their names; and stand at ease
Or gallop for what must be joy.
No field glasses pursue them home. /And not a field-glass sees them home/
Stopwatches make no prophecies.   /Or curious stop watch prophesies/
Only the groom, or the groom's boy   /and the groom's boy/
With bridles in the evening come.

The first stanza seems to have come easily:

> The eye can hardly pick them out
>   shelter in
> From the cold shade they ~~select~~ —
> Till wind distresses
> ~~To shelter in~~   tail and mane:
> Then, on the far side of the field,
> We see them standing, nose to nose

The first line remained to the end exactly as first written. It embodies both the subject of the poem and its dominant perspective: the horses are far off, lost to sight, as their past is. Most of the details of the final version are there: the pair of distant horses, standing close to one another, sheltering in the shade, while the wind disturbs their hair. After a second draft, Larkin writes out what becomes the published version of the stanza, except for its final line. There is a firm sense

of the subject and its possibilities implicit in the poem's opening,
quickly come to.

Here, as throughout the drafting of the poem, the rhyming pattern
is absent in the first version. This is not to say that the poet is
solely concerned with narrative line or imagery: phrases that carry
important feelings for the overall impact of the poem are evolved and
retained. When the narrative line shows shape, modifications are
made to produce rhymes. In this first stanza, the metrical pattern
and the rhyme scheme (a, b, c, a, b, c) for the whole poem are
discovered. In addition, other features emerge: "in" and "on" are
imperfect rhymes; they have weak natural stress, but are placed in
positions where metrically a firm stress is implied. This sets up the
natural, muted feel of rhyme and metre that is characteristic of the
poem as a whole.

The horses are not revealed to be race horses in the first stanza.
That they were famous but now forgotten, becomes the theme of the
next stanza attempted:

> Fifteen years ago, they were
> More famous than most men, pursued
> By cameras, field-glasses and cars,
> Ham-sandwiches, and newspaper:
> On Epsom Downs, at Newmarket
> Their names were bandied in the bars.

Larkin redrafted this second stanza, using the original first three
lines as the last, to give a new direction to the poem. Attention
turned to the disturbance of human life produced by the horses as
objects of betting — an emphasis taken up again in the fifth and
sixth stanzas of the original draft version — "But money rode them,
led them in" and "Broke three people in one day". In essaying these
stanzas, Larkin at first wrote "They lived in terms of men, hedged
in/By bet and bid". We see him trying to plot the direction of the
poem. Beside one rejected version of his original second stanza, there
is one of his notes to himself:

> magic of names — names
> woven into human world —
> names passed into encyclopedias
> — horses, free at last, become
> horses? Do they remember? ?
> the burst of speed

Much of this is taken up later; though the poem was to find its own resolution in slightly different and decidedly more subtle terms.

The manuscript continues:

> Through
> ~~In~~ thirty-three and -four, perhaps
>   distances sufficed
> Two dozen ~~afternoons contain~~ (?)
>   fable   far
> To ~~make~~ them, ~~fabled lest~~ afternoons
> Of Cups and Stakes and Handicaps.
>   when   ~~jogged~~ slid by
> Their names, ~~though ours passed on unnoticed~~,
>
> Parasols and silks
> ~~The silks and parasols~~, mauves and greys.
> What did they make of them?
>
> Their names, that might have gone unnoticed,
> ~~Eternally inlay those Junes~~
> ~~Inlay Now~~ inlay those classic Junes
> Thereby ~~Since~~

There is some groping, as evidenced by the large amount of alteration. When Larkin reaches the phrase that, after two rejected attempts, was to become (with its craft metaphor) "To inlay faded classic Junes", he stops as though he has found what he wanted, and the next version of the stanza is virtually the published one, with the "classic Junes" concluding the last line. We see in fact how much the process of composition involves the discovery of phrases or details that at once evoke the world of horses but also carry the emotional movement of the poem.

The next two stanzas attempted to continue the theme of the horses being dominated by human concerns, and in particular by money and betting. Finally eliminated, they were heavily worked over, particularly in the search for the type of everyday detail that was to be a feature of Larkin's poetry from this time on: "a cheaper suit/A better smoke"; "pawned coats, a week's advance of pay" are among the phrases tried out.

The money/betting theme is reintroduced more decidedly in the drafting of the last two stanzas, with "pencilled bets" in the penultimate stanza and "Like colts again: they trot for joy/And not for bets" in the final stanza. These phrases were eliminated early in the drafting; and as soon as the phrase concerning "memories" emerged, it was transformed into its final version "Do memories plague their

ears like flies?", and became the first line, thus bringing the theme
of memory into prominence, and returning the poem to the visual
image with which it opened: the scene provides the simile, as so often
in Larkin's mature poetry.

The reference to the horses trotting like "colts" brings back the
suggestion, explored earlier, that they will be like other horses again.
The phrase is transformed later to "gallop (if they do) for joy", and
ends up as "gallop for what must be joy". In these changes, there is
a movement away from any presumption to understand the horses'
feelings; and the final perspective, as throughout the published poem,
is a human one.

A key metaphor, delicately muted, but given prominence by its
placing across two stanzas is "they/Have slipped their names". It
appears at first as "But this stiff cloth,/Long since slid from their
backs", where the saddle blanket is given a vague figurative extension. Its suggestions become more specific in "this stiff cloth/ Of
reputation"; but it is then changed to "The cloth of gold has slipped
their backs", to become "the cloth of fame" in the next draft. It
emerges in a new form as the conclusion to the stanza:

> Till the fever and the money had slipped and gone
> From their backs like a stable-cloth.

Finally, as the drafting moves on to the closing stanza, the phrase becomes a link between the two stanzas, and the metaphor becomes
submerged in "they/Have slipped their names"; while any mone-
tary reference, linking it to the money/betting theme, disappears.
Indeed, Larkin had associated the cloth successively with "reputation", "gold", and "fame", only to eliminate all of these in favour of
"names", with its more elusive suggestions of his frequent theme of
identity. In the same way, in searching for an image of fruitfulness
for the conclusion of "The Whitsun Weddings", Larkin arrived at
"packed like squares" after trying out "spread like fields" and "packed
like fields".[1]

"At Grass" is unusual in that, although there is the notation "(fin
3.1.50)" that customarily marks the completion of a poem in Larkin's
notebooks, it did not appear in print in something close to this "finished" form, as did most other poems. Larkin remarked: "It was
always my practice to transfer a poem from manuscript to the typewriter, usually at the point at which a coherent and consecutive version had emerged; this did not mean that that version was final. It
may be that more changes were made to 'At Grass' at this stage than

is usual . . ."[2] For the published version he took five of the nine stanzas, altering some phrases before the poem appeared in *XX Poems* in April 1951.

These later alterations of phrase are few, and they are noted beside the version given earlier. In stanza two of the published poem, "Yet, fifteen years ago" is taken from one of the deleted stanzas and substituted, as a linking phrase, for "Through thirty-three and -four". In the third stanza, "stop press columns" is revived from one of the drafts to replace "sports editions"; while "far afternoons" in the same stanza becomes "faint afternoons". At the conclusion, "Only the groom and the groom's boy" rather than "Only the groom or the groom's boy" tidies up the grammar, as the rhyme required the plural "come"; while "No field-glasses pursue them home/Stop watches make no prophecies" is rephrased "And not a field-glass sees them home,/Or curious stop-watch prophesies", presumably to avoid the broken movement at the end of the poem that a series of unlinked clauses would give. Only one alteration seems the work of independent second thought: the "new Spring rain" of the first stanza had been with the poem from the beginning, though "rain" had little emotional function for the poem as a whole. The line now reads "And stands anonymous again", where "anonymous" links forward to the phrase "their names are artificed" in what is now the next stanza, and takes up a note that is in tension with the dominant concern with fame.

The reorganization of the poem for publication can be seen as the final stage in its focusing. The eliminated stanzas have to do with the involvement of the horses in the world of men and the disturbances caused by betting. This theme, which at one stage of the drafting seemed to dominate the poem, does not appear in the published version. A similar elimination occurred in the drafting of "The Whitsun Weddings", where the poem at one point described the couples climbing on to the train and speculating on how their marriages would go.[3]

Larkin's mode of composition in this poem is completely characteristic. He begins at the beginning, composing line by line, with very few leaps ahead, even to the end of the stanza. W.B. Yeats, in drafting, made notes to himself of images he would use.[4] Stephen Spender, on the evidence of the notebook in which he composed his early poems ("Sketch Book III" at the Lockwood Memorial Library in Buffalo) would produce drafts of considerable length, which were then pruned of passages and phrases. This is borne out in his own essay "The Making of a Poem".[5] Dylan Thomas, in writing his later poems, would set words and phrases about the page, and the poem would grow around them. In the case of Yeats and Thomas particu-

larly, the mode of composition is indicative of the orientation towards
the poem. For Yeats, images were the major structural device of his
poems, in terms of which the emotional movement of the poetry was
carried forward. Thomas worked "*out* of words"[6] and his poems were
a form of verbal orchestration.

It is noteworthy that, as Larkin's stanzas evolve, the thought and
narrative line lead the writing, and details and phrases are sometimes
developed without regard for the rhyme scheme. This contrasts with
the procedures of some poets who employ traditional forms, and who
allow the rhyme scheme to suggest the phrasing.

We see in all this corroboration of the importance of narrative, conscious thought, declarative statement and particular detail in Larkin's
work. The actual is present in its own right in his poetry, and not as
a surrogate for something else. His poems seek to evoke the everyday
world and to make statements about it. They are in no way oblique.
The forms are traditional, and do not have an overall subordinating
power, as in Eliot's *Four Quartets* (to cite an extreme example).

Indeed, Larkin's way of proceeding and the coherence of his poetry
in the earliest drafts contrasts with what is known of the processes
of composition of several other important twentieth-century poets.
T.S. Eliot, evidently reflecting on his own experience, said that "a
poem, or a passage of a poem, may tend to realize itself first as a
particular rhythm before it reaches expression in words, and . . . this
rhythm may bring to birth the idea and the image . . ."[7]

Larkin spoke out against the notion that the reader knows better
than the writer what the poem means; and the very coherence of his
mode of composition attests to its being a very conscious process.
The stance of the poet, in his mature poems, is invariably that of
someone making observations about a scene or event, arguing, drawing conclusions. It is a very British orientation to the material of the
poem, to be encountered in the topographical poetry of Denham or
Dyer, and in the work of Barnes and Hardy, of Edward Thomas, and
of Auden, MacNeice and Betjeman.

The notebooks give an unusual insight into the work of a poet as
he formed his idiom. In addition, the books give us a very complete
picture of the process of composition over a number of years. In
respect of this kind of interest, the notebooks are among the most
important literary documents of their period.

Equally revealing for the reader (or listener) today are recordings
of the poet reading his own work. Each of Larkin's mature books of
poetry was recorded by him in its entirety, with the poems in the order
in which they appear in the books. In an interview reproduced on

the cover of the first album, he discussed the particular illumination that such readings can give: "I suppose that an actual reading of a poem by its author can be helpful: you can hear where he puts the stresses, whether he sounds ironic or flippant or serious. You go back to the text with a firmer grasp on what he meant . . . I think tone of voice does something for the colloquial ones." He also remarked (with the suggestion of agreement) "There's a book that argues that every poet writes for his own voice . . ."[8] Hearing Larkin read, one can appreciate the force of this contention.

His aim (rather unusual when he made the first recording in October, 1958) was "to sound like someone talking, rather than the laboured snail's pace style some people have, full of breathing."[9] This in itself generates a particular emotional tone and defines our sense of the emotional attitudes of the poet. In the reading of "Maiden Name", the lovely, low-toned, conversational manner conveys a feeling of distanced resignation that heightens our sense of the loss of the beauty of the past. As always with Larkin, in the reading there is a drawing back from emotion that has the effect of strengthening it. The handling of pace is very important to the impact of the readings — that easy change of pace and voice that was so expressive in his apparently flat middle-class English speech. However intricate the form, Larkin's voice moves with perfect naturalness through it — a mark of the way in which the music of the poems is attuned to the rhythms of ordinary speech. Indeed, one can say of his style that, however distinctive it is, it seems, when he reads, perfectly natural — the only possible form of expression.

Concerning some of the later poems, he gave on the recordings comments on how they were written or how they were to be taken. "Mr. Bleaney" he recalled as having arisen from personal experience; while "Dockery and Son" was not seen as a poem of regret but of puzzlement. "Broadcast" was, he confessed, "as near as I get in this collection to a love poem". He expressed his preference for poems based on "unsorted experience", while admitting that "Faith Healing" (one of his most powerful poems) had its origin (as did "At Grass") in a documentary. For "The Whitsun Weddings", he recalled having the sense that it would make a poem if he could do no more than re-create the experience that seemed that afternoon to give promise of a poem.[10]

Most of these comments are on a very obvious level; and, while Larkin gave us many memorable remarks about the kinds of poetry he disliked or the ways in which he thought poetry should be read, he said very little about the process of writing poetry. Perhaps this was understandable, as he believed that it was "fatal to decide, intellectually, what good poetry is because you are then in honour bound to try to write it, instead of the poems that only you can write." ("Statement", *RW* 79) Indeed, while his style is unmistakable, he did not seem to regard the attainment of an individual style as an end in itself: "What I should like to write is different kinds of poem that might be by different people."[11] For him the poet's business was "externalising and eternalising his own perceptions in unique and original verbal form." ("Subsidizing Poetry", *RW* 89) This process was a slow one: "Longer ones take weeks or even months." ("An Interview with *Paris Review*", *RW* 58) The traditional formal elements were important to him: "meter and rhyme . . . I doubt really if I could operate without them";[12] and he later said, "Writing poetry is playing off the natural rhythms and word-order of speech against the artificialities of rhyme and meter" ("An Interview with *Paris Review*, *RW* 71) — a remark that echoes what Robert Frost said in "The Figure a Poem Makes".

The conception of writing conveyed by these remarks is that of a process consciously controlled, while the function of rhetorical devices is seen as instrumental to the process rather than of its essence. Yet, as he said, "I seem to have spent my life waiting for poems to turn up."[13] There is nothing particularly original in admitting to the vagaries of inspiration. However, in *The Poetry Book Society Bulletin* for February 1964, when *The Whitsun Weddings* was the Society's choice, he gave a very acute discussion of those elements of creation that lie outside the artist's control:

> If something must be said, it should be about the poems one writes not necessarily being the poems one wants to write. Some years ago I came to the conclusion that to write a poem was to construct a verbal device that would preserve an experience indefinitely by reproducing it in whoever read the poem . . . In so far as it suggested that all one had to do was pick an experience and preserve it . . . it was much oversimplified . . . The longer one goes on . . . the more one feels that some subjects *are* more poetic than others, if only that poems about them get written whereas poems about other subjects don't . . . This means that most of the time one is engaged in doing, or trying to do, something of which the value is doubtful and the mode of operation unclear . . . The days when one could claim to be the priest of a mystery are gone . . . Yet writing a poem is still not an act of the will. The distinction between subjects is not an act of the will. Whatever makes a poem successful is not an act of the will. In consequence, the poems that actually get written may seem trivial or unedifying, compared with those that don't. But the poems that get written, even if they do

> not please the will, evidently please that mysterious something that
> has to be pleased . . . there must be among the ingredients that go
> towards the writing of a poem a streak of curious self-gratification,
> almost impossible to describe except in some such terms, the presence
> of which tends to nullify any satisfaction the will might be feeling at a
> finished job . . . To write a poem is a pleasure: sometimes I deliberately
> let it compete . . . with other spare-time activities . . . Yet doesn't
> this perhaps conceal a subconscious objection to writing?   ("Writing
> Poems", *RW* 83–4)

His often rather aggressive insistence on the importance of pleasure for
both reader and writer has annoyed some of his high-minded readers;
but the passage brings into focus the often discommoding role in
creation of those elements of the self that lie beyond the reach of the
will. There is a recognition that the poet does not *elect* his themes or
subjects, and cannot impose his own sense of what is important on
what he writes. As Larkin put it elsewhere: "Very little that catches
the imagination . . . can get its clearance from either the intelligence
or the moral sense. And equally, properly truthful or dispassionate
themes enlist only the wannest support from the imagination. The
poet is perpetually in that common human condition of trying to feel
a thing because he believes it, or believe a thing because he feels
it." [14] One suspects that those who read literature as a embodiment
of values or as an unqualified unitary expression of our whole bodily
and mental being — or as any of the dozen things that literature is
supposed to do that would be better done in a church or a revival
meeting or a philosophy seminar — will not find these remarks of
Larkin to their taste. Yet he points to one of the most mysterious
and paradoxical features of literature, for both writer and reader. An
awareness of the shaping of the idiom in which Larkin operated and
of the things that that idiom will permit is enhanced by a study of
his notebooks and recordings.

Chapter 11

STRATEGIES AND CONTAINMENTS

The style of poetry that Larkin chose to write in his mature years was very much in tune with his literary preferences — a poetry with a clear, declarative structure of narrative, statement or argument. He seemed, indeed, to assert, both in his criticism and in the poems themselves, that this was the natural form for poetry to take, and that, in poetry at its best, the use of language had much in common with our use of language in everyday, practical activities. This runs counter to the modernist conception of poetry, where the qualities (other than diction) that distinguished poetry from the linguistic usages of philosophy, science and practical discourse were constantly emphasized and explored. A flaunting of the modernist sense that "poetry of statement" was a contradiction in terms was the deliberate intent of some contributors to *New Lines* (1956).

In the poetry of Mallarmé, to cite an example at an opposite extreme to that of Larkin, the narrative, declarative, and, indeed, frequently the syntactic elements are subdued, and the poetry does most of its work through the immediate interplay of words and their associations and through rhythm and localized imagery. A sense that poetry should operate in this sort of way was adopted by Eliot and the early modernists; and Lawrence Durrell, one of the more wholehearted, latter-day exponents of the modernist conception of poetry, saw syntax as the enemy of poetry. W.H. Auden, in contrast, found in Hardy a model alternative to Eliot just because Hardy brought "syntax" back into poetry.[1] In line with this, and in contrast with modernist views, Auden conceived of the poem as a literary artifact that said something that the reader might or might not find true, and that demanded as, for instance, in "September 1st, 1939", agreement or disagreement of the reader. In his poetry and that of his generation we encounter the return of "subject" to poetry, in contradiction to the modernist contention that poems are not *about* anything. Auden's poetry works through a realization of the world in which the poet is situated and through the interplay of evoked detail. It is powerful just in so far as he makes us feel that the England of his day is the inalienable setting for his vision of things — a vision discovered, the reader is made to feel, through a contemplation of the details of the scene.

This is the manner of Larkin's poetry, which reaches back conservatively to the poetry of Auden and Hardy. Despite the delicate and often intricate verbal artistry, his poems are structured in terms of the interplay of evoked detail rather than through an orchestration of imagery or verbal effects (as was the case with much of the poetry of Dylan Thomas). In this aspect of his poetry, which may be characterized as metonymic rather than metaphoric, Larkin shares in the art of the novelist. On the other hand, much of his verbal artifice is aimed at the construction and control of "voice" — the creation of a sense of something being *said* about experience by a particular speaker in a particular way.

Larkin's poetry is done no service by analysis that runs counter to his idiom. The "light industry" of exegesis and criticism that he decried might be identified with the New Criticism, whose analyses of imagery and ambiguity were well attuned to the rhetoric of the early modernists whom the New Critics admired. Similarly, there is little use of intertextuality (conscious or unconscious) in Larkin's work: the reference to other literatures as a dimension of understanding — even so obvious as that made by Eliot's "The Journey of the Magi" — was anathema to him:

> "One is constantly trying to measure the effects of what you have written on someone starting from cold who may not have the experience you have had. This may not sound very significant, but it does cut out an extraordinary number of things which are quite common in other poetry. It cuts out obscurity. It cuts out references to literature and mythology which you cannot be sure they know. It means you are writing fairly simply in the language of ordinary people, using the accepted grammatical constructions and so on. That is my practice."[2]

Aside from his undistorted syntax, Larkin used regular metres and rhyming stanzas (in contrast with the free verse encountered in modernist poetry) though he often muted his rhythms and employed partial rhymes. The form of his most ambitious poems, such as "Church Going" or "The Whitsun Weddings", is what might have been referred to in the nineteenth century as the "reflective poem", in which an incident in the poet's life leads him to make certain general reflections. This is a very traditional type of poem in English; and its form, in prose, is a frequent one for the "essay". It should finally be observed that the images of Larkin's poetry have primarily the status of objects observed in the scene in which the poem is set, though they are generally given a submerged metaphorical extension, as (for instance) with the locked door in "Dockery and Son". They do not belong to a world of symbolism developed by the poet, and they are seldom, if ever, introduced into the poems primarily for their symbolic value. The conclusion of "High Windows" is a noticeable exception to this.

The choice of this type of poetry would have been explained by Larkin first of all as the choice to write what the general reader could understand and enjoy. He would have admitted, too, that he wrote poems that he himself could understand and enjoy; though, as we have seen, he observed that he ended up writing the poems that seemed to want to be written, in contrast with others that somehow refused to get written. ("Writing Poems", *RW* 83–84)

Yet the practice of steadily writing any type of poetry says something about one's sense of experience, of what poetry is like, and of how poetry relates to experience. At the very least, Larkin's poetry evinces a belief in the value of rationality, clarity and control, and, by implication, asserts that these are values to be cultivated. In addition, there is the suggestion, borne out by the poetry, that for Larkin these qualities may not have been so easy to attain as his consummate deployment of them suggests. The assertion of control through form is frequently associated with a thematic exploration of the elusiveness of choice and control. "Dockery and Son" again affords an example, where the strict form weaves a web of order through a characteristically complex variation of inter-locking rhymes, while the poem explores the extent to which we are indeed able to choose and control what we become.

However, the formal aspects of Larkin's poetry assert something more: that experience is amenable to being understood, grasped, or explored in important ways through a medium that cultivates the qualities of rationality, clarity and control. They assert, too — by corollary — that experience itself has an innate rationality and that what is important in it may be rendered clearly and in terms of images derived from our common experience, and having the meaning they have in that experience. His poetry enforces a sense that our world is to be understood in the terms in which it immediately presents itself to us; and, with characteristic British empiricism, that whatever meaning experience may have is to be found within experience and not by appeal to something outside experience. In particular, the apparently undistortive quality of Larkin's medium seems to deny the

need to *impose* a vision on reality in order to make it understandable
or acceptable: its order, it is implied, lies in reality itself.

Larkin's poems have the air of being "discovered" in experience.
This is, of course, in keeping with a dominant conception of poetry
since the Romantic period — that its validation lies in the fact that
the poet finds his sense of things *invested* in the world around him.
Place and incident are tremendously important to Larkin. So many
poems begin with an incident that seems to force the poet (and
reader) to look again and reflect. Again the poetry seems to suggest that sometimes (to use the words of Wallace Stevens) "the world
arranges itself in a poem"[3] and that what is being offered is what
Larkin called "unsorted experience".[4] In addition, it seems to assert
that our relationship to experience in understanding it is that of making rational statements about it — a view not embraced by all great
poets of the past.

Yet, if Larkin seems to "find" the poems in reality, and arranges
them so that the reader feels he also "finds" them, there is a strong
element of "steering" in the control evinced in the poems. Larkin's
seemingly undistorted presentation of the details of reality gives authenticity to the structuring of the poems, so that the details seem
unforcedly to imply the poet's sense of things; and the unmetaphoric
nature of Larkin's poetry reinforces the sense that there is no active
structuring. The feeling is strengthened by the pressure towards nom-
inalization, as in his frequent use of double adjectives and adjectival
phrases, which have the effect of implying that perceived attributes
are indeed fixed attributes of the objects and scenes observed. In
many poems the presence of the Larkinesque figure is a means of
directing the reader's response through a dramatically realized selection of incident and attitude, as in "Church Going" and "Dockery and
Son". Larkin's sense concerning "The Whitsun Weddings" that his
experiences had only to be written down to make a poem might seem
at odds with the careful structuring of relationship between speaker
and incident in the poem, with its dramatized changes of perspective
and its controlled expansion of figurative language. Even in poems
where the voice is the neutral authorial voice, experience does not
seem to surround the speaker with a dense, unsorted otherness, but
comes to us in the clear but controlling perspective of the speaker.

Indeed, the presence of the self-dramatized figure is an important
aspect of the emotional economy of the poems. It is a commonplace
that the Larkinesque speaker places himself at a distance, looking in
on experience — or looking back on it. One impression that this conveys is that Larkin is an outsider to the great emotional events of life

— a self-image that he cultivated. The choice of an observing speaker as a rhetorical device corresponded to a need to distance emotion and control it before it could be dealt with poetically. A notable example is "Lines on a Young Lady's Photograph Album", where the speaker is distanced from the emotional object of the poem by the device of having her appear only through the photographs he contemplates. However, from the reader's point of view, this presentation of emotion in a distancing perspective is undoubtedly what many have felt as a shortcoming in Larkin's poetry, despite the emotional power of poems like "Faith Healing", where Larkin seems secure enough in his relationship to his material to face it directly.

The movement of argument and tone in the poems is very carefully contrived — too carefully contrived sometimes, one feels, as in "Reasons for Attendance" for instance; and the reader may sense that the tight control and rationality may be there because the poet feels that his capacity to exercise these qualities in experience is threatened. A pattern frequently encountered in Larkin's poetry is of beginning in an undisturbing situation that in no way seems to threaten the speaker's sense of the world or himself. Yet something threatening does emerge, and the poet is forced to deal with the threat to his composure; and he does this with an ever tightening argument that leads to a series of generalizations (sometimes qualified, but deployed in such a way that the assertion of the generalizations rhetorically overwhelms the qualifications). This is the pattern of "Dockery and Son", "Church Going" and "An Arundel Tomb". It could be said with some truth that the "arguments" of the poems constitute their irrational *raison d'être* — the repeated assertion that experience and its assaults on our emotional security can be "contained" in this way.

There is, indeed, in many of the poems a certain deviousness to the rhetoric, which is masked by the very even tone. Larkin said of the conclusion to "Dockery and Son": "I'm very proud of these lines. They're true. I remember when I was writing it, I thought this is how it's got to end."[5] "Life is first boredom, then fear" may have seemed to the writer to be the way that, for him, the poem had "got to end"; but it may not seem to all readers that the poem in fact demanded this ending. The line is consonant with the experience of the poem, but it does not embody a view that the poem seems to make inevitable. "Church Going" is not marred by authorial intrusion of this kind; though the speaker strains the tone a little at the beginning with his "up at the holy end". However, its rhetorical strategies are more complex towards the end of the poem. Many may remember the lines "it held unspilt/So long and equably what since is found/Only in

separation — marriage, and birth,/And death" — a rather humbled
and dignified compliment to the church. They come, however, not
as unqualified assertion but as an explanatory clause in a question.
Within the logic of the poem's ostensible argument, there is only a
passing commitment to the statement; but within the rhetoric of the
poem, it stands out as memorable.

Larkin's poems are frequently structured so as to invite or assume
agreement or complicity with attitudes that are implied by means of
what is taken for granted in passing. Indeed, the images of everyday
reality come to us not merely with the expectation of recognition, but
with the expectation of assent to a particular attitude that the images
evoke for speaker and reader. The structure of tone in the poems is
in part built on this structure of assents — which are not necessarily
universally shared assents. Some of the "misreadings" encountered in
discussion of Larkin's poetry arise from an absence of the appropriate
assent by the reader, as in the case of "Naturally the Foundation will
Bear Your Expenses", commented on by Larkin himself.[6]

The expectation of assent goes beyond the enlisting of agreement
that is not ostensibly invited, as in "Church Going", where the expectation implies a special relationship between speaker and reader. The
movement from "I" to "we" as the poem progresses (a movement repeated in "Dockery and Son") involves a careful manipulation of tone
and incident so that the reader passes without noticing from the position of observer to that of assenting respondent. The "we", stated
or implied, is not always for Larkin "everybody" or "most people:
there is frequently a feeling of being drawn into a privileged assenting
group. The action of "The Whitsun Weddings" is not merely observed by a speaker whose mode of perception is different from that
of the participants in the weddings; the speaker's stance implies that
the reader, for whom the experiences of the afternoon are interpreted,
is not himself of the same social group as the members of the weddings, even though the "we" to which the poem modulates comprises
the poet and the newly-weds.

A remarkable rhetorical turn that comes close to eating one's cake
and having it is at the conclusion of "An Arundel Tomb" — "What
will survive of us is love". As was remarked earlier, it is preceded by
the qualifying disclaimer "to prove/Our almost-instinct almost true";
yet, as the final line of the poem, it resounds in the mind as the
poem's resolution — and as the poet's longed for resolution. This,
indeed, is arguably the intent: to leave us torn between the transcendence we wish for and our awareness of its impossibility. The mode
is one frequently encountered in Larkin's poetry, where an implied

rejected condition is employed so that the attendant consequent may be placed with tempting directness before the reader, who nonetheless is invited to *accede* in its rejection. In "The Building" the lines "for unless its powers/Outbuild cathedrals, nothing contravenes/The coming dark" evoke a nostalgia for the power that cathedrals once seemed to have, while implying rejection of both that power and any power "the building" itself might appear to have.

Indeed, we constantly encounter Larkin manipulating the rhetoric of his poems so that we are led to reach out for something beyond the perceived unsatisfactoriness of experience, while at the same time — and this is Larkin's strength — we are forced to recognise how limited are the possibilities of rising above our condition. The starkest recognitions are in "Faith Healing", "Reference Back" or "Love Songs in Age"; but the implied longing for transcendence is there in so much of his poetry.

A poem may be viewed as a structure to contain or come to terms with concerns that are persistently pressing for the poet. Death, the passage of time, the way in which experience passes from us, have always been the themes of poetry. They were particularly urgent ones for a poet like Larkin, who recognized no possibility of consolation in anything outside experience. There is a great preoccupation in his poetry with the individual life as unity or construct — with what we make *out of* it, and with what we make *of* it when we look back on what has happened in it. This too is a common enough theme in Western literature; but for Larkin it is related to a particularly intense concern with identity, with the way we come to be what we are, and with the extent to which we choose what we become, as in "Mr. Bleaney", "Wild Oats", "Dockery and Son", "Reasons for Attendance" or "Afternoons". The concern with identity, with a secure sense of one's relationship to the world is manifested in the already observed emphasis on control and on the clear individuation of elements of experience encountered in the poetry, and also in the dramatization of the poet as an observer looking out on experience. The mere act of perception with clarity has the effect of "placing" experience, of controlling it, of asserting the perceiver's identity *vis à vis* it.

Larkin's themes are presented with disturbing candour. Yet, even though, as he put it, "Deprivation is for me what daffodils were for Wordsworth" ("An Interview with the *Observer*", *RW* 47), it would be wrong to deny the element of self-transcendence found in Larkin's poetry. "Ambulances", ostensibly a frightening and bleak poem, attains through its recognitions just such a self-transcendence — the aspect of Larkin's poetry that has made it so deeply heartening to so many readers.

Though the poem does not begin with the recreation of a particular experience, it finds its subject in the events of everyday life. Into the world of "children strewn on steps or road/Or women coming from the shops/Past smells of different dinners" obtrudes the ambulance, the threatening reminder of sickness and death. "All streets in time are visited"; and, "Closed like confessionals", they seem to carry a secret to which we are not privy. The turning moment of the poem involves a glimpse that affords a momentary entry into that secret, as those around

>   . . . see
> A wild white face that overtops
> Red stretcher-blankets momently
> As it is carried in and stowed,
>
> And sense the solving emptiness
> That lies just under all we do,
> And for a second get it whole,
> So permanent and blank and true.

Getting it whole — seeing the truth in its fullness, seeing how the desultory facts of our lives fit in with the fact of death, is a kind of transcendence — a rising above being trapped in the events of our lives or in our immediate preoccupation with our "own distress".

This effect is reinforced by the phrase "solving emptiness", which suggests both a dissolving and the solving of a problem whose nature has eluded us. The poem then moves to an apprehension of death as loss of individuality and human attachment, characteristic of Larkin, and closes with the humbling:

>   Far
> From the exchange of love to lie
> Unreachable inside a room
> The traffic parts to let go by
> Brings closer what is left to come,
> And dulls to distance all we are.

Awareness, and humility in the face of that awareness, is what the poem finds in experience; and, for poet and reader, these become modes, however diminished, of transcending the limitations of experience. Recognition of truth, for Larkin, is a means of rising above the self and its concerns.

Recognition is what "Nothing to be Said" offers:

> The day spent hunting pig
> Or holding a garden-party,
>
> Hours giving evidence
> Or birth, advance
> On death equally slowly.
> And saying so to some
> Means nothing; others it leaves
> Nothing to be said.

The tone of calm acceptance is the poem's attainment; its stillness in the face of the unacceptable, its mode of triumph. The same stillness is encountered in two poems of death — "Dublinesque" and "The Explosion". Both conclude in images of great beauty, fragility and tenderness, as though the very fragility of human loveliness were its redeeming and enduring feature:

> As they wend away
> A voice is heard singing
> Of Kitty, or Katy,
> As if the name meant once
> All love, all beauty.   ("Dublinesque")

The pathetic, undeliberate gestures of love with which both poems conclude seem, in their openness and vulnerability, to transcend the very conditions they lament.

In 1964 Larkin said that he had come "to the conclusion that to write a poem was to construct a verbal device that would preserve an experience indefinitely". ("Writing Poems", RW 83) Many of Larkin's most poignant poems are about preserving the past, or involve reference to doing so: "Lines on a Young Lady's Photograph Album", "Maiden Name", "Love Songs in Age", "Home is So Sad", "An Arundel Tomb", or "Forget What Did". The gestures of preservation are gestures towards a transcendence; and, in their recognition of our longing to hold on to the loveliness of the past and find in our love for it something that will render it permanent, they seem to make their own beauty and consolation. These gestures of preservation are sometimes associated with a denial that anything may be held on to or reached back to, as in "Reference Back" or "Love Songs in Age"; yet the denials seem only to make the gestures more poignant.

The stillness of "Dublinesque" and "Nothing to Be Said" is a quality encountered frequently in Larkin's poetry as a desired good: in

"Coming" ("On longer evenings/Light, chill and yellow,/Bathes the serene/Foreheads of houses"); in the movement of "Days"; in the verbless stasis of "MCMXIV"; and most notably in "At Grass", where the idyllic final days of the horses is contrasted with the fervid acclaim that success once brought them. The horses' peace is associated with the sense that "they//Have slipped their names" and stand "anonymous again", free of fame and all the troubles of identity. A similar association is made at the beginning of "The Whitsun Weddings", where the speaker, his usual train missed and "all sense/Of being in a hurry gone", recalls that "All afternoon, through the tall heat that slept/For miles inland,/A slow and stopping curve southwards we kept." That same sense of freedom from pressures involved in being oneself is found in "Here", in the notion of "unfenced existence" that lies beyond human habitation. To be free of one's name, of the pressures of identity, offers the possibility of transcending concerns with identity — what one is and how one came to be what one is — that haunt so much of Larkin's poetry. The early "Absences" concludes exultantly: "Such attics cleared of me! Such absences!" There is a moment of stillness in "Dockery and Son" before the speaker encounters the disturbing recognitions: "The lawn spreads dazzlingly wide./A known bell chimes. I catch my train, ignored."

The word "ignored" carries both the suggestion of attention avoided and the suggestion of being forgotten. The ambivalence corresponds to an ambivalence that loneliness and isolation have for Larkin. Loneliness was a frightening condition for him as a young man, as it was for his hero, John Kemp, in *Jill*; but in *A Girl in Winter* it becomes an aspect of the human condition to be accepted. In "Talking in Bed", the inevitable loneliness that resides in the fact of our being separate human beings is explored; and the sense of isolation encountered in face of a wish for closeness is rendered starkly in "Reference Back". Yet, in "Here", "loneliness clarifies"; while, in "The Whitsun Weddings" and "Church Going", the speaker's understanding of events is associated with his being alone.

The obverse of loneliness — togetherness or love — is what some readers have found lacking in Larkin's poetry; yet an awareness of love and of its power is there in so many of Larkin's poems, if only as a sense of the gap between what we can imagine and what life affords. Indeed, in "Faith Healing", "Love Songs in Age" or "Broadcast", love becomes a measure of our lives, of how they fall short of our hopes and our sense of life's potentiality. For some, such poems seem to exist merely to offer their denials; and this no doubt has been responsible for much of the feeling that Larkin sells life short. Yet, as Larkin himself remarked: "I suppose I always try to write the truth and I wouldn't want to write a poem which suggested that I was different from what I am . . . I think that one of the great criticisms of poets of the past is that they said one thing and did another, a false relation between life and art."[7]

We may say then that truth and its recognition, along with stillness and anonymity and freedom from concerns with self, exist not merely as values in Larkin's poetry, but as modes of self-transcendence. Love, "that much-mentioned brilliance", remains a mode of transcendence acknowledged and continually yearned for, yet whose easy attainment and universal efficacy is carefully denied.

For all this, one must admit that there seem to exist in Larkin's poems certain strategies that appear compulsive and destructive in a finally negative way, sometimes disturbing the economy of the poems in which they occur. As Dan Jacobson wrote: "Flippant or self-wounding impulses play an essential part in the inner emotional dramas which many of his important poems act out; the poems couldn't exist without them. The famous 'Church Going' is a case in point; so is the truthful and terrible 'The Old Fools' . . . In poems like these, flippancy and derision are taken wholly into the very different 'element' which is peculiarly Larkin's, into the particular 'imaginative note' he manages to strike with so much plangency."[8] This is in many cases true; yet one is left with the question of the extent to which these strategies are contained — or containing: "contained", in the sense that they take their place in the total resolution of feeling that is the poem; "containing" in the sense that they contribute to that resolution which is the poem's *raison d'être*. The answer is often elusive, depending as it does in "The Old Fools" on one's feeling about the modulations of tone. Ian Hamilton said to Larkin in 1964: "A number of poems in *The Less Deceived* seem to me to carry a final kick in the head for the attitudes they have seemed to be taking up. In a poem like *Reasons for Attendance*, say, where you have that final 'Or lied'; somehow the whole poem doubles back on itself. What I want to know is how conscious you are of your poems plotting a kind of elaborate self-imprisonment." Larkin's reply was that "poems are artificial in the sense that a play is artificial. There are strong second act curtains in poems as well as in plays . . ."[9] Such poems include "Poetry of Departures", "Places, Loved Ones", "Toads" and "Reasons for Attendance"; and the ostentatious self-deflation, accompanied by the shock of an affront to customary pieties, was undoubtedly a "Movement" gesture. Some of these poems work by deflating the quasi-autobiographical figure who is the speaker of the poem. This vein is continued in "Self's the Man", "A Study of Reading Habits", "Wild Oats", "Send No Money", "Sympathy in White Major" and "Annus Mirabilis". Sometimes customary pieties are attacked front-face, as in "Home Is So Sad" or "This Be The Verse" ("They fuck you up, your mum and dad"); and it is the attack on these pieties (such as work, home, parenthood) that had a lot to do with the aversion felt for some of these poems. Yet the valid objection to "Reasons for Attendance", it was suggested earlier, is that the reversal at the conclusion does not serve to resolve the elaborate rhetorical play with argument at the centre of the poem, but seems rather to disguise the absence of such a resolution at any point in the poem. "Self's the Man" closes with a similar reversal, which, among other things, might seem intended to forestall questions as to what attitude we are to take to the vulgarly dismissive, cocky tone of the speaker.

It seems likely that Larkin was not entirely aware of some of the effects of the rhetorical complexity of his poems. The question that arises, in the minds of many readers of "Deceptions", is whether "fulfilment's lonely attic" refers merely to the "fulfilment" that occurred in the "lonely attic" of the poem or whether it applies to fulfilment in general. The ambiguity does not seem fruitful for the poem; and, if it is unintended, it is arguably self-revelatory. Similarly, concerning the indirections of the concluding eight line sentence of "Mr. Bleaney", one would be disappointed to feel that its baffling syntax was not a rhetorical feature that the author wished to have there: the relationship of the speaker to Mr. Bleaney's previous environment seems to have little point unless we in some sense feel that he is trapped in his own life too.

"If My Darling" can give rise to disconcertingly ambivalent reactions; though it was evidently intended to be "funny rather than self-derogatory". Larkin seemed to agree that it was "telling the girl that if she really knew me she'd know what a terrible person I am", commenting rather old-fashionedly, "I think we all think that, with girls."[10] Those who find the poem distasteful no doubt feel that, under the guise of fantasy, there is a certain gratuitousness in the unpleasantness of the poem:

> She would find herself looped with the creep of varying light,
> Monkey-brown, fish-grey, a string of infected circles
> Loitering like bullies, about to coagulate;
>
> Delusions that shrink to the size of a woman's glove
> Then sicken inclusively outwards. She would also remark
> The unwholesome floor, as it might be the skin of a grave,

From which ascends an adhesive sense of betrayal,
A Grecian statue kicked in the privates, money,
A swill-tub of finer feelings.

The same might be said of "Send No Money" or "A Study of Reading Habits". There seems to be some need to bring the poems round to certain feelings that are not always contained by the structure of resolution that the poem makes; and these feelings are associated, one senses, with fears and preoccupations too pressing to be talked about in a way that brings them into focus, but also too pressing not to be talked about at all. Though some of Larkin's satirical poems, like "Wild Oats" or "Self's the Man", that leave one feeling uncomfortable, have to do with women or sexuality, it is not these topics, one feels, that give rise to the uncertainty or aberrations of tone, but rather the threat to the poet's identity that these subjects bring with them.

Even the famous "Toads" has a trace of unpleasantness in its implied self-denigration. "Vers de Société" can be seen as a poem about how sadly ready we are in later years to accept company rather than face loneliness or our lack of capacity to generate self-rewarding activity. Yet its ostensibly satirical strategy involves the speaker (with whom the poet seems to identify) in accepting an invitation whose prospect has been made to appear totally disgusting. Such situations were not a part of Larkin's life, one believes; but the need to write poems in which they were rehearsed seems to have stayed with him.

"Vers de Société" deals with the conflicting calls of solitude and society. While loneliness is viewed ambivalently throughout Larkin's work, in "Best Society" solitude is presented as a form of selfishness: "Our virtues are all social" is stated axiomatically, but with a tone of defensive rejection. In at least two poems, "Places Loved Ones" and "Love", loving someone is seen as a form of selfish possession or intrusion. It is surprising how many of Larkin's poems deal with the theme of selfishness (often in relation to sexual relationships) and surprising how many of them were found uncollectable by the poet or have been found unsatisfactory by his readers: "To My Wife"; "Best Society"; "Continuing to Live"; "Places Loved Ones"; "Reference Back"; "Counting"; "Self's the Man"; "None of the books have time"; "Wild Oats"; "Love"; "Sympathy in White Major"; "Vers de Société"; "The Life with a Hole in it". He seems to have made an unfortunate connection, common enough in the English middle-class of his and earlier generations, between enjoying or fulfilling oneself and selfishness. In 1979 he remarked: ". . . being in love is a very difficult business anyway because almost by definition it means putting yourself at the disposal of someone else, ranking them higher than yourself". ("An Interview with the *Observer*", *RW* 54) He then went on to quote his poem "Love" as illustration. The comment shows his customary acumen; though it seems a perverted acumen. Offered (as it is) in conjunction with the remark "I often wonder why people get married" (*RW* 54), it presents a rather unusual perspective.

These poems project a conflict that Larkin appears never to have quite got into focus; and it is ironical that this poet who somewhat ostentatiously never married should have left behind so many poems about marriage — and so many that seem irremediably crippled. Marriage emerges as a threat to identity and a competition for control rather than an enhancement of identity. Equally, as in "Reasons for Attendance" or "Send No Money", Larkin seems to have remained troubled by the notion that the life of art or contemplation can be sustained only by foregoing "real" satisfactions, such as sexual gratification; while there is often the suggestion of an attendant corollary, that foregoing those "real" satisfactions is because of delusion or pusillanimity. Acompanying all this is an underlying passive attitude to experience, as though, in this area of experience at least, one was somewhat helpless before things that happen to one. This was a feature of his character John Kemp in *Jill*; and, indeed, this whole imbroglio of feeling is little changed in his later work from what it was in *Jill* — and seems still as defeating.

In contrast to the self-wounding impulses, one must note the proclivity for the conventionally poetic, from which Larkin freed himself with such difficulty — though not completely, it would seem. "The dedicated" (again, a poem about love) from *In the Grip of Light* is an embarrassing example that Larkin chose to reprint in *XX Poems* in 1951:

> Some must employ the scythe
> Upon the grasses,
> That the walks be smooth
> For the feet of the angel.
> Some keep in repair
> The locks, that the visitor
> Unhindered passes
> To the innermost chamber.

The effort to be lyrical at the end of "Arrival" (written in 1950) causes the poem to collapse:

> For this ignorance of me
> Seems a kind of innocence.
> Fast enough I shall wound it:
> Let me breathe till then
> Its milk-aired Eden,
> Till my own life impound it —
> Slow-falling; grey-veil-hung; a theft,
> A style of dying only.

A liking for this kind of thing seems to have stayed with Larkin and to have received a furtive respect throughout his career, like a denied need that kept creeping in as an uncontained reaching for transcendence. "First Sight" in *The Whitsun Weddings* and "Cut Grass" in *High Windows* teeter on the edge of the conventionally poetic. Even in the harsh "The Old Fools", when he reaches for an image of the identity that death will destroy, the rhetoric comes close to offering a slightly outmoded literary coinage: "the million-petalled flower/Of being here".

It has been noted elsewhere that in "The Whitsun Weddings", "Dockery and Son" and "The Old Fools" — three of his most ambitious poems — he works the imagery in terms derived from the settings of the poems, until he reaches his culminating images, which seem chosen from more traditional stock: "like an arrow-shower/Sent out of sight" ("The Whitsun Weddings"); "they rear/Like sand-clouds" ("Dockery and Son"); or "The peak that stays in view" ("The Old Fools"). This effect was evidently a matter of deliberate choice. Yet it was not as though Larkin could not find in his loved everyday scenes the unqualifiedly beautiful. How much more densely poetic are some of the earlier images in these poems; how compellingly lovely are the images of England in "MCMXIV". He manages things better at the end of "Church Going"; and nowhere more effectively than in "Broadcast", where he takes an image that is part of the scene and invests it with all the power and beauty and vulnerability of an object of love:

> Leaving me desperate to pick out
> Your hands, tiny in all that air, applauding.

There is in much of Larkin's poetry, as in Auden's, a relishing for their own sake of sonorities and of phrases memorable in themselves:

> A serious house on serious earth it is,
> In whose blent air all our compulsions meet,
> Are recognised, and robed as destinies.

This tendency was, admittedly, less pronounced in the later work. A close examination of poems such as "Dockery and Son" and "The Old Fools" reveals too how he relished complexity of form in a rather old-fashioned sense, triumphing over it to generate the feeling of a voice addressing us with intimacy and naturalness.

The excursions into the conventionally poetic might be seen as a failure of emotional containment — gestures that do not, in all their aspects, take their place properly in the economy of the poem. These gestures are, in a sense, what the gestures of self-wounding seem in part to be guarding against — the poet's longing for a transcendence that truth will not allow. Larkin comes back to the Keatsian dichotomy in discussing his own poetry: "every poem starts out as either true or beautiful. Then you try to make the true ones seem beautiful, and the beautiful ones true . . . 'Send no money' is true. 'Essential beauty' is beautiful. When I say beautiful, I mean the original idea seemed beautiful. When I say true, I mean something was grinding its knuckles in my neck and I thought: God, I've got to say this somehow."[11] This tension must exist for all poets; but not every one of them would find it presenting itself in those fairly cut and dried terms.

Perhaps this has something to do with the relationship to experience encountered in so many of Larkin's poems. As in "Church Going" and "Dockery and Son", the speaker is often surprised by experience and the revelations it brings; but he attempts to place himself in a dispassionate position regarding the experience, discussing it with himself, looking back on it — almost recollecting it in tranquility. At times, as in "Reasons for Attendance" or "Poetry of Departures" or "Mr. Bleaney", the process is itself dramatized as one that leads to a conclusion that is ambiguous. Nonetheless, the process is one of argument — often by the speaker with himself — leading frequently to a conclusion that takes the form of a secure generalization. The pressure is towards clarity and control and an enactment of acceptance by understanding. The ordered forms, the logical syntax, the way in which the objects of our everyday world enter into the poems in their normal roles, all contribute to the sense of control. So too, in most instances, does the dramatization of the speaker in a situation of retrospective reflection. We do not have the sense of experience overwhelming the speaker (and, by implication, the reader) and of his groping his way out of it or standing in awe of its mystery. The poems do not especially seek to dramatize the intransigence of experience, its multi-facetedness and its resistence to order, as does, say, the poetry of Ted Hughes or Sylvia Plath. Larkin's poetry corresponds to a conception of poetry very different from that of the young Dylan Thomas, who said: "an image must be born and die in another . . . Out of the inevitable conflict of images . . . I try to make that momentary peace which is a poem."[12] For Larkin, the emphasis is on perception and understanding. Our everyday world is rendered back to us almost as it seems to us in our daily commerce with it, yet transformed by acceptance. In that, indeed, lies both the wide appeal and the power of Larkin's poetry.

CONCLUSION

The success of Larkin's poetry with those who read it for pleasure and consolation must be seen as a measure of its centrality; and
the appeal that it had for the relatively uninitiated must have been
a source of gratification to Larkin and a vindication of his sense of
what the arts should be. Yet an examination of his life and some of
the positions enunciated in his poetry as well as in his prose must
make us ask what is the basis for that centrality. Despite the powerful recognitions that his work offered, there were alarmed reservations
concerning his attitudes to many received pieties: home came in for
sceptical disavowals; marriage and love were approached with circumspection; children were seldom mentioned and seemed to be disliked
by the poet; hope itself, some felt, was depicted as an aspect of the
delusions whereby we live; while death was starkly what it was. Indeed, as Larkin became popular, poems like "Church Going" were
manoeuvred into the context of religious affirmation, disheartening
though this was to their author. Yet Larkin's poetry was widely embraced with love, not merely admiration; and, with the publication of
his *Collected Poems*, he attained a readership such as only Housman
and Betjeman have been afforded in this century.

No doubt the appeal of Larkin's poetry to what one might term
the uninitiated reader was that, despite its affronting certain pieties
and despite the tentativeness of its affirmations, his work marked a
break with the alienated literature of the early twentieth century. In
contrast to *Dubliners*, for example, Larkin's poetry portrays ordinary
people and their feelings as decent and not shabby. He said of Barbara
Pym's novels:

> I like to read about people who have done nothing spectacular, who
> aren't beautiful and lucky, who try to behave well in the limited field of
> activity they command, but who can see, in little autumnal moments
> of vision, that the so called "big" experiences of life are going to miss
> them; and I like to read about such things presented not with self
> pity or despair or romanticism, but with realistic firmness and even
> humour.[1]

What he liked to read about was very much what he liked to write about. In describing Barbara Pym's novels, he was describing the world of his own poetry and the honesty with which it reaches out to us in its recognition of how comparatively humble all our destinies are.

In keeping with this, Larkin's poetry is not a poetry of encompassing vision but a poetry of recognitions. So many of his important poems, such as "Church Going", "The Whitsun Weddings", "Dockery and Son" and "Ambulances", involve encounters in which experiences, bland enough in themselves, take the poet by surprise with the recognitions that they impel. Although these recognitions may have a tentativeness and may occur in seemingly diminishing contexts, they come with the tentativeness and sense of limitation that attends them in most people's lives. Yet, in themselves, these recognitions involve the "great questions": who we are; how we come to be what we are; the role of choice in our lives; the extent to which our lives may be transformed by experiences; the acceptance of the fact that life does not always answer to our hopes; the inevitability of aging and death. That Larkin does not respond to these recognitions with clear and uplifting certainties, but sometimes goes out of his way to question the possibility of such certainties, was no doubt the cause of much early criticism of his work. That he himself seems humbled and questioning in the face of experience is possibly a source of the wide response that his poetry has come to evoke. Above all, there is throughout his poetry a cherishing of ordinary experience, even in its smallness.

The recreation of voice — heard "in the flesh" so to speak in his own very effective readings — is one of the great triumphs of Larkin's poetry; and that voice is the vehicle for the attitudes that permeate the poetry — the unassuming, matter of fact facing of experience that some have found emotionally barren but that reveals itself as stoical and moving in its honesty. The modulations of voice, which Larkin could recreate with such skill, are crucial to the control of our response to the poems, whose narrative structure is as much one of changing tone as of changing event. The voice is also a manifestation of the authorial presence that contributes so importantly to the sense of authenticity created by the poems. The Larkin persona, at first a device for self-deflation, becomes the focus of the reader's response as he is drawn into the speaker's argument with himself.

The recognitions that are so rewarding in Larkin's poetry seem strengthened by a holding back from emotion that is encountered throughout his work; and, in his best poetry, this is associated with an honesty and a humility of doubt that strengthens its emotional impact. If this holding back was a personal proclivity, it is transformed into a significant gesture in the structure of his art. Yet there are poems where the tendency to draw away from emotion or to call things baldly what they are, seem manifestations of predispositions that Larkin cannot bring into a satisfying focus. The emotional ambience of such poems is usually one that involves a particular concatenation of concerns: identity; love; sexual satisfaction; selfishness; gratifications that have been missed. These are the feelings explored in his satirical poems, such as "Self's the Man", or "The Life with a Hole in it", or "Send No Money". The powerfully engaging self-doubt of his major poems becomes a self-wounding doubt in the satirical poems — poems that in their reflexive back-lash seem to strike at the values Larkin most cherished. Many of them are conducted, surprisingly, in terms of conventional sexual stereotypes or in terms of stereotypical conceptions of strength and weakness as the basis of the ability or inability to obtain desired satisfactions. Here one senses that very pressing concerns with identity lead to a drawing back from involvement in human relations, because such involvement is a threat to identity. The poems convey a feeling of that threat, but they do not come to terms with it in any satisfying way.

However, if the important recognitions that Larkin's poetry affords are made in a context of guardedness and an inconoclastic denigration of anything that smacked of the transcendent or of high-mindedness, this was not entirely personal to Larkin, but was a feature of the cultural situation in which he wrote. If "Church Going" marked a subdued and accepting conclusion of a century of agonizing over the death of traditional Christian belief, it in nonetheless a poem that recognises what has gone before. The iconoclasm of the Movement and its preoccupation with the bogus was in part a product of the attempt to stand free of the detritus of a hundred years of attempts to make up for the awareness that "Our religion has materialised itself in the fact . . . and now the fact is failing it", as Matthew Arnold put it.[2]

Though "Church Going" is a cultural milestone in this respect, Larkin reaches back into tradition for sustaining valuations, as in "Church Going" itself and in "MCMXIV" and "An Arundel Tomb". Those events and ceremonies that make for "regenerative union" in "Show Saturday", in "The Whitsun Weddings", in "To the Sea", and again in "Church Going", are ones that the church "held unspilt/So long" or belong to traditional patterns of life that reach back to an age when belief had not gone. Indeed, there is a strong and odd nostalgia for family life, expressed by implication or in passing, in poems such as "Reference Back", "Afternoons" and even "Home is so Sad", which is at odds with the overt rejections of "I Remember, I Remember" and "This Be the Verse". Despite his liking for being alone, Larkin seemed to find his most powerful valuations in events that reflect social cohesiveness. This paradoxical undercurrent of conservatism, which became obvious as Larkin grew older, had much to do with his popularity. It goes along with his masterful containment of doubt in poetic structures that reach towards certainty and closure — something that contributes so much to the characteristic Larkin tone.

The power to write in this way was not attained with the directness and obviousness that some of Larkin's later cut-and-dried assertions concerning poetry might lead one to surmise. The idiom and the emotional stance of his poetry was arrived at in a cultural atmosphere very different from that generated by his own mature work. We have only to look at the lives and work of certain American poets almost of his generation — of John Berryman, Robert Lowell, Delmore Schwartz, Randall Jarrell and Theodore Rhoethke — to see at work powerfully shaping attitudes to life and art that were the legacy of modernism. Two of these poets committed suicide and all were emotionally disturbed or required psychotherapy. It is clear that, beyond any artistic considerations, their lives were permeated by the assumption that, for a sensitive person, the contemplation of the human condition was an agonizing experience. Larkin himself spoke against this view of the contemporary poet's relation to experience — what he called "Mr. Alvarez and the Necessary Nervous Breakdown"[3] theory of poetry; yet the lives of his American near contemporaries seem almost an enforced exemplification of that theory.

The feeling that the human condition is unbearable to contemplate is one that permeates the work of T.S. Eliot, which played such an important role in shaping the conception of poetry in the English-speaking world in the first half of the twentieth century. This is particularly true of *The Waste Land* (1922), *Sweeney Agonistes* (1932), *The Family Reunion* (1939) and *Four Quartets* (1943). Eliot's Lazarus figures, who have a vision that they cannot communicate to others less sensitive than themselves, are a modern version of the Romantic poet, whose fate it was to be set apart by his agonizing vision. This sense of the world and the poet's role in it became dominant during the World War II — the years in which Larkin was searching for his identity as a poet.

The book from Larkin's generation that most closely followed the role depicted for the poet by Eliot and that presented a vision most akin to Eliot's was Lowell's *Lord Weary's Castle* (1947). *In the Grip of Light* is not in the class of Lowell's book; yet it is permeated by the same sort of visionary ambition. The new Romanticism of the nineteen-forties, to which *In the Grip of Light* belonged, seemed to some of its practitioners to be a reaction to the social-political poetry of Auden and his generation; but it also involved a resurrection of the modernist ambition to generate a world-explaining vision in the face of the death of traditional beliefs, and it cultivated the reverence for traditional attitudes found in Eliot's later work and in the poetry of Yeats.

Larkin seems never to have admired the work of Eliot or Pound or to have been influenced by their programme for poetry, with its strong emphasis on the cultural duty of the poet. He began as an follower of Auden; and in Auden's work in the nineteen-thirties we encounter a break with the modernist conception of the autotelic nature of poetry in favour of a more humanistic orientation. Yet, like almost all British writers during the war years, Larkin was drawn away from Auden's poetry to the new Romanticism — in his case through his conversion to the poetry of Yeats after his meeting with Vernon Watkins. The grandeur and wonder of Yeats seems the obverse of the vision of an unredeemed world of fragmentary meanings that is encountered in *The Waste Land*; yet Yeats was the author of "The Second Coming", and his affirmations in poems such as "Lapiz Lazuli" have an almost consciously willed quality, made as they were out of a longing as great as Eliot's for some transcendent unifying vision.

For Larkin the conversion to Yeats was not merely a stylistic misdirection: it was a misdirection in his orientation towards experience. Yeats's achievement is not in question; but, as a model, his poetry is an invitation to impute to experience a grandeur that derives from a sense of things that lie outside the realm of that experience. In that respect, an admiration for Yeats involved a dehumanization of experience because it tended to separate the admirer from the emotional truth of his own experiences. This is what Larkin found when he rediscovered Hardy's poetry. Hardy showed him how his own world of everyday experience in its untransformed humanity could become the world of his poetry.

For the poet, the finding of his idiom is the discovery of his world — the discovery of his mode of shaping experience and of the experiences that it is important to him to shape. The circuitous cultural passage from *The North Ship* and Yeats through *In the Grip of Light* and

XX Poems and the Movement was the journey that Larkin had to make to find his "proper ground". It brought him, in the words of E.M. Forster, to "connect the prose and the passion": the passion that is felt, if held back, in all his work; and the prose of the everyday things that he loved.

The example of Hardy was crucial in this, leading Larkin to that direct commerce with his own experience that was to be the great strength of his mature poetry. The great change comes, gropingly at first, in the barren years of the late nineteen-forties. "At Grass" marks the break-through. The recognitions that provided the basis for Larkin's major achievement came with the poems of 1953 and 1954; and their philosophical ambience is explored in "Church Going", a pivotal poem for Larkin, and one that marks a moment of cultural recognition as importantly as did *The Waste Land* in 1922. The agonized awareness of the ultimate groundlessness of human beliefs and valuations, which had been a mark of the poetry of both Yeats and Eliot, is replaced by a subdued reflection on "what remains when disbelief has gone".

A particular significance of the Movement for Larkin was that it involved a self-conscious rejection of high-toned experiences as the material of art, to make way, in Larkin's work, for experiences and concerns previously regarded as trivial or mundane, but that nonetheless make up the fabric of our lives. It was Larkin's special gift to see how the important events of most lives take place in a framework of the unextraordinary. That sense of things had its full flowering in *The Whitsun Weddings*, where Larkin seems free to abandon the aggressive posture of many of the poems in *The Less Deceived*. The aggressive/defensive tone remains mainly in the satirical poems, some of which, one senses, are marred by the fact that they bring into play emotions that Larkin found hard to get into focus. Indeed, one way of viewing these poems is as attempts by Larkin to avoid seeing his emotional predicaments for what they were.

The defensiveness encountered in some of the satirical poems seems to manifest itself as a permeating conservatism in many of the poems in *High Windows*, in some of which, such as "Livings III", "The Card Players", "Vers de Société", or "Going, Going", the self-wounding impulses seem to merge with a misogyny. The world of those who "Push through plate-glass swing doors to their desires" ("Here") must have appeared to have become a world of uncaring affluence that in itself seemed threatening.

This later conservatism was associated with the very violent attack on modernism in *All What Jazz?*, the obverse of which was the well-mannered conservatism of most of the reviews collected in *Required Writing*, which sold so well. The conservatism of the attack on modernism and of several later associated assertions seemed almost a denial of the way in which his own poetry in the nineteen-fifties had at first affronted many readers' expectations concerning poetry. The welcome change that Larkin brought to the idiom and emotional atmosphere of British poetry at that time contained conservative elements, but was nonetheless a radical change: a change of attitude, of range of subject matter, of language — of the whole idiom of poetry. The conservative elements that were a part of this radical change involved a rejection of the oblique, metaphorical, often arcanely allusive poetry of modernism. These conservative elements had been a feature of Larkin's work from the beginning; and, in this sense, it could be argued (as Larkin did) that his views had not changed at all. However, the emphasis with which these views were articulated had. Presented as an acknowledgement of the needs of the common reader, his conservatism was what Larkin, in his later years, chose to rejoice in. The reasons for this were in part personal and in part a reaction to the cultural revolution of the nineteen-sixties that seemed to reveal potentialities in modernism that Larkin found threatening and that were at odds with the emphasis on control in his work.

Larkin, in *The Less Deceived*, had shown his own sense of the complexity of our relation to the actual and the complexity of our expression of that relation, in his self-doubting personae, in his frequent use of oxymoron, and in the reversals with which several of the poems conclude. In some of the poems in *High Windows* there is an implication of the chaotic nature of experience, such that it is not to be contained by the clear and controlled characterizations that are encountered in most of Larkin's famous and successful poems, where there is a pressure towards closure and a concomitant unambivalent reification of the objects of experience. Nonetheless, in much of Larkin's practice and in his writing about poetry, there is a repudiation of twentieth-century concerns with the complexity of our apprehension of experience and of our attempts to contain it in poetic form. Larkin turned away from a recognition of the essentially artificial nature of poetic form and the concomitant problems of its relation to the experiences engendered by and embodied in a work of art, choosing to emphasize what is being articulated in that form. In his later pronouncements, at least, he gave the impression of wanting to feel that traditional forms (and traditional musical harmonies and scales) are natural and that the clarity of traditional art is a product of its naturalness.

The artistic conservatism of Larkin's poetry after 1956 was undoubtedly a source of much of his success with ordinary readers of poetry. It broke down the sense that serious art was necessarily highbrow and difficult of approach. It went along with an embracing of traditional English values and a comfortable and comforting sense of what was traditionally English, itself touched with nostalgia. The scenes and situations of British middle-class life were evoked and cherished; and even the ambivalence concerning "home" was, one senses, widely shared. The puritanical drawing back from emotion, particular in relation to the opposite sex, which remains as an unresolved perplexity in so many of Larkin's poems, was a part of the British middle-class cultural heritage to which many readers must have responded; and it seems probable that poems such as "Wild Oats" and "A Study of Reading Habits" may have had as much to do with Larkin's popularity as "Church Going" or "Faith Healing". It is nonetheless difficult not to feel uncomfortable at encountering his essentially conservative attitudes in the context of a dismissal of modern art, praise of Mrs. Thatcher, and poems such as "Going, Going", "Homage to a Government" and "Posterity".

Such discomfort goes along with a sense of a growing elusiveness of the author. As time went by, Larkin increasingly presented a defensive "official" version of himself to the literary world — mildly philistine, with no-nonsense views on what literature should be and on the relation between author and reader. He was at pains to emphasize what, in the main, was true — that his views on these matters had not changed. Yet his art had changed; and the relation of that art to his public had changed — in large measure because of the effect that his work had had on the public perception of literature. *The Less Deceived* and its author seemed, in their day, intent on affronting public preconceptions of what literature should be. *High Windows* seemed ready to take what was, in most circles, afforded it: a place in the pantheon.

There was a more genuine conservatism that came to permeate Larkin's work. He was clearly by no means ignorant of foreign poetry, as he pretended to be; and his cut-and-dried views on modernism hid a very sensitive and informed awareness of twentieth-century literature. While his taste in the visual arts seemed quite unforcedly conservative (and there is no evidence of his opinions about classical music), the well-mannered later pieces in *Required Writing* attest to a sophistication and a broadness of culture at odds with the simplistic positions apparently entertained by their author. Nonetheless, the well-bred nature of these essays is a manifestation of an aspect of the later Larkin that was "official" in another sense of the word. He had not only become an established literary figure in his lifetime; the assistant librarian who had written *The Less Deceived* had become the head of a large university library and a distinguished figure in the world of library administration. The Movement rebel found himself a part of the Establishment; and this must have reinforced the hardening of attitude that seems to have come with Larkin's reaction to the cultural developments of the late sixties.

Indeed, Larkin was a much more paradoxical figure than has generally been admitted. This does not invalidate his poetry, and may have been the source of some of its power. Certainly, there were experiences, as has been seen, that he seemed unable to bring into clear focus. Yet he was increasingly concerned to present himself and his art as involved in a very simple relation to his reader — one in which a sophisticated sense of the arts was the road to obfuscation. The discovery of his idiom was not seen in terms of cultural history or the inherently complex relationship of the writer to a serious public. Instead, it was presented as it came to him — that he had to wait until he read Hardy before the penny dropped and he saw his way clear of all the modern Yeatsian nonsense. And, of course, he successfully reached the kind of public that he felt a poet should reach — and largely for the reasons he gave. Yet, in its day, the philistine, no-nonsense stance of the Movement had been a sophisticated one developed by educated young men who were reacting to the artistic establishment of their day. There was nothing naive about Larkin and what he had done; and the vehement insistence that he had no time for foreign poetry or that he didn't know who Borges was became as much a protection of his position as an expression of it.

Yet for all these reservations, the power of Larkin's work as a whole remains undeniable. It takes us into a world that is distinctively his own, yet one that resembles our everyday world. This world is presented so as to imply a particular perspective — a perspective reinforced by the tightly containing rationality and the clear sense that reality is what, in common sense, it seems to be, that is characteristic of his work. It might be argued that there is a limit to the experiences that this ordered and domesticated world can contain, and that it presents the locus of our emotional life as one protected from the more devastating aspects of existence. Yet Larkin's poetry is, as he protested, strongly emotional; and rightly read it is deeply heartening, with its honesty, its compassion and its love of the particular events and places that go to make up our lives. Its power lies in the fact that it locates the tremendous archetypal events and concerns of humanity in their full force in our everyday suburban setting, with all the diminution and all the immediacy that this implies.

Bibliography

A complete list of Philip Larkin's publications up to 1976 is to be found in *Philip Larkin: A Bibliography (1933-1976)* (London: Faber, 1979) by B.C. Bloomfield. It is to be hoped that an up-to-date version of this may be appearing soon. A list of secondary sources up to 1984 is given in "Philip Larkin: Secondary Sources, 1950-1984" by Mike Tierce in *Bulletin of Bibliography*, 43, 2 (June 1986) 67-75. Full information on material past that time is to be found in reference sources such as *Cumulative Book Index*, *MLA International Bibliography* and *The Year's Work in English Studies*. What is offered here is a listing of Larkin's books and records and a selection of pieces not collected by him, along with a selection of writing that, it is felt, may most assist study of his work. Additional material is cited in the references.

Books

POETRY

The North Ship (London: The Fortune Press, 1945; new edition, with Introduction and additional poem, London: Faber, 1966)

XX Poems (Belfast: Privately Printed, 1951)

The Fantasy Poets No. 21: Philip Larkin (Eynsham: Fantasy Press, 1954)

The Less Deceived (Hessle: The Marvell Press, 1955)

The Whitsun Weddings (London: Faber, 1964)

The Explosion (London: Poem-of-the-Month Club, 1970)

High Windows (London: Faber, 1974)

Femmes Damnées (Oxford: Sycamore Press, 1978)

Collected Poems, ed. A. Thwaite, (London: Faber, 1988)

NOVELS

Jill (London: The Fortune Press, 1946; new, slightly revised edition, with Introduction, London: Faber, 1964)

A Girl in Winter (London: Faber, 1947)

OTHER PROSE WORKS

All What Jazz? (London: Faber, 1970; 2nd ed. (with new material) Faber, 1985) (Jazz Criticism)

Required Writing (London: Faber, 1983) (Literary Criticism, Interviews and Jazz Criticism)

EDITED BY LARKIN

The Oxford Book of Twentieth-Century English Verse, chosen, with Preface, by Philip Larkin (Oxford: Clarendon Press, 1973)

Poetry Supplement compiled by Philip Larkin (London: Poetry Book Society, 1974)

UNCOLLECTED PROSE (A Selection)

"No more fever", *Listen* II, I (Summer 1956) 22–6. (A review of *The Shield of Achilles* by W.H. Auden) (Reprinted in *Philip Larkin: A Tribute* (London: Marvell Press, 1988))

"Separate Ways", *Manchester Guardian* (30 November 1956) 14. (A review of *A Case of Samples* by K. Amis and other books)

"No fun any more", *Manchester Guardian* (18 November 1958) 4. (A review of *The Chequer'd Shade* by J. Press)

"Poetry beyond a joke", *Manchester Guardian* (19 December 1958) 4. (A review of *Collected Poems* by J. Betjeman)

"Not the place's fault", *Umbrella* I, 3 (Spring 1959) 107–12. (Reprinted in *An Enormous Yes* (Calstock: Peterloo Poets, 1986))

"Betjeman En Bloc", *Listen* III, 2 (Spring 1959) 14–22. (A review of *Collected Poems* by John Betjeman) (Reprinted in "Philip Larkin: A Tribute" (London: Marvell Press, 1988))

"Texts and Symbols", *Guardian* (27 November 1959) 11. (A review of *Cypress and Acacia* by Vernon Watkins and other work)

"Poetry 1962: context — Philip Larkin", *London Magazine* I, II n.s. (February 1962) 27–54.

(A review of *Christina Rossetti* by L.M. Packer and *The Rossetti-Macmillan Letters*) *Listener* LXX, 1826 (March 26, 1964) 526.

"Stevie, good-bye", *Observer* (23 January 1972) 28. (A review of *Scorpion and Other Poems* by S. Smith)

"The state of poetry — a symposium: Philip Larkin", *The Review* 29–30. (Spring-Summer 1972) 60.

"Foreword" to *An Unsuitable Attachment* by B. Pym (London: Macmillan, 1962)

Uncollected Interviews (A Selection)

"Four young poets: Philip Larkin", *Times Educational Supplement* 2147 (July 13, 1956) 933.

"Speaking of Writing XIII: Philip Larkin", *The Times* (20 February 1964) 16.

"Four Conversations" (Ian Hamilton) *London Magazine* n.s. IV, 8 (November 1964) 64–85.

"A poet on the 8.15" (John Horder) *Guardian* (May 20, 1965), 9.

"A sharp-edged view" (Frances Hill) *Times Educational Supplement* 2974 (May 19, 1972) 19.

"Philip Larkin — a profile" (Dan Jacobson) *The New Review* I, 3 (June 1974) 25–9.

"The True and the Beautiful", *London Magazine* 20, 1 & 2 (April/May 1980) (Reprinted in *Viewpoints: Poets in Conversation*, ed. J. Haffenden (London: Faber, 1981))

Published Recordings

Listen presents Philip Larkin reading The Less Deceived (Listen LPV 1, Hessle: The Marvell Press, 1959)

Philip Larkin reads and comments on The Whitsun Weddings (Listen LPV 6, Hessle: The Marvell Press, c. 1965)

Philip Larkin: High Windows (Argo PLP 1202, London c. 1975)

Douglas Dunn and Philip Larkin (London: Faber, 1984)

Historically Important Anthologies and Collections containing poems by Larkin

Oxford Poetry 1942–1943, ed. Ian Davie (Oxford: Blackwell, 1943)

Poetry from Oxford in Wartime, ed. William Bell (London: The Fortune Press, 1945)

Springtime [one] ed. G.S. Fraser and Iain Fletcher (London: Owen, 1953)

Poets of the 1950's, ed. D.J. Enright (Tokyo: Kenkyusha, 1955)

New Lines, ed. Robert Conquest (London: Macmillan, 1956)

The New Poetry, ed. A. Alvarez (Harmondsworth: Penguin, 1962)

Writing about Larkin

Monographs

Timms, David — *Philip Larkin* (London: Oliver & Boyd, 1973)

Kuby, Lolette — *An Uncommon Poet for the Common Man* (The Hague: Mouton, 1974)

Brownjohn, Alan — *Philip Larkin* (London: Longman for the British Council, 1975)

Day, Roger — *Philip Larkin* (Milton Keynes: Open University Press, 1976)

Petch, Simon — *The Art of Philip Larkin* (Sidney: University of Sidney Press, 1981)

Motion, Andrew — *Philip Larkin* (London: Methuen, 1982)

Latré, Guido — *Locking Earth to Sky: A Structuralist Approach to Philip Larkin's Poetry* (Frankfurt am Main, 1985)

Whalen, Terry — *Philip Larkin and English Poetry* (London: Macmillan, 1986; Vancouver: University of British Columbia, 1986)

Hassan, Salem K. — *Philip Larkin and his Contemporaries* (London: Macmillan, 1988)

Rossen, Jane — *Philip Larkin: His Life's Work* (London: Harvester Wheatsheaf, 1989)

Portions of Books (A selection)

Alvarez, A. — Introduction to *The New Poetry* (London: Penguin, 1962)

Bedient, C. — *Eight Contemporary Poets* (London: Oxford, 1974)

Brown, M. — *Double Lyric* (New York: Columbia, 1980)

Falck, C. — "Philip Larkin" in *The Modern Poet* ed. I. Hamilton (London: Macdonald, 1968)

Heaney, S. — "Englands of the Mind" in *Preoccupations* (London: Faber, 1980)

Lindop, G. — "Being Different from Yourself: Philip Larkin in the 1970s" in *British Poetry Since 1970* eds. P. Jones & M. Schmidt (Manchester: Carcanet, 1980), 46–54.

O'Connor, W.V. — *The New University Wits* (Carbondale: Southern Illinois, 1963)

Powell, N. — *Carpenters of Light: A Critical Study of Contemporary British Poetry* (New York: Barnes, 1980)

Rosenthal, M.L. — *The New Poets: American and British Poetry Since World War II* (New York: Oxford, 1967)

Thurley, G. — *Ironic Harvest* (London: Arnold, 1974)

Thwaite, A. — "The Poetry of Philip Larkin" in *The Survival of Poetry* ed. M. Dodsworth (London: Faber, 1972)

— *Twentieth-Century English Poetry* (London: Heinemann, 1978)

Tomlinson, C. — "Poetry Today" in *The Pelican Guide to English Literature* Vol. 7 ed. B. Ford (London: Penguin, 1961)

Wain, J. — *Professing Poetry* (London: Macmillan, 1977)

COLLECTIONS OF MATERIAL BY VARIOUS AUTHORS

Phoenix 11/12: *Philip Larkin Issue*, ed. H. Chambers (Autumn/Winter, 1973/4)

Larkin at Sixty, ed. A. Thwaite (London: Faber, 1982)

An Enormous Yes, ed. H. Chambers (Calstock: Peterloo Poets, 1986)

A Tribute to Philip Larkin, ed. G. Hartley (London: Marvell Press, 1987)

Philip Larkin: The Man and His Work, ed. D. Salwak (London: Macmillan, 1988)

Critical Survey, 1989, 1, 2. (Special Larkin Number)

ESSAYS AND REVIEWS (A Selection)

(Material included in books and collections listed in other sections is not listed here.)

Bateson, F.W. — "Auden's (and Empson's) Heirs" *Essays in Criticism* VII (January 1957) 76–80.

Bayley, J. — "Larkin and the Romantic Tradition" *Critical Quarterly* 26, 1–2 (Spring-Summer, 1984) 61–66.

Cox, C.B. — "Philip Larkin" *Critical Quarterly* 1 (Spring, 1959) 14–17.

Everett, B. — "Philip Larkin: After Symbolism" *Essays in Criticism* XXX (1980) 227–242.

— "Larkin and Us" *London Review of Books* (Nov. 4–17, 1982) 4, 20, 6–9.

Ford, M. — "Loneliness Clarifies: A Study of the Longer Poems of Philip Larkin" *English Studies in Canada* 6 (1980) 323–332.

Greer, G. — "A Very British Misery" *Manchester Guardian Weekly* Oct. 30 1988, 28.

Hamburger, M. — "Philip Larkin: A Retrospect" *Poetry Nation Review* (1987) 14 ,4 , 71–80.

Hamilton, I. — "Phil the Lark" *London Review of Books* 10, 18 (Oct. 13, 1988) 3–5.

James, C. — "Somewhere Becoming Rain" *New Yorker* July 17 1989, 88–92.

Morrison, B. — "Larkin, Sin and Death" *Times Literary Supplement* (Oct. 14–20) 4, 463, 1151–2.

Press, J. — "The Poetry of Philip Larkin" *The Southern Review* XIII, 1 (January 1977) 131–146.

Reibetanz, J. — " 'The Whitsun Weddings': Larkin's Reinterpretation of Time and Form in Keats" *Contemporary Literature* 17 (1976) 529–540.

Scrimingeour, P.D. — "Philip Larkin's 'Dockery and Son' and Julian Hall's *The Senior Commoner*" *Notes & Queries* (June 1986) 33 (231)(2) 193.

Thwaite, A. — "A Great Parade of Single Poems" *Listener* 89 (1973) 472–474.

Tolley, A.T. — "The Making of 'At Grass'" *Arc* 12/13 (Summer/Fall 1984) 118–128.

Tomlinson, C. — "The Middlebrow Muse" *Essays in Criticism* VII (1957) 208–217.

Wain, J. — "Engagement or Withdrawal ?" *Critical Quarterly* VI, 2 (Summer, 1964) 167–178.

Walcott, D. — "The Master of the Ordinary" *The New York Review of Books* June 1 1989, 37–40.

Background

Bergonzi, B. — "After 'The Movement'" *Listener* 66 (1961) 284–5.

Conquest, R. — "Modernity in Poetry" *Departure* 4, 10, 6–8.

Hewison, Robert — *In Anger: Culture in the Cold War 1945–60* (London: Weidenfeld & Nicolson, 1981)

Morrison, Blake — *The Movement* (London: Oxford University Press, 1980; 2nd ed. 1986)

Davie, Donald — "Remembering the Movement" in *The Poet in the Imaginary Museum* (Manchester: Carcanet, 1977)

Cotton, John — *Oscar Mellor: The Fantasy Press* (Hitchin: Didman Press, 1977)

Hartley, Jean — *Philip Larkin, the Marvell Press and Me* (Manchester: Carcanet, 1989)

Sinfield, Alan (ed.) — *Society and Literature: 1945–1970* (London: Methuen, 1983)

Tolley, A.T. — "The Fortune Press and the Poetry of the Forties" *Aquarius* 17/18 (1986/87) 92–100

References

INTRODUCTORY

1. Larkin, P. — "Poetry Beyond a Joke" (a review of *Collected Poems* by J. Betjeman), *Manchester Guardian* Dec. 19, 1958, 4.

CHAPTER 1

1. "Not the Place's Fault", *Umbrella* I, 3 (Spring 1959) 111 (Reprinted in *An Enormous Yes* ed. H. Chambers (Calstock: Peterloo Poets, 1986)).
2. "Not the Place's Fault", 111.
3. "Not the Place's Fault", 112.
4. "Not the Place's Fault", 111.
5. "Not the Place's Fault", 112.
6. Amis, K. — "Remembering a Friend" in *Philip Larkin: The Man and His Work* ed. D. Salwak (London: Macmillan, 1989), 4.
7. Letter to J.A. Johnson, December 29, 1964. Quoted in *The Development of Philip Larkin's Poetry* by J.A. Johnson (Thesis submitted at North Dakota State University: Fargo, 1965)
8. "Not the Place's Fault", 112.
9. "Not the Place's Fault", 112.
10. *Poetry Book Society Bulletin*, 40 (Feb. 1964).
11. Meyer, M. — "John Heath-Stubbs in the Forties", *Aquarius* 10 (1978), 12–13.
12. Amis, K. — "Oxford and After" in *Larkin at Sixty* ed. A. Thwaite (London: Faber, 1982), 27.
13. *Eight Oxford Poets* eds. M. Meyer & S. Keyes (London: Routledge, 1941), vii.
14. Jacobson, D. — "Philip Larkin — a profile", *The New Review* I, 3 (June 1974), 26.
15. "Oxford and After", 25.
16. Hamburger, M. — *A Mug's Game* (Cheadle Hulme: Carcanet, 1873), 79.
17. "Oxford and After", 27.
18. "Oxford and After", 28.
19. Horder, J. — "Poet on the 8.15", *The Guardian* May 20, 1965, 9.
20. *John Heath-Stubbs: An Interview* (with A.T. Tolley), *Aquarius* 17 & 18 (1986–87), 119.

21. Larkin, P. — Foreword to typescript of *Chosen Poems 1941* (unpublished). Quoted by A. Thwaite in "Introduction" to *Collected Poems* by Philip Larkin (London: Faber, 1988), xix.

CHAPTER 2

1. Jacobson, D. — "Philip Larkin — a profile", *The New Review* I, 3 (June 1947), 26–27.
2. Wain, J. — *Sprightly Running* (London: Macmillan, 1962), 188.
3. "Philip Larkin — a profile", 27.
4. Bloomfield, B.C. — *Philip Larkin: A Bibliography* (London: Faber, 1979), 24; and Larkin, P. — Letter to A.T. Tolley, 30th September, 1982.
5. Motion, A. — *Philip Larkin* (London: Methuen, 1982), 46.
6. Amis, K. — "Oxford and After", in *Larkin at Sixty* ed. A. Thwaite (London: Faber, 1982), 27.
7. Woolf, V. — *Orlando* (London: Penguin, 1946), 14.
8. *Orlando*, 145.
9. Letter to J.B. Sutton, 20 Sep. 1945. Cited in *Philip Larkin: His Life's Work* by J. Rossen (London: Harvester, 1989)
10. "Publishing Larkin", by Charles Monteith in *Larkin at Sixty*, 39.
11. "Oxford and After", by Kingsley Amis in *Larkin at Sixty*, 28.
12. "Publishing Larkin", 39.
13. "Publishing Larkin", 39.
14. "Philip Larkin — a profile", 27.
15. "Four Conversations", Ian Hamilton, *London Magazine* n.s. (Nov. 64), 75.
16. "Raymond Gardner interviews Dr. Larkin about his Approach to Life and Poetry", *The Guardian* Mar. 31, 1973, 12.

CHAPTER 3

1. "Poet on the 8.15" — Interview with Philip Larkin by John Horder, *The Guardian* May 20, 1965, 9.
2. Larkin, P. — "Texts and Symbols", *The Guardian* Nov. 27, 1959, 11.
3. Wain, J. — *Professing Poetry* (London: Macmillan, 1977), 178.
4. Larkin, P. — Letter to A.T. Tolley, November 18, 1981.
5. Ferguson, P. — "Philip Larkin's *XX Poems*: The Missing Link", *Agenda* XIV, 3, 64.
6. "Four Conversations", Ian Hamilton, *London Magazine* n.s. 4, 8 (Nov. 1964), 77.

7. Jacobson, D. — "Philip Larkin — a profile", *The New Review* I, 3 (June 1974), 28.
8. "Four Conversations", 77.
9. Motion, A. — *Philip Larkin* (London: Methuen, 1982), 26.
10. "Four Conversations", 77.

CHAPTER 4

1. "Poet on the 8.15" — Interview with Philip Larkin by John Horder, *The Guardian* May 20, 1965, 9.
2. Larkin, P. — Letter to A.T. Tolley, 30th Sept. 1982.
3. Worsley, T.C. in *New Statemen & Nation* Dec. 10, 1949 (quoted in Hewison, R. — *In Anger* (London: Weidenfeld & Nicolson, 1981), 5).
4. Jacobson, D. — "Philip Larkin — a profile", *The New Review* I, 3 (June 1974), 27.
5. Motion, A. — *Philip Larkin* (London: Methuen, 1982), 35.
6. Timms, D. — *Philip Larkin* (Edinburgh: Oliver & Boyd, 1973), 35.
7. Motion, 36; *and* Thwaite, A. — "The Poetry of Philip Larkin" in *The Survival of Poetry* ed. M. Dodsworth (London: Faber, 1970), 43.
8. Ferguson, P. — "Philip Larkin's *XX Poems*: The Missing Link", *Agenda* XIV, 3, 56 (Remark by Larkin from "Two Poets Promenading", *Radio Times* Aug. 16, 1973, 11).
9. "Four Young Poets: Philip Larkin", *Times Educational Supplement* 2147 (July 13, 1956), 933.
10. Alvarez, A. — *The New Poetry* (London: Penguin, 1962), 26.
11. "Philip Larkin — a profile", 27.
12. "Philip Larkin — a profile", 27.
13. "Four Conversations", Ian Hamilton, *London Magazine* n.s. 4, 8 (Nov. 1964), 72.
14. Bloomfield, B.C. — *Philip Larkin: A Bibliography* (London: Faber, 1979), 33.
15. Haffenden, J. — "The True and the Beautiful: a conversation with Philip Larkin", *London Magazine* 20, 1 & 2 (April/May 1980), 90.
16. Timms — *Philip Larkin*, 69.
17. Eliot, T.S. — "Andrew Marvell" in *Selected Essays* (London: Faber, 1951), 293.

CHAPTER 5

1. Hartley, A. — "Poets of the Fifties", *The Spectator* Aug. 27, 1954, 261.
2. Hartley, A. — "Critic Between the Lines", *The Spectator* Jan. 8, 1954, 47.
3. Scott, J.D. — "In the Movement", *The Spectator* Oct. 1, 1954, 399.
4. "In the Movement", 400.
5. Wain, J. — *Sprightly Running* (London: Macmillan, 1962), 145.
6. Wain, J. — *Preliminary Essays* (London: Macmillan, 1957), 159.
7. Letter to J.A. Johnson, December 19, 1965. Quoted in *The Development of Philip Larkin's Poetry* by J.A. Johnson (Thesis submitted at North Dakota State University: Fargo, 1965)
8. "Robert Lowell: interviewed by F. Seidel in *Robert Lowell: A Collection of Critical Essays* ed. T. Parkinson (Englewood Cliffs: Prentice-Hall, 1968), 19. (Interview reprinted from *The Paris Review* 25 (Winter-Spring, 1961).)
9. "Four Conversations", Ian Hamilton, *London Magazine* n.s. 4, 8 (Nov. 1964), 72.
10. Hamburger, M. — "Philip Larkin: A Retrospect" in *Testimonies* (Manchester; Carcanet, 1989), 312.
11. "Poet on the 8.15" — Interview with Philip Larkin by J. Horder, *The Guardian* May 20, 1965, 9.
12. Larkin, P. — "Separate Ways" (a review of *A Case of Samples* by K. Amis) *Manchester Guardian* Nov. 30, 1956, 14.
13. Larkin, P. — "Exhumation" (review of *The Buried Day* by C. Day Lewis) *The Spectator* May 20, 1960, 742.
14. Haffenden, J. — "The True and the Beautiful: a conversation with Philip Larkin" *London Magazine* 20, 1 & 2 (April/May 1980), 93.
15. "The True and the Beautiful", 93.
16. Yeats, W.B. — *The Autobiography of William Butler Yeats* (New York: Collier, 1965), 77.
17. "Four Conversations", 73–74.
18. Hartley, A. — "Natural Piety", *The Spectator* June 8, 1956, 801.
19. Fraser, G.S. — "A New Tone", *New Statesman & Nation* Jan. 21, 1956, 79.
20. [Anon.] — "Poetic Moods", *Times Literary Supplement* Dec. 16, 1953, 762.
21. Fuller, R. — [Review of *The Less Deceived*] *London Magazine* III (April 1956), 85.
22. Wright, D. — "A Small Green Insect Shelters in the Bowels of My Quivering Typewriter", *Encounter* Oct. 1956, 75.

23. "The True and the Beautiful", 92.
24. Conquest, R. — "A Proper Sport" in *Larkin at Sixty* ed. A. Thwaite (London: Faber, 1982), 33.

CHAPTER 6

1. Haffenden, J. — "The True and the Beautiful: a conversation with Philip Larkin", *London Magazine* 20, 1 & 2 (April/May 1980), 92.
2. James, C. — "Kingsley Amis — a profile", *The New Review* 1, 4 (July 1974), 23.
3. *Philip Larkin Reads* The Whitsun Weddings, *Listen* LPV6.
4. *Philip Larkin Reads* The Whitsun Weddings.
5. *Philip Larkin Reads* The Whitsun Weddings.
6. "Four Conversations", Ian Hamilton, *London Magazine* n.s. 4, 8 (Nov. 1964), 76.
7. Petch, S., *The Art of Philip Larkin* (Sidney: Sidney University Press, 1981), 65.
8. Jacobson, D. — "Philip Larkin — a profile", *The New Review* 1, 3 (June 1974), 27–28.
9. "The True and the Beautiful", 96.
10. Rosen, J. — *Philip Larkin: His Life's Work* (London: Harvester, 1989), 25.
11. Hartley, J. — *Philip Larkin, The Marvell Press and Me* (Manchester: Carcanet, 1989), 95.
12. "Four Conversations", 71.
13. "Four Conversations", 71.

CHAPTER 7

1. "Four Conversations", Ian Hamilton, *London Magazine* n.s. 4, 8 (Nov. 1984), 74.
2. Pym, B. — *A Very Private Eye* (London: Macmillan, 1984), 244.
3. Larkin, P. — "Not like Larkin", *The Listener* Aug. 17, 1972, 209.
4. Haffenden, J. — "The True and the Beautiful: a conversation with Philip Larkin", *London Magazine* 20, 1 & 2 (April/May 1980), 95.
5. Larkin, P. — "Not the Place's Fault", *Umbrella* I, 3 (Spring 1959), 109.
6. "Poet on the 8.15" — An Interview with Philip Larkin by John Horder, *The Guardian* May 20, 1965, 9.
7. Kazin, A. — *On Native Grounds* (New York: Harcourt, 1942; Anchor, 1956), 174.
8. Frost, R. — "The Figure a Poem Makes" in *Selected Poems of Robert Frost* (New York: Holt, 1963), 2–3.

9. "Raymond Gardner Interviews Dr. Larkin About His Approach to Life and Poetry", *The Guardian* May 31, 1973, 12.

CHAPTER 8

1. *Philip Larkin Reads* The Whitsun Weddings, *Listen* LPV6.
2. "Poet on the 8.15" — Interview with Philip Larkin by J. Horder, *The Guardian* May 20, 1965, 9.
3. Amis, K. — *Lucky Jim* (London: Penguin, 1961), 24. (Original publication: Gollancz, 1954).
4. Amis, K. — "Oxford and After" in *Larkin at Sixty* ed. A. Thwaite (London: Faber, 1982), 24.
5. James, C. — "On His Wit" in *Larkin at Sixty* ed. A. Thwaite (London: Faber, 1982), 104.
6. Letter to M. Bowen, Oct. 27, 1984. See *Philip Larkin: his life and work*, Catalogue of Exhibition at B.M. Jones Library, Hull, 17–8.
7. Pleasants, Henry — *Serious Music and All That Jazz* (New York: Simon & Schuster, 1971), 46.

CHAPTER 9

1. Larkin, P. — "No Fun Any More" (review of *The Chequered Shade* by J. Press) *Manchester Guardian* Nov. 18, 1958, 4.
2. Eliot, T.S. — "The Metaphysical Poets" in *Selected Essays* (London: Faber, 1951), 289.
3. "Poet on the 8.15" — An Interview with Philip Larkin by J. Horder, *The Guardian* May 20, 1965, 9.
4. Lodge, D. — "Philip Larkin: The Metonymic Muse" in *Philip Larkin: The Man and His Work* ed. D. Salwak (London: Macmillan, 1989), 120 (from *The Modes of Modern Writing* by D. Lodge (London: Arnold, 1977)).
5. Eliot, T.S. — "Tradition and the Individual Talent", in *Selected Essays* (London: Faber, 1951) 22.
6. "Four Conversations", Ian Hamilton *London Magazine* n.s. 4, 8 (Nov. 1964), 71.
7. Larkin, P. — "Not Literary Enough" (review of *A Charm Against the Toothache* by J. Heath-Stubbs), *Poetry & Audience* 21, (June 10, 1954), 2.
8. Larkin, P. — Contribution to "Poetry 1962: context", *London Magazine* n.s. 1, 11 (Feb. 1962), 31.
9. Davie, D. — "Larkin's Choice", *Listener* Mar. 29, 1973, 420.
10. Scupham, P. — "A Caucus-race", *Phoenix* 11/12, 177 & 182.

11. Grigson, G. — Review of *Faber Book of Modern Verse, New Verse* 20 (Apr.-May, 1936), 26.

12. "A Great Parade of Single Poems" — An Interview with Philip Larkin by A. Thwaite, *Listener* Apr. 12, 1973, 473.

13. Larkin, P. — "Preface" to *The Oxford Book of Twentieth-Century English Verse* (Oxford: Clarendon Press, 1973), v–vi.

14. "A Great Parade of Single Poems", 473.

15. Larkin, P. — "Graves Superior" (review of *Steps* by R. Graves), *Manchester Guardian* Dec. 2, 1958, 4.

16. Larkin, P. — "Glimpses from a Poor Year of Poetry" (review of *Collected Poems* by E. Muir), *The Guardian* Apr. 29, 1960, 10.

17. Larkin P. — "Reports on Experience" (review of *Poetry for Supper* by R.S. Thomas), *Manchester Guardian* Sept. 5, 1958, 4.

18. James, C. — "On His Wit" in *Larkin at Sixty* ed. A. Thwaite (London; Faber, 1982), 98.

19. Larkin, P. — "Poetry Beyond a Joke", a review of *Collected Poems* by J. Betjeman, *Manchester Guardian* Dec. 19, 1958, 4.

20. Larkin, P. — Contribution to "Reputations Revisited", *Times Literary Supplement* Jan. 21, 1977, 67.

21. "Four Conversations", 76–77.

22. Eliot, T.S. — "Tradition and the Individual Talent", 14.

23. Pym, B. — *A Very Private Eye* (London: Macmillan, 1984), 299.

24. Haffenden, J. — "The True and the Beautiful: a conversation with Philip Larkin", *London Magazine* 20, 1 & 2 (April/May 1980), 88–89.

25. Everett, D. — "Art and Larkin" in *Philip Larkin: The Man and His Work*, 130.

26. Eliot, T.S. — "Hamlet" in *Selected Essays* 3rd. ed. (London: Faber, 1951) 145.

CHAPTER 10

1. Crozier, A. — "Thrills and Frills" in *Society and Literature: 1945–1970* ed. A. Sinfield (London: Methuen, 1983)

2. Larkin, P. — Letter to A.T. Tolley, Sept. 30, 1982.

3. Rossen, J. — *Philip Larkin: His Life's Work* (London: Harvester, 1989), 57.

4. Bradford, C. — "Yeats's Byzantium Poems: A Study of Their Development", *PMLA* LXXV (March 1960).

5. Spender, S. — "The Making of a Poem" in *The Making of a Poem* (London: Hamish Hamilton, 1955).

6. Thomas, D. — *Selected Letters* (London: Dent, 1966), 115.

7. Eliot, T.S. — "The Music of Poetry" in *On Poetry and Poets* (London: Faber, 1957), 38.
8. Liner notes to *Philip Larkin reads* The Less Deceived, *Listen* LPV1.
9. Liner notes, *Listen* LPV1.
10. *Philip Larkin Reads* The Whitsun Weddings, *Listen* LPV6.
11. Larkin, P. — "Not Like Larkin", *Listener* Aug. 17, 1972, 209.
12. "Four Conversations", Ian Hamilton, *London Magazine* n.s. 4, 6 (Nov. 64), 73.
13. "Not Like Larkin", 209.
14. Larkin, P. — Contribution to "Poetry 1962: context", *London Magazine* n.s. 1, 11 (Feb. 1962) 32.

CHAPTER 11

1. Auden, W.H. — "A Literary Transference", *Southern Review* VI (Summer 1940).
2. "Raymond Gardner Interviews Dr. Larkin About His Approach To Life and Poetry", *The Guardian* Mar. 31, 1973, 12.
3. Stevens, W. — "Adagia" from *Opus Posthumous* (New York: Knopf, 1957) 165.
4. *Philip Larkin Reads* The Whitsun Weddings, *Listen* LPV6.
5. Haffenden, J. — "The True and the Beautiful: a conversation with Philip Larkin", *London Magazine* 20, 1 & 2 (April/May 1980), 84.
6. "Four Conversations", Ian Hamilton, *London Magazine* n.s. 4, 8 (Nov. 1964), 76.
7. "Four Conversations", 75.
8. Jacobson, D. — "Philip Larkin — a profile", *The New Review* 3 (June 1974), 28.
9. "Four Conversations", 74.
10. *Philip Larkin Reads* The Less Deceived, *Listen* LPV1.
11. "The True and the Beautiful", 84.
12. Thomas, D. — "Letter to Henry Treece", in *Selected Letters of Dylan Thomas* (London: Dent, 1966), 191.

CONCLUSION

1. Quoted in "Publishing Larkin" by C. Monteith in *Larkin at Sixty* ed. A. Thwaite (London: Faber, 1982) 42–3.
2. Arnold, M. — "The Study of Poetry" in *The Portable Matthew Arnold* ed. L. Trilling (New York: Viking, 1949), 299.
3. Larkin, P. — "Poets in a fine frenzy and otherwise", *The Guardian* Feb. 13, 1969, 7.

Index

NOTE: There are separate entries for authors and other literary figures and organisations, and for periodicals and anthologies. Books by specific authors, poems, and prose pieces that are not whole books, are listed under authors, in that order. Only books, plays or pieces of prose *named* in the text are indexed; but all poems quoted from or mentioned are indexed. The Index covers only the text from "Introductory" to "Conclusion", and not prefatory or appended material. Names that appear in quoted material are not indexed.

Pages containing discussion of a particular item are indicated by putting the page number in **bold type**.

INDEX